DENVER

ROCKY MOUNTAIN GOLD

by Thomas J. Noel

Denver: Rocky Mountain Gold

a pictorial and entertaining commentary on the growth and development of Denver, Colorado.

by Thomas J. Noel

for Vi Kamiya Noel

Publishers:
Larry P. Silvey
Douglas S. Drown

Editor:
Ellen Sue Blakey

Associate Editor:
Peggi Ridgway

Art Director:
Rusty Johnson

Assistant Art Director:
James Michael Martin

Current Photographer:
Roger Whitacre

Project Director:
Tim Colwell

Reliance running team gets fired up for the firemen's competition, 1889.

Denver: Rocky Mountain Gold is sponsored by The Denver Chamber of Commerce.

Copyright 1980 by Continental Heritage Press, Inc., P. O. Box 1620, Tulsa, Oklahoma 74101. All rights reserved.

Library of Congress Catalogue Card Number: 80–66339

ISBN: 0–932986–12–9

Denver: Rocky Mountain Gold is one of *The American Portrait Series* published by Continental Heritage Press. Others include:

Charlotte: Spirit of the New South
Cleveland: Prodigy of the Western Reserve
Columbus: America's Crossroads
Des Moines: Capital City
Detroit: American Urban Renaissance
Fort Worth: The Civilized West

Houston: A History of a Giant
Los Angeles Two Hundred
The San Antonio Story
San Diego: California's Cornerstone
San Jose: California's First City
The Saint Louis Portrait
The Tulsa Spirit

Benefactors and Sponsors

The following Denver area firms, organizations and individuals have invested toward the quality production of this historic book and have thereby expressed their commitment to the future of this great city and to the support of the book's principal sponsor, The Denver Chamber of Commerce.

ABS Construction Management
AT&T — Long Lines
Air Rentals, Inc.
Allstate Insurance Company
Ambrose & Company
American Express Co.
*American Salesmasters, Inc.
Anadarko Production Company
Arthur Andersen & Co.
*Atlantic Richfield/Anaconda
Aurora Business Center
Bacon & Schramm, Inc.
Edwin W. Baker, Jr.
Bartholomew & Company
Bayly Martin Fay Inc. of Colorado
Bays Equipment, Inc.
Beech Aircraft Corporation
Behrent Engineering Company
R. H. Bell Co.
Dan Berich Inc.

Blinder Robinson & Co., Inc.
*Blue Cross and Blue Shield of Colorado
Boddington Lumber Co.
The Boeing Company
Charles J. Borg
Boulevard Colorado National Bank
*Boyd Distributing Company, Inc.
R. L. Branish
*The Brown Palace Hotel
Broyles, Allebaugh & Davis, Inc.
Builders Service Bureau, Inc.
*Burlington Northern, Inc.
Burns Realty & Trust Co.
N. Allen Burt
N. B. Burt
CH2M Hill Engineers
*Capitol Federal Savings and Loan Association
John H. Caton
*Central Bank of Denver
Champion Packaging
Lloyd G. Chavez
Harold L. Cherry
*The Children's Hospital
Circle Air Freight Corp.
Coldwell Banker Commercial Real Estate Services
The Collins Corporation

Colorado Container Corp.
*Colorado National Bank
Colorado National Mortgage Company
Colorado Petroleum Products Co.
Commission on Community Relations, City and County of Denver
Connecticut General Life
*Conoco Inc.
*Continental Airlines
Coopers & Lybrand
Craig's Distribution & Consolidation Co.
Dahl Sales
Dain Bosworth Incorporated
Davis Graham & Stubbs
Denver Consumers & Maddox Ice Service Co.
*The Denver Dry Goods Company
Denver Technological Center Executive Offices
Developments International Inc.
Downings
Denver Board of Water Commissioners
Drive Train Industries, Inc.
Duncan and Duncan, Realtors
Duncan-Allen, Insurors
Dutch Property Investments, Ltd.

Elcar Fence & Supply Co.
*Empire Savings
Exeter Drilling Northern, Inc.
Fairmont Hotel
*The Fairmount Cemetery Association
Fidelity National Title Insurance Company
First Denver Insurance Agency, Inc.
First Denver Mortgage Co.
*The First National Bank of Denver
First Parkview Coporation
Flying Tiger Line Inc.
*Frankel Manufacturing Company
*Frederic Printing
*Frontier Airlines
Garrett-Bromfield & Company
Gary Energy Corporation
*The Gates Rubber Company
Ann L. Goodro
Great-West Life
Great Western Construction Ltd.
C. R. Grice Associates, Inc.
Gulf Mineral Resources Co.
Rod Hall Company
A. S. Hansen, Inc.
The E. F. Hauserman Company
Harrison Western Corporation

DEN

CITY OF T

Claus Heppner & Associates
The C. F. Hoeckel B. B. & L. Co.
Houston International Minerals Corporation
Howard Needles Tammen & Bergendoff
Impact Environmental Consultants Ltd.
Information Handling Services
Jager & Company, Inc.
Jesuits of Denver
*Johns-Manville Corporation
*The Jolly Rancher Candy Company
*KBTV, Channel 9
*KOA Radio
*KOA TV
Keebler Company
*King Soopers, Inc.
Lakewood Ford, Inc.
Elaine E. Lakin
James E. Lakin
Clifford J. Lane
Lewis Associates, Inc.
*Howard Lorton Galleries
Machine Payroll Accounting Service, Inc.
Manufacturers Financial Services
*Martin Marietta Denver Aerospace
*May D&F
McGladrey-Hendrickson & Co.
*The A. E. Meek Trunk and Bag Co.
Metro Brokers
*The Midwest Steel & Iron Works Company
Mile Hi Employment Agency
*Mile High United Way, Inc.
*Mountain Bell
National City Bank of Denver
*C. A. Norgen Co.
Nu-West, Inc.
*Olinger's
Pacific West Exploration Co.
Peat, Marwick, Mitchell & Co.
Pennzoil Exploration & Production Co.
Pentax Corporation
Petroleum Information Corporation
Gerald H. Phipps, Inc.
Amos A. Plante
Port-O-Flex, Inc.
*Porter Memorial Hospital
Stuart M. Porter
*Presbyterian/Saint Luke's Medical Center
Priest Keenan Consultants
Allan G. Provost
*Public Service Company of Colorado
James E. Rawley and Co.
Realty World Corp. of Colorado and Wyoming
Regis College
Thomas R. Richards
Rine Mackenzie Smith
Melvin J. Roberts
*Robinson Dairy
*Rocky Mountain Empire Sports, Inc.
Rodriquez & Assoc., P.C., Certified Public Accountants
Rolm Corporation
*Rose Medical Center
*Frederick Ross Company
Sage Capital Corporation
*Saint Joseph Hospital
*Samsonite Corporation
*Seal Furniture & Systems, Inc.
*Sears
Security Life of Denver
Sheraton Denver Airport
Shwayder Real Estate Academy
J. H. Silversmith, Inc.
W. A. Smith and Associates
Sonnenblick-Goldman Corp.
Todd C. Stansfield
*Stearns-Roger Corporation
Steiner Corp.
Walton L. Stinson
*Sundstrand Corporation
The Susquehanna Corporation
Swingle Tree Company
Teaque Equipment Co.
Touche Ross & Co.
*United Airlines
*United Bank of Denver
*University of Denver
*Van Schaack & Company
Vanatta and Spelts, P.C.
Vantex Properties
Vinson Supply Company
Bill Wall Homes
Warren & Sommer Incorporated
*Watersaver Company, Inc.
Evelyn Weingardt
Richard Weingardt Consultants, Inc.
*Western Airlines
Western Electric
*Western Federal Savings
Western Filter Company
Allen I. Williams, Jr.
*Wright & McGill Co.
Zadelhoff & Associates, Ltd.

*Denotes Corporate Sponsors. The histories of these organizations and individuals appear in a special section beginning on page 186.

...e District Court of the United States for the Southern District of New York.

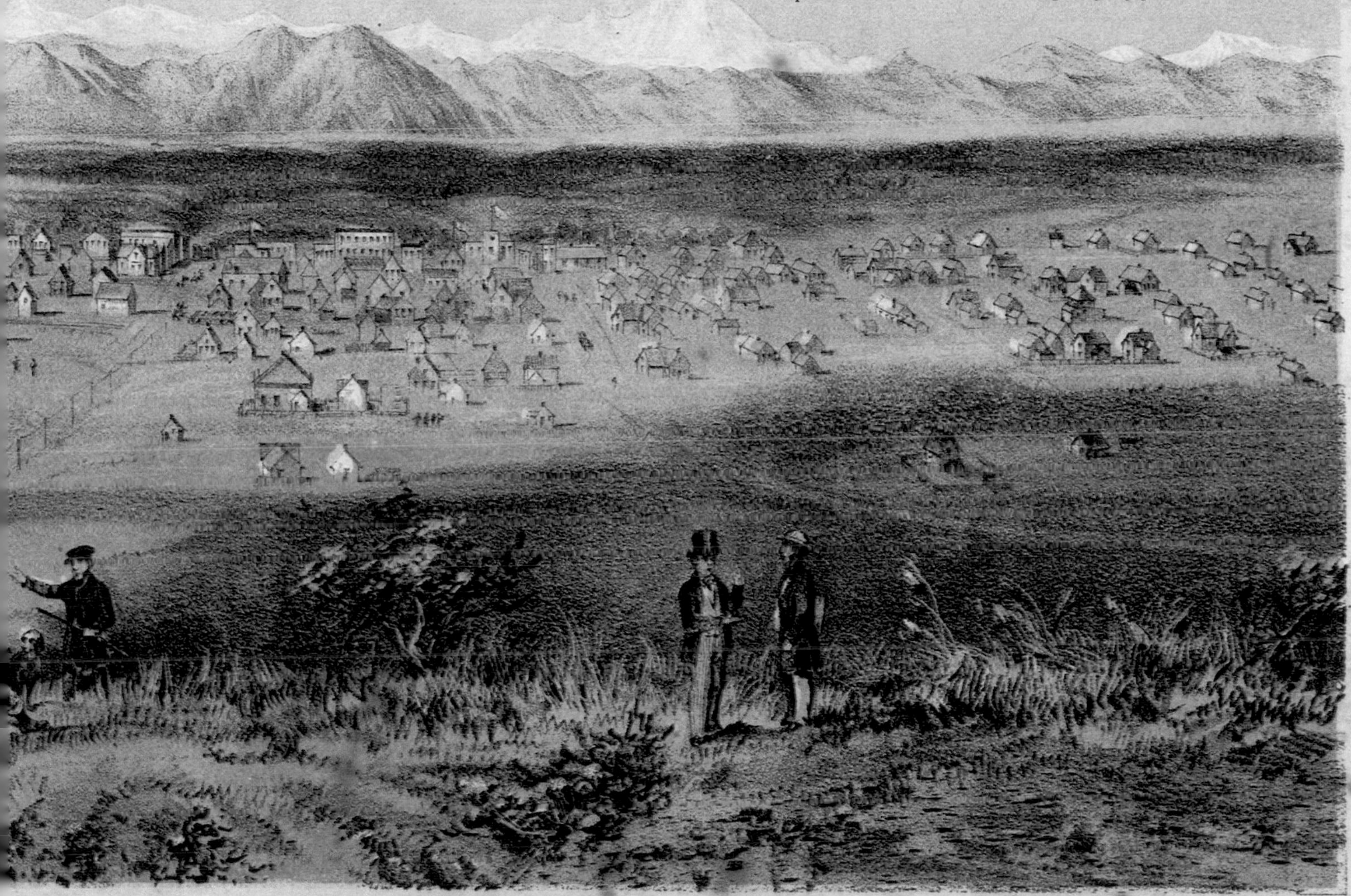

A. E. Mathews, Del.

R,

LAINS.

Seventeenth Street, with Union Station at its feet and the State Capitol at its head, became Denver's commercial hub by the early 20th century. Today, Seventeenth Street has become the booming Wall Street of the Rockies.

Contents

Cheyenne Indian village life on the present-day site of Denver, from a diorama in the Denver Museum of Natural History.

Wagons circle up in early-day street scene in Denver, 1865.

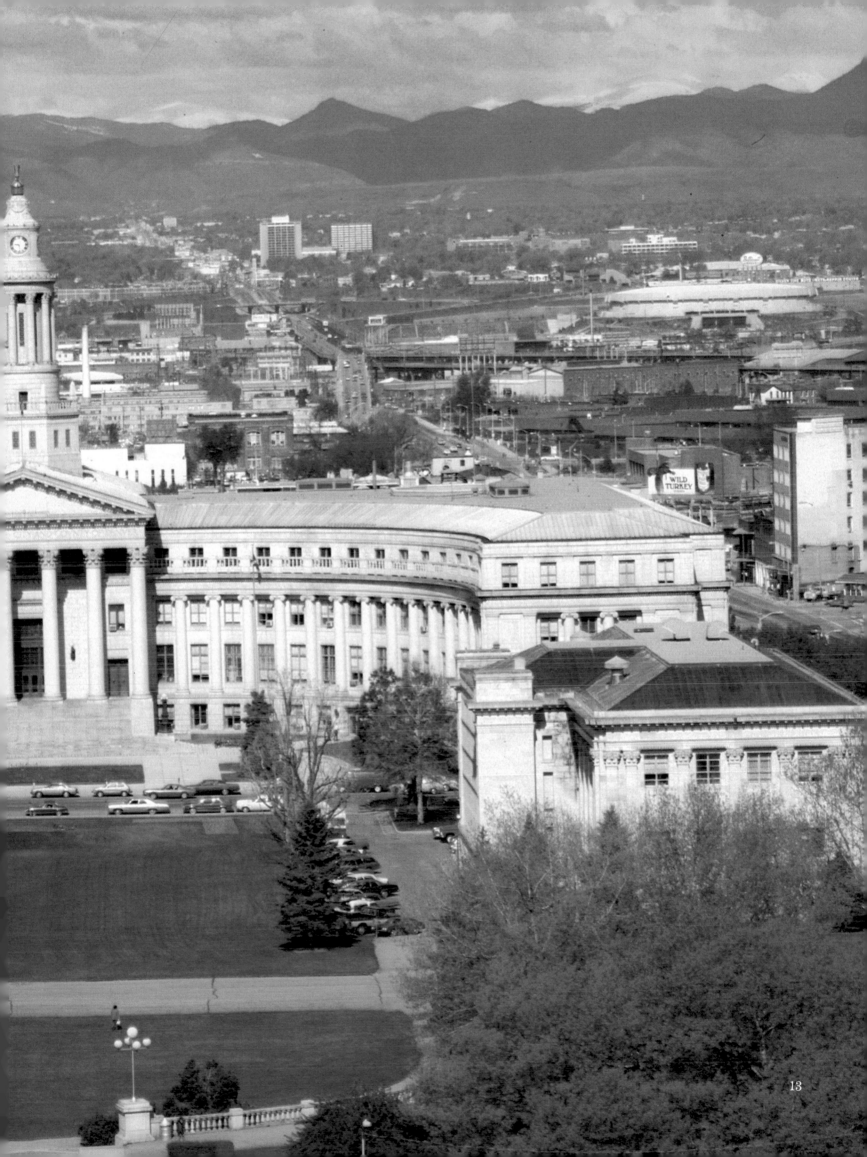

Major Stephen Long was the first to chart the Denver region in detail. On his map, Longs Peak is labeled Highest Peak, Pikes Peak is James Peak, Cherry Creek is Vermillion Creek and the Colorado High Plains are branded the Great American Desert.

PROLOGUE

Dawning

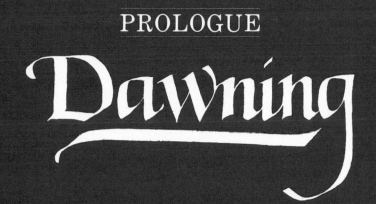

In washing away the mountains, rivers carried traces of placer gold that would tease Spanish, French and English explorers for centuries.

Ages before the townbuilders came, gold settled at the confluence of Cherry Creek and the South Platte River. It was one of many minerals washed down from the mountains. Over millions of years, it was deposited by magma-heated solutions from the gaseous and liquid core of the earth. The golden ores veined the ancestral range that existed before the present Rockies about 300 million years ago. Water, wind and ice wore down the peaks of this earlier range while inland oceans tore away their foothills. Some 40 million years after they surfaced, the ancestral Rockies were gone. Rivers carried some of their sediment eastward, creating the gently sloping High Plains. On this alluvial fan of melted mountains, the future site of Denver lay underwater for millions of years, rising as the mountains sank.

About 65 million years ago, volcanoes and other geologic disturbances gave birth to the present Rocky Mountains. Sediment from these mountains and from the ancestral range slowly filled the seas and lakes of the Denver Basin. At the Basin's western edge, the tilted hogbacks and red sandstone foothills rimmed the geologic bowl. Slowly over the eons, plants and animals emerged from the waters of the Denver Basin. (Tiny fossils and huge dinosaur bones have been found and other ancient fauna and flora had been compressed into coal and oil deposits that are now more valuable to Denver's economy than silver and gold.)

The South Platte River, which originates in the mountain valley known as South Park, carried traces of gold a hundred miles downstream to the future site of Denver. Sparkles in the sand teased Spanish, French and American explorers for two centuries before the gold rush.

Europeans had first discovered the South Platte in 1739 when a party of Frenchmen led by Pierre and Paul Mallet followed it into the future state of Colorado. They named the broad, shallow tributary of the Missouri the *Plate* (flat). The Mallets did not follow the Platte (as the Americans spelled it) far enough to find that it was not flat at its headwaters where it tumbled out of the Colorado Rockies.

That discovery awaited Major Stephen H. Long of the United States Army Corps of Topographical Engineers. In 1820 President James Monroe ordered Long and a small group—including a botanist, zoologist, geologist and an artist—to follow the South Platte to its source. After reaching Saint Louis, the Long Party steamboated up the Mississippi to the Missouri and then up the Missouri to its confluence with the Platte. Long followed the Platte until it divided into the North and South Platte. Sticking with the south fork, the American explorers reached its confluence with Cherry Creek on July 5, 1820.

The South Platte was bigger then—before dams and ditches and retaining walls—and ran fast, cool and delicious. In the river's cottonwood fringes, the Long party found Indian campsites and fascinating plants, birds and animals. Dr. Edwin James, the naturalist, marveled at the brilliant blue columbine, Rocky Mountain bighorn sheep and water ouzels. The party admired (but did not climb) the flat-topped peak later named for Major Long. A few days later, James did become the first recorded climber of Pikes Peak which lies 60 miles south of present-day Denver.

Rebuffed by the rugged South Platte Canyon, the Long Expedition headed back East. Long had failed to find the Colorado headwaters of either the South or the North Platte. And he discouraged settlement by labeling the High Plains the "Great American Desert" that might make a good reservation for Indians, but was uninhabitable by a people depending upon agriculture for their subsistence.

Yet to the south, another people were settling the Rio Grande River valley and planting villages on land just as arid as Long's desert. Both areas received less than fifteen inches of moisture annually, but the Spanish-Americans found that sufficient for farming and ranching in Southern Colorado.

Only itinerant hunters, trappers and traders followed Long's trail for the next four decades. During the heyday of the beaver pelt trade, they built forts just downriver from present Denver. (Forts Vasquez, St. Vrain, Lupton and Jackson are gone now, except for the Colorado Historical Society's adobe reconstruction of Fort Vasquez, where visitors can see remnants of the fur trade era.)

A hundred miles south of Denver, another river burst from the mountains with enough snow melt to carry it across the plains to the Mississippi. This was the Arkansas. Between the Arkansas and South Platte valleys, a ridge of ponderosa pine was the watershed for a creek which amazed plainsmen by flowing toward the mountains. Early travelers named it Cherry Creek for its wild chokecherries and followed it down the Divide to the Platte.

Reaching the confluence of the river and the creek, white men found that red men had been camping there for years. The Indians favored the spot particularly in the fall when they feasted on sunflower seeds, chokecherries and plums and obtained box elder sap for sweetening.

Francis Parkman, the historian, toured the South Platte in 1846. He found the four fur forts largely abandoned, their adobe walls cracked and crumbling. Nearby, Parkman's party found many cold Arapaho campfires and killed a snake with fourteen rattles.

Parkman lingered at the cottonwood grove at the mouth of Cherry Creek. There, the blue-blooded Bostonian noted Cherry Creek's "abundance of wild-cherries, plums, gooseberries and currants" and its lack of water. His party had to dig holes in the creek bed to find water for themselves and their horses.

Sometimes, late in the year, the South Platte also shrivelled up and hid underground from the hot sun and thirsty winds. Only a bed of sand bordered by cottonwoods remained. The junction of these puny waterways seemed an unlikely place to build a city.

In 1849, California gold infected Americans with what Mark Twain called the get-rich-quick-disease. The depression of 1857 left the country even more susceptible to gold fever. A year later, when a few yellow crumbs washed out of the Platte, a mass migration gave birth to Denver. During the gold rush, the South Platte became the major trail into Colorado.

Major Stephen H. Long led the first official U.S. exploration of the Denver region as commander of the expedition to Pikes Peak country, 1820.

Home of the Arapaho

NATIVE LIFE: The Arapaho Indians camped on the site of Denver (left) for decades before the gold rush. Little Raven (center) mingled freely with the city's white settlers (below).

A band of Arapaho continued to camp at the confluence of Cherry Creek and the South Platte for several years after the gold seekers settled the area in 1858. The Arapaho were a distinctive tribe with light skins and prominent Roman noses, (sometimes called the "big nose people"). Arapaho warriors left their women and children in Denver while they made war on the Utes in the mountains. After returning, the Arapaho invited white Denverites to their dog feasts and Ute scalp dances.

Little Raven, an Arapaho chief, was a familiar sight in early Denver. He often left his own handsomely decorated Denver teepee to talk with the whites in their strange square houses.

Friendly relations deteriorated when many Arapaho refused to sign the Fort Wise Treaty of 1861. Three years later, the Colorado Volunteers slaughtered many Arapaho and their Cheyenne allies at Sand Creek. Afterwards the Arapaho were shoved out of Colorado and onto reservations. Chief Little Raven complained in vain to the American Indian Commis-sioners, "It will be a very hard thing to leave the country that God gave us. Our friends are buried there, and we hate to leave these grounds…. That fool band of soldiers that cleared out our lodges and killed our women and children. That is hard on us. This is hard on us. There at Sand Creek—White Antelope and many other chiefs lie there; our women and children lie there. Our lodges were destroyed there, and our horses were taken from us there, and I do not feel disposed to go right off to a new country and leave them."

Twentieth-century Indians have returned often settling in the Capitol Hill neighborhood. In the 1970s, some moved out of the Eagle Lodge rehabilitation center, into traditional summer quarters in the front yard.

Over a century after the gold rush, the Mile High City is still booming. Since World War II, a million newcomers have settled in the 5,045-square-mile metropolitan area (Denver, Adams, Arapahoe, Boulder, Douglas, Gilpin and Jefferson counties). In 1980, the seven-county population swelled to more than 1.6 million with a predicted 2.4 million by 2000. According to a recent study, today's newcomers come in the largest numbers from California, Texas, Illinois, New York and Kansas, in that order. Once again, Denver glitters as it did in the golden beginning.

A smartly-dressed miner posed for one of the earliest
tintypes taken in Denver, about the time of the 1859
gold rush.

CHAPTER 1

> *"There is a company of five men working within two hundred yards of this place...today they have taken $5 out of a single pan of ore."*

olden rumors had drifted out of the Rocky Mountains for three centuries before the 1859 rush to Colorado. In 1540, Coronado followed the Rio Grande River north from Mexico looking for the legendary Cities of Cibola. He may have seen Colorado's gold-laced peaks shimmering on the horizon, but he turned east to the High Plains. Another Spaniard, Father Francisco Silvestre Velez Escalante, reported "open veins" of gold and silver in his diary of the 1776 pioneer expedition to cross the Colorado mountains.

Men of many nations had divined gold in the Rockies. Le Page du Pratz published *Histoire de la Louisiane* in Paris in 1758. It included a map showing a "mine d'or" on the upper Arkansas and mountain streams that "rolled down gold dust." Jonathan Carver, an English explorer, wrote that the Indians "of the Shining Mountains have gold so plenty among them that they make their most common utensils of it."

James Purcell, who left his Bardstown, Kentucky, carpentry shop to trap and trade in the Rockies, filled his "possibles bag" with gold from the headwaters of the South Platte. The American army explorer Zebulon Pike heard the story from Purcell in Santa Fe in 1806. When Pike's report was published in 1810, the world had another clue to the region's riches. Other army explorers, including John C. Fremont and Randolph B. Marcy, also reported rumors of the heavy, yellow metal.

Rumor became fact when William Greeneberry Russell's 1858 discovery of gold triggered the Colorado gold rush. Russell was a lanky, genteel Georgian. He might have been remembered—had he not found gold—for his dapper appearance. Others west of the Mississippi might hide behind bushy moustaches and wild whiskers, but not Green (as he liked to be called). He waxed and tweaked his lip hair into perfect points and braided his reddish beard into two neat pony tails.

Panning for gold

Green Russell's party found the paydirt that caused the Pikes Peak gold rush and gave birth to Denver in 1858. Russell also made a major discovery in Russell Gulch near Central City and wrote home to Georgia on June 17, 1859:

> *"The prospects in the veins or mountain diggings, as they call them here, is improving. There are now about 75 sluices in operation, all washing the ore taken from the veins, which is paying variously from $5 to $50 per day to the hand....There is a company of five men working within 200 yards of this place, on a vein which they lately discovered, and yesterday they carried the ore to the branch, washed it in a common box sluice, and made $125; and today they have taken $5 out of a single pan of ore."*

Green came from the gold belt of North Georgia where he grew up working family claims with his father. Gold had been found on Cherokee Indian land in 1828, two years before the tribe was shoved west on their "Trail of Tears" to the Oklahoma Indian Territory. Within a decade, their Georgia lands had been mined for an estimated $20 million.

Green had married into the gentle, civilized Cherokee nation. His wife's kinfolk chose him to lead an 1848 expedition to the California gold fields. Traveling overland along the Arkansas River to the Rockies, Green spotted promising outcroppings along the Front Range. But that year, it was California or bust.

Visions of Colorado's red sandstone foothills and gray granite peaks stayed with Green as he prospected the Sierra Nevada Mountains. He and his brothers returned to Georgia with plenty of California paydirt. Green bought a plantation, his brother Levi went to medical school in Philadelphia, and another brother, Oliver, mined the Georgia hills. Of an evening, the brothers remembered the Rockies. The money panic of '57 made their decision easier. During the gray Appalachian winter, Green and his two younger brothers began organizing a party of friends and relatives to prospect the Pikes Peak country.

In February of 1858, the Russells left Auraria, their home in the Lumpkin County gold region. After traveling to the Mississippi, they picked up the Arkansas River road to the West. They followed the Arkansas to a rendezvous in June with some old Cherokee friends from the Indian Territory.

John Beck, leader of the Cherokees and a Baptist preacher, insisted on Sabbath rests for both men and beasts. But when the company reached Bent's New Fort on June 12, the parson could not keep the boys from sampling Bent's booze. "We partook, at a cost of $1 per pint," reported the party's scribe, Luke Tierney, whose *History of the Gold Discoveries of the South Platte* appeared the following year. After drinks all around inside the fort, Oliver Russell was persuaded to bring out his travel-worn fiddle. Hours later, after the constellations had swung across the sky, Green listened as the mountain men, Mexicans, French Canadians and Indians of the fort shared yarns about the Shining Mountains. They spoke of Spanish mines and arrastras, of lost bonanzas littered with Spanish armor and skeletons. Long after Coronado gave up the search, New Spain's Seven Cities of Cibola remained an unforgettable hallucination. Not whether—but where—the gold lay in Colorado was the question in men's minds.

From a Georgia neighbor, Samuel Ralston, the Russells had a first-hand clue. Near where Green had seen croppings on his way to California, Ralston and a party of Cherokees had found color in 1850. They washed it from Ralston Creek, in the present-day Denver suburb of Arvada. With Ralston Creek in mind, the Russells left Bent's Fort. They followed the Arkansas to Fountain Creek and then cut north to the headwaters of Cherry Creek, prospecting as they went. They were Bible readers and believers in the Book of Job:

Surely there is a vein for silver,
And a place for gold where they find it.

Their patience, like that of Job, was eventually rewarded. Five miles south of today's Franktown, the Georgians found a few gold flakes. A huddle of shacks called Russellville went up within a few months, but its founders pushed on, looking for a bigger strike. Their creekside site in Douglas County became one of Colorado's first ghost towns.

Near Cherry Creek's confluence with the Platte, the Georgians found another tease of yellow in the sand. Green guided his men two miles up the Platte to Mexican Diggings, an 1857 Mexican-American enterprise. Only a few rumors survive of this operation which may have been the first non-Indian settlement in Denver.

At Mexican Diggings, the Georgians extracted some glistening grains from the Platte before moving three miles upriver to the mouth of Dry Creek. Dartmouth Avenue in Englewood now crosses the Platte where the three Russells and the ten men still with them washed out about seven ounces of gold during the first week in July. In those days, it was worth about $200. They called their diggings Placer Camp, never guessing it would become the cradle of the Colorado gold rush.

Placer Camp gold soon played out, and the Russells probed further up the South Platte before moving north to test Clear Creek, Ralston Creek,

A double log cabin shared by the Russell brothers and John Smith, a mountain man, was reportedly the first house in Denver. The sketch was made by one of the cabin's builders, Dr. Levi J. Russell.

FROM THE MAGIC LANTERN: Photographs painted with oil colors became lantern slides, preserving Denver (below), Russell Gulch (center) and General William Larimer in front of his cabin (bottom) in 1859.

A painting of Auraria in 1859 included strangely shaped cottonwood trees along the banks of Cherry Creek, as well as an oddly shaped Pikes Peak in the background.

Probably the city's first white settler, William McGaa was living on the site of Denver when Russell, Larimer and the other founding fathers arrived. As McGaa claimed title to Denver through his Indian in-laws, he was made an officer of both the Denver and Auraria town companies and had a major street named after him. The furry-tongued McGaa, who was usually in his cups, boasted about fathering the city and naming streets after some of his squaws—Wewatta, Wazee and Champa. He became such an embarrassment to respectable Denverites that they renamed McGaa Street–Holladay Street–and tried to forget this rough-hewn mountain man.

Boulder Creek and other Front Range canyons well into Wyoming. In September, the discoverers returned to their Dry Creek camp. They found a half-dozen tents and a swarm of men re-working their Placer Camp diggings. John Easter and a party from Lawrence, Kansas Territory, were laying out the town of Montana City.

Unwittingly, the Russells had triggered one of the largest and fastest mass migrations in history. Within three years, 35,000 would stream across the Great American Desert to establish a new territory. Word of the Placer Camp discovery was carried to the Missouri River towns by Indians and mountain men. Outfitters and storekeepers ballooned the $200 discovery into the Pikes Peak gold rush. By September 20, 1858, even the *New York Times* declared, "There is no longer any doubt of the auriferous region and its wonderful wealth." The *Times* notwithstanding, the '58 gold rush was largely goldless. Montana City evaporated. (All that survives is a tiny cabin relocated in Grant-Frontier Park, just south of Evans Avenue on the Platte. School children panning there today have about as much luck as the '58ers.)

Downstream at the Platte's confluence with Cherry Creek, another expedition from Kansas established the St. Charles Town Company in the fall of '58. Across the creek, the Russells constructed a double log cabin with old John Smith, a trader married into the Arapaho tribe. Smith and his sidekick William McGaa claimed land ownership through their squaws.

On October 30, 1858, part of the Russell Party, Smith, McGaa and other optimists formed a town company. Dr. Levi Russell named it Auraria (Latin for gold) after his hometown in Georgia. Auraria (where the Auraria Higher Education Center and Ninth Street Historic Park are now located) became the first permanent settlement within the modern metropolis.

Brilliant sunshine and a warm autumn coddled the Aurarians. In the clear air, golden aspen blazed on the foothills. One nippy morning, the

Russells saw white dust on the panorama framed by Longs and Pikes Peaks. As weeks of cabin building wore on, the snow crept down the mountains. When the first wet flakes reached Auraria, the Russells shivered and remembered Georgia.

With $500 in dust, Green and Levi started back to visit the homefolks, buy supplies and recruit men for a return in the spring. Oliver stayed, wintering in the Auraria cabin. On their way east that November, the Russells met a burly character at Bent's Fort. He called himself General Larimer, a title he had earned in the state militia of his native Pennsylvania. He was headed for the mines with a group from Leavenworth. The general seemed terribly curious. He was better at asking questions than at answering them. He kept asking if towns had sprung up. They had no idea that Larimer was determined to upstage the Russell's Auraria with his own town. "On our first night [at Auraria]," wrote Larimer's son, Will, "my father, without consulting anyone outside of our own Leavenworth Party, packed his blankets and some provisions, left camp and crossed the creek to pick out a new site.... When we finally reached the eastern side of Cherry Creek, we found him near the bank with a camp fire awaiting us. He had 4 cottonwood poles crossed, which he called the foundation of his settlement and claimed the site for a town." This was the St. Charles site, which Larimer jumped, quieting protestors with whiskey and shares of his Denver city town company. A veteran of Pennsylvania, Nebraska and Kansas town promotion, the general was a shrewd town boomer. He named his settlement Denver for Kansas Territory Governor James W. Denver, who had authorized the creation of Arapahoe County in the gold fields of western Kansas.

As donating agent of the Denver City Town Company, Larimer also gave town lots to Governor Denver. (Unknown to Larimer, Governor Denver had resigned by then to become commissioner of Indian affairs and did not visit his namesake until 1882, by which time his lots had gone to someone else.) Larimer also gave land to friends who were establishing the Leavenworth and Pikes Peak Express Company. The general knew that this stage company would make or break the aspiring "cities" of the Pikes Peak region.

On November 22, 1858, Larimer and his associates

A jumped claim called Denver

After jumping a claim on Cherry Creek, General William Larimer crossed four cottonwood sticks to stake out a town. On November 19, 1858, he wrote to the mayor of Leavenworth,

"This town, 'Denver City', is situated at the mouth of Cherry Creek where it forms its confluence with the South Platte. This is the point where the Santa Fe and New Mexico road crosses to Fort Laramie and Fort Bridger, also the great leading road from the Missouri River: in short, it is the center of all the great leading thoroughfares and is bound to be a great city."

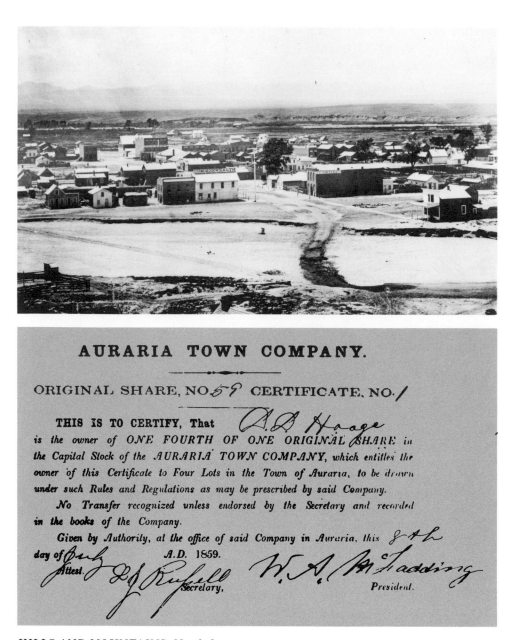

AURARIA TOWN COMPANY.

ORIGINAL SHARE, NO *59* CERTIFICATE, NO. *1*

THIS IS TO CERTIFY, That *O. D. Hooge* is the owner of *ONE FOURTH OF ONE ORIGINAL SHARE* in the Capital Stock of the *AURARIA TOWN COMPANY*, which entitles the owner of this Certificate to Four Lots in the Town of Auraria, to be drawn under such Rules and Regulations as may be prescribed by said Company.

No Transfer recognized unless endorsed by the Secretary and recorded in the books of the Company.

Given by Authority, at the office of said Company in Auraria, this *8th* day of *July* A.D. 1859.

Attest
L. J. Russell
Secretary.

W. A. McFadding
President.

HILLS AND MOUNTAINS: Nestled against the foothills was Auraria, seen in the early 1860s (top) with the dry bed of Cherry Creek in the foreground and the South Platte in the background; in 1859, shares (above) were issued in the capital stock of Auraria Town Company. Also in 1859, John H. Gregory (below) discovered gold in Clear Creek Canyon, which lured 10,000 argonauts into the mountains.

formed the Denver City Town Company. They platted the streets to parallel the river and the creek in an ambitious grid of 345 blocks, each divided into 32 lots 25 feet wide and 125 feet deep.

Larimer's dreams soon outgrew even this gigantic grid. On December 14, 1858, he waded across the icy South Platte and staked out the town of Highland. On the hill east of Denver, Larimer and his son Will mapped out another addition. Although Larimer had boasted that Denver's salubrious climate would revive even those on the edge of the grave, he and Will staked out Mount Prospect Cemetery. Soil was soon broken in this pioneer boneyard for gunshot victims and their murderers—in case the vigilantes caught them. (Today most of the bones are gone from the site of today's Denver Botanic Gardens and Cheesman Park.)

When the Russells returned in May of '59 with more Georgians, they found General Larimer, a Yankee, in charge. They also discovered that Auraria, formerly the larger settlement, was losing population and business to Larimer's Denver City Town Company. Denver's supremacy had been established when the first stagecoach came in the spring of '59. Hotels, saloons and other Auraria businesses crossed the creek to Denver to huddle around the stage depot built on a site donated by Larimer.

Green did not linger in Auraria but took his men prospecting up Clear Creek Canyon. The Georgians found it flooded with 10,000 argonauts and Horace Greeley, editor of the *New York Tribune*. From the rumor-ridden swarm of miners, Green learned that the diggings had been a bust until a Georgian by the name of John H. Gregory found gold on the North Fork of Clear Creek in February. By June, the hasty rise of Central City, Blackhawk, Nevadaville and other camps and towns made Gregory Gulch the most populous settlement in the Rockies.

Green sought out Gregory and found an illiterate, smelly character, a shaggy-headed, wild-eyed "cracker." Sudden wealth had excited Gregory. He wandered around muttering such things as, "Now my wife can be a lady and my young'uns can git educated." Then he sold his discovery claim and disappeared.

Other prospectors flitted around the Front Range like miller moths around a candle in June. Camps and towns popped up on Boulder Creek and on the headwaters of the South Platte and the Arkansas. Their gold gravitated to Denver where miners sold it to the Clark, Gruber and Company mint or shipped it east on the stage.

Four miles southwest of Gregory Gulch, Green found paydirt in Russell

Gulch. Realizing the crucial need for water to drink, to wash out ore and to supply the mountain towns, Green and others formed the Consolidated Ditch Company. Green was its president. He also established the community of Russell Gulch, where a thousand people soon congregated to scrape out as much as $35,000 a week in gold.

After a fall blizzard blanketed Russell Gulch, Green retreated to Auraria. There he met with Larimer and others to establish a territorial government. They elected Robert W. Steele, Green's partner in the ditch company, as governor of Jefferson Territory. (Jefferson Territory, however, was never recognized by the United States.)

General Larimer oversaw the 1859 establishment of the People's Government of Denver. He taxed town company shareholders to make

IN THEM THAR HILLS: Some 10,000 gold seekers traveled through Denver (left) to the Gregory Gulch Diggings in 1859 (top). Sluices (above) were commonly used in early-day placer mining.

Wheelbarrow McGraw hoped to gold plate his wheelbarrow by soaking it in Cherry Creek and then collect potato-sized nuggets in the mountains.

Cherry Creek Emigrant's Song

We expect hard times, we expect hard fare,
    Sometimes sleep in the open air;
We'll lay on the ground and sleep very
    sound,
    Except when Indians are howling
    around.

CHORUS:
Then ho boys ho, to Cherry Creek we'll go.
    There's plenty of gold
In the West, we are told,
    In the new Eldorado.

We'll rock our cradles around Pike's Peak
    In search of the dust, and for nuggets
    seek;
If the Indians ask us why we are there,
    We'll tell them we're made as free as
    the air.

The gold is there, 'most anywhere.
    You can take it out rich with an iron
    crowbar,
And where it is thick, with a shovel and pick
    You can pick it out in lumps as big as a
    brick.

At Cherry Creek if the dirt don't pay,
    We can strike our tents most any day.
We know we are bound to strike a streak
    Of very rich quartz among the
    mountain peaks.

Oh dear girls, now don't you cry,
    We are coming back by and by;
Don't you fret nor shed a tear,
    Be patient wait about one year.

Rocky Mountain News
June 18, 1859

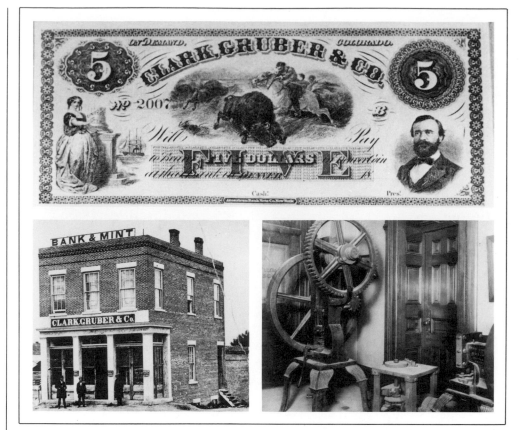

SIGNS OF GOLD: Clark, Gruber and Company printed gold notes (top) as well as producing $2.50, $5, $10 and $20 gold pieces. The minting machinery (above right) is now in the Colorado Heritage Center. The company's building (above left) stood at the corner of Sixteenth and Market Streets. After private mints were outlawed in 1864, the federal government took over the job in its Denver Mint; Clark, Gruber and Company became the nucleus of the First National Bank of Denver.

improvements and to puff the "city" in prospectuses and a lithographed map. Larimer also strove to unite Denver with rival Auraria. By moonlight on April 5, 1860, the towns celebrated a merger on the Larimer Street bridge. Auraria became West Denver and Highland became North Denver.

By the spring of 1860, the camp at the confluence had become an instant city of 4,749. Most of the newcomers on the streets did not recognize Green Russell, and he was not one to brag that his discovery had brought them there. Most of them were from Kansas, Nebraska, Iowa, Indiana, Illinois and Ohio. They were Yankees suspicious of a Georgian's drawl. The Russells learned to speak even less than usual.

A louder leader—General Larimer—sought to take charge. When President Abraham Lincoln and the federal government created Colorado Territory in 1861, the General scurried to Washington to solicit an audience with President Lincoln. As the founder of Denver City and Colorado's Republican Party, Larimer judged himself the obvious choice for the first territorial governor. But William Gilpin, an early and strong supporter of Lincoln, got the presidential nod.

That spring, a four-horse stage rolled up to Denver's Tremont House. Governor Gilpin emerged bowing, smiling and shaking hands. From a flag-decked balcony of the Tremont, Gilpin gave his inaugural address. Rebellion, he roared, would not be tolerated. Colorado would be loyal to Abraham Lincoln and the Union. On the fringe of the crowd, Levi Russell listened intently.

Quietly, Green, Levi and Oliver began selling their Colorado assets. They visited Russell Gulch—by then a booming community of 2,500—for the last time and told friends that they were planning a prospecting venture in southern Colorado. Actually, they hoped to slip out of

THE COUNTRY GROWS: After regular stage service began in May 1859, Denver emerged as the transportation hub of Colorado Territory. The Holladay Overland Mail and Express Co. Depot (left) on Market Street became Wells, Fargo and Company in 1866. Market Street was once called Holladay Street after the stagecoach company whose brick building still sits at its Fifteenth Street intersection. Pike's Peakers claimed mail at Denver's Overland House where the stage stopped. Because of the stiff 25-cent mail fee, many miners opened and read their letters, then returned them to the postmaster, claiming the letter was not for them and asking for their quarter back. In 1861, William Gilpin (below) was appointed first governor of Colorado Territory by his friend and political ally, President Abraham Lincoln.

Yankee-dominated Colorado before the inevitable war began. They left with other Georgians, including five of the Placer Camp pioneers. Their allegiance to the rebellious South cost the Russells fame and fortune in Colorado. When Green reached Georgia, he raised a company and fought Yankees to the end.

By 1872, Green figured the war was far enough behind him. He took his family by ox team over the old Arkansas River route hoping to find some old friends and collect old debts in Denver. Neither panned out. He left the foreign city that had arisen on his claims and headed once more for Georgia. Violent chills and fever struck him in Oklahoma. He died August 14, 1877 and was buried by strangers in the school yard of Briarwood, Oklahoma. Only his family and his old friends, the Cherokee, mourned.

Larimer had expired two years earlier on his farm outside Leavenworth. After failing to be appointed governor of Colorado Territory, he had run for mayor after Denver was officially chartered on November 7, 1861. Again Larimer lost. He denounced Denver's "lack of comforts" and rejoined his wife and family in Leavenworth. Shortly afterwards, as the Civil War intensified, he joined the Union Army and fought primarily to get a rank more august than captain. When the war ended, he retired to the family farm where he died in 1875.

Larimer's death was mourned in Denver, where the main street bore his name and he was honored as the city's founder. For Green, the rebel, there was only a forgotten campsite on Cherry Creek and a gulch and ghost town near Central City. But while the discoverer and the claim jumper deserted Denver, others went to work at the confluence of the river and the creek to build a city.

CHAPTER 2

Argonauts & early days

"*Brandy is intended for medicine, rainy days, and Fourth of July, and should always be used VERY sparingly...*" advised Byer's 1859 Gold Rush Guidebook. *It was also suggested: "Your ruffled shirts, standing collars and all kinds of fine clothing had better be left in your wardrobe at home. Discard all cotton or linen clothing; adapt yourself at once to woolen and leather; provide yourself with woolen underclothes...you may also leave your razor for you won't use it."*

William Newton Byers, founder of *Colorado's first newspaper, the* Rocky Mountain News.

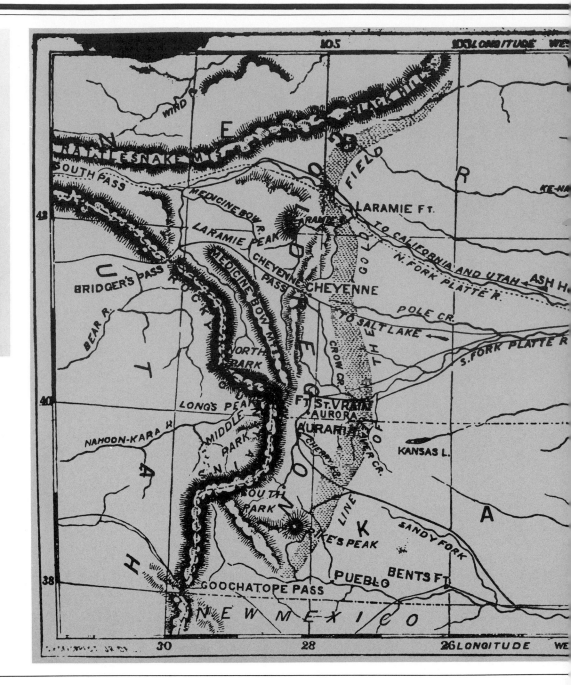

Miss Rose Kingsley, an English visitor, saw Denver in 1871 and marveled, "It looks just as if it had been dropped out of the clouds accidentally, by someone who meant to carry it further on, but got tired, and let it fall anywhere."

Denver had few visible means of support, little reason to become a city. It lacked the navigable waterways that usually explain cities, and other settlements were closer to the mines. In the decade after the gold rush, Denver faced the same problems that left the prairies and the mountains littered with ghost towns. Yet Miss Kingsley reported that the mile-high town was "one of the most successful of all the new cities of the West."

Why did Denver survive? How did it surpass many rival towns that also aspired to be the metropolis of the Rockies?

Gold in the nearby hills and the strategic location at the junction of the river and the creek led early miners to pitch their tents and build cabins on the site. But neither economic nor geographic factors alone explain why the town lived and flourished. Skilled promoters, energetic townbuilders and a proud and active population made the difference. Once

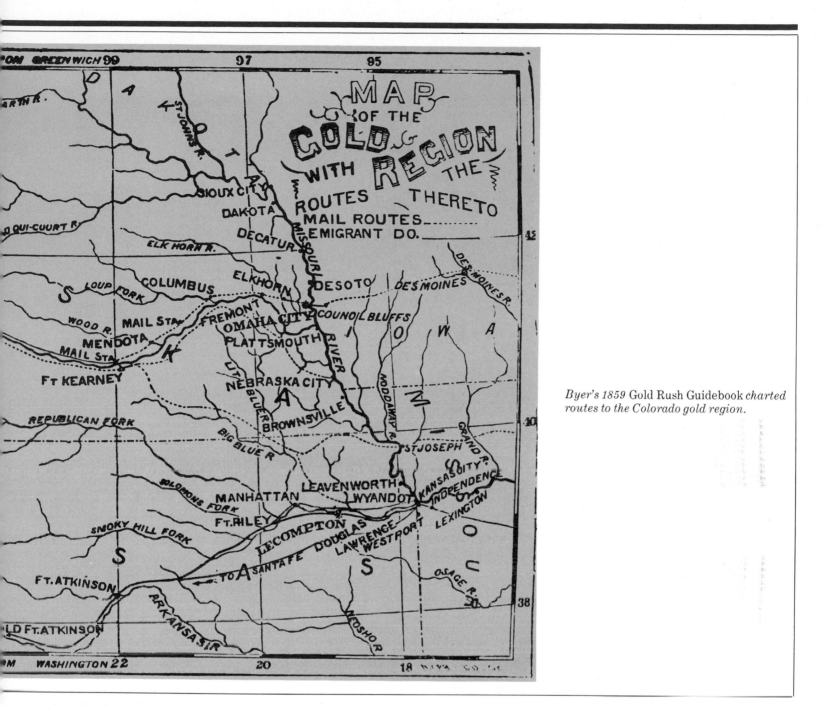

Byer's 1859 Gold Rush Guidebook *charted routes to the Colorado gold region.*

civic leaders identified problems and proposed solutions, Denverites, by and large, invested in their community. These human factors enabled the frontier crossroads to defy the odds and become a city.

Denver was blessed with capable townbuilders. Russell and Larimer planted the twin seeds of Auraria and Denver and watched them grow together. Before leaving the infant town, they met a young newspaperman from Omaha, William Newton Byers, who adopted the foundling. He became the community's watchdog and promoter. Except for a scandalous love affair, Byers might have been mayor and governor. He was a vigorous, self-educated man, encyclopedic in his interests and in his vision. He was involved in practically every aspect of urban growth. He carried the wine for the first party to climb Longs Peak. He experimented with grape vines and fruit trees. His newspaper covered everything — stray dogs, troublemakers, railroads and tourism.

Byers was born in 1831 to an Ohio farm family that later moved to Iowa. Young Bill thought the family farm no place for him. At nineteen, he went West with a surveying party bound for California. After bouncing around the West coast for several years, he settled in Omaha, a gateway

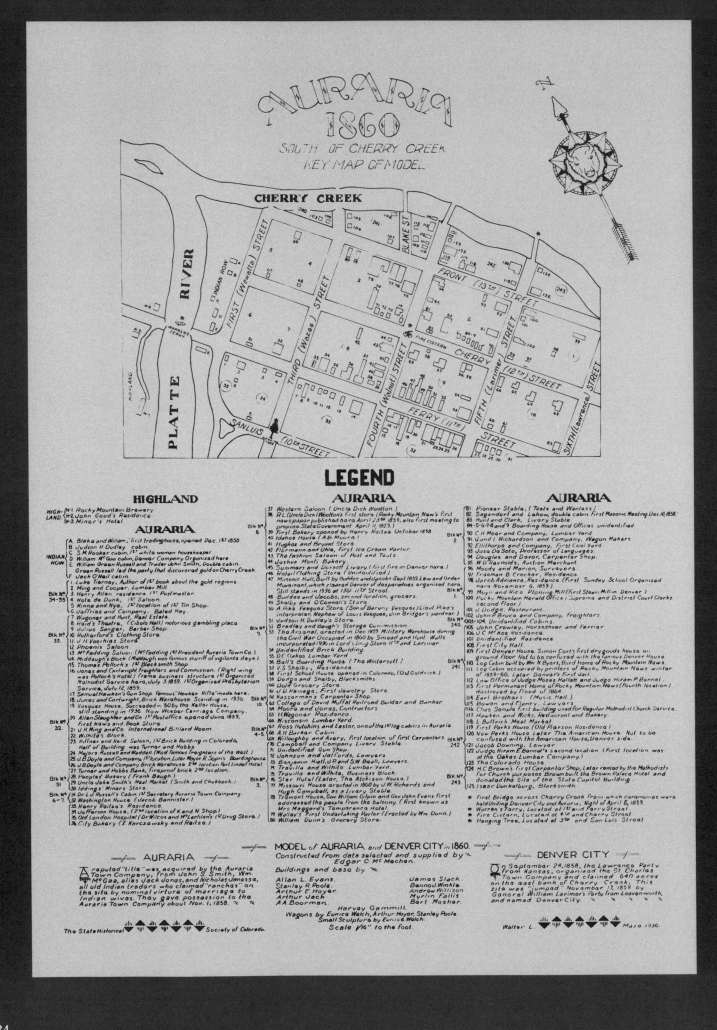

AURARIA 1860

SOUTH OF CHERRY CREEK
KEY MAP OF MODEL

LEGEND

HIGHLAND

HIGHLAND.
H-1 Rocky Mountain Brewery
H-2 John Good's Residence
H-3 Miner's Hotel

AURARIA

INDIAN ROW
A. Blake and William, First trading house, opened Dec. 1st 1858
B. Judson H. Dudley cabin.
C. S.M. Rooker cabin, 1st white woman housekeeper.
D. William McGaa cabin, Denver Company Organized here
E. William Green Russell and Trader John Smith, Double cabin. Green Russell led the party that discovered gold on Cherry Creek
F. Jack O'Neil cabin

Blk No 34-35
1 Luke Tierney, Author of 1st book about the gold regions
2 Ming and Cooper, Lumber Mill
3 Henry Allen residence 1st Postmaster
4 Hote de Dunk, 1st Saloon
5 Kinna and Nye, 1st location of 1st Tin Shop.
6 Jaffries and Company, Baled Hay
7 Wagoner and Hunt, Real Estate.
8 Reid's Theatre, ("Cibola Hall") notorious gambling place
9 Julius Sanger, Barber Shop.

Blk No 33.
10 Rutherford's Clothing Store
11 J.H. Voorhies Store
12 Phoenix Saloon
13 McFadding Saloon (McFadding 1st President Auraria Town Co.)
14 Middaugh's Block (Middaugh was famous sheriff of vigilante days.)
15 Thomas Pollock's 1st Blacksmith Shop
16 Jones and Cartwright Freighters and Commission. (Right wing was Pollock's Hotel.) frame business structure 1st Organized Methodist Service here, July 3, 1859. 1st Organized Presbyterian Service, July 12, 1859.
17 Samuel Hawken's Gun Shop, famous "Hawken Rifle" made here.

Blk No 32.
18 Jones and Cartwright, Brick Warehouse Standing in 1936
19 Vasquez House, Succeeded in '60 by the Keller House.
20 Allen Slaughter and Co. 1st Postoffice opened June 1859, First News and Book Store
21 J.H. Ming and Co. International Billiard Room

Blk No 31
22 Wilhite's Block.
23 Hillmer and Reid Saloon, 1st Brick Building in Colorado, Half of Building was Turner and Hobbs
24 Majors Russell and Waddell. (Most famous Freighters of the West)
25 J.B. Doyle and Company, 1st location, Later Mayor R Sopris Boardinghouse
26 J.B. Doyle and Company Brick Warehouse 2nd location Fort Lindell Hotel
27 Turner and Hobbs Bank, fireproof brick 2nd location.
28 Peoples' Bakery (Frank Baugh.)
29 Uncle Jake Smith's Meat Market (Smith and Chubbock.)

Blk No 6-7.
30 Iddings' Miners Store
31 Col Dr L J Russell's Cabin 1st Secretary Auraria Town Company.
32 Washington House (Jacob Bannister.)
33 Henry Reitze's Residence.
34 Jefferson House, (2nd location of K and N Shop)
35 Old London Hospital (Dr Wilcox and McLachlan's 1st Drug Store.)
36 City Bakery (E. Karczewsky and Reitze.)

AURARIA

37 Western Saloon (Uncle Dick Wootton)
38 R.L (Uncle Dick) Wootton's first store (Rocky Mountain News's First newspaper published here April 23rd 1859, also first meeting to propose State Government April 11, 1859.)
39 First Bakery opened by Henry Reitze October 1858.

Blk No 2
40 Idahoe House (A.B. Moore.)
41 Hughes and Bryant Store.
42 Florman and Uhle, First Ice Cream Parlor.
43 The Fashion Saloon of Rust and Teals.
44 Joshua Monti Bakery
45 Summers and Dorsett Livary (first fire in Denver here.)
46 Retail Clothing Store (Unidentified.)
47 Masonic Hall, built by Budden and Jacobs Sept 1859, Law and Order Movement, which cleared Denver of desperadoes organized here. Still stands in 1936 at 1361 11th Street.
48 Budden and Jacobs, second location, grocers.
49 Shally and O'Connell's Store.
50 A Pike Vasquez Store (Son of Barony Vasquez) Lieut Pike's interpreter. Nephew of Louis Vasquez, Jim Bridger's partner.
51 Judson H Dudley's Store.

Blk No 240.
52 Bradley and Baugh's Storage Commission.
53 The Arsenal, erected in Dec 1859 Military Warehouse during the Civil War Occupied in 1860 by Smead and Hunt. Walls incorporated in Kim Lord's Drug Store 11th and Larimer.
54 Unidentified Brick Building
55 D.C. Oakes Lumber Yard

Blk No 241.
56 Ball's Boarding House (The Winterzett.)
57 V.S Shelby, Residence
58 First School House opened in Colorado, (O.J Goldrick)
59 Dodge and Shelby, Blacksmiths
60 Dold Grocery Store
61 J.D. Ramage, First Jewelry Store.
62 Kassorman's Carpenter Shop
63 College of David Moffat Railroad Builder and Banker
64 Moore and Jonas, Contractors
65 H.Wagoner Residence
66 Wisconsin Lumber Yard
67 Ross Hutchins and Easter, one of the 1st log cabins in Auraria
68 A.H. Barker Cabin.
69 Willoughby and Avery, First location of first Carpenters

Blk No 242.
70 Campbell and Company Livery Stable.
71 Unidentified Gun Shop
72 Johnson and Jaffords, Lawyers
73 Benjamin Hast, J.R and S.W Beall, Lawyers.
74 Travilla and Wilhite, Lumber Yard.
75 Travilla and Wilhite, Business Block.
76 Star Hotel (Lefer, The Atchison House.)
77 Missouri House erected in 1860 by J.R Richards and Hugh Campbell, as a Livery Stable

Blk No 243.
78 Tremont House, Gov William Gilpin and Gov John Evans First addressed the people from the balcony. (First known as Mrs Maggard's Temperance Hotel.
79 Wolley's First Undertaking Parlor (Erected by Wm Dunn.)
80 William Dunn's Grocery Store.

AURARIA

81 Pioneer Stable, (Teals and Wanless)
82 Sagundorf and Lehow, double cabin First Masonic Meeting Dec 10, 1858
83 Hunt and Clark, Livery Stable
84-85-76 and 9 Boarding House and Offices unidentified
86 C H Moor and Company, Lumber Yard
87 U and I. Richardson and Company, Wagon Makers
88 Ellithorpe and Company, First Coal Yard
89 Jose De Soto, Professor of Languages.
90 Douglas and Dover, Carpenter Shop.
91 W D Reynolds, Auction Merchant
92 Moody and Marion, Surveyors
93 Freeman B Crocker, Residence
94 Jacob Adriance, Residence (First Sunday School Organized here November 6, 1859.)
95 Moyr and Rice Planing Mill (First Steam Mill in Denver)
96 Rocky Mountain Herald Office (Supreme and District Court Clerks second floor.)
100 J Dodge, Restaurant.
102 John P Bruce and Company, Freighters.
103-104 Unidentified Cabins
105 John Crowley, Horseshoer and Farrier
106 U C McKea Residence
107 Unidentified Residence
108 First City Hall.
109 First Denver House, Simon Cort's first dry goods house on ground floor Not to be confused with the famous Denver House.
110 Log Cabin built by Wm N Byers, third home of Rocky Mountain News.
111 Log Cabin occupied by printers of Rocky Mountain News winter of 1859-60, Later Denver's first Jail
112 Law Office of Judge Moses Hallett and Judge Hiram P Bennet.
113 First Permanent Home of Rocky Mountain News (Fourth location) destroyed by flood of 1864
114 Earl Brothers (Music Hall.)
115 Bowen and Clancy, Lawyers
116 Chas Semple first building used for Regular Methodist Church Service.
117 Hawken and Wicks, Restaurant and Bakery
118 L Bulfrich Meat Market
119 First Parks House (Old Pierson Residence)
120 New Parks House Later The American House Not to be confused with the American House, Denver side.
121 Jacob Downing, Lawyer
122 Judge Hiram E Bennet's second location (First location was at the Oakes Lumber Company)
123 The Colorado House.
124 H C Brown's first Carpenter Shop, Later rented by the Methodists for Church purposes Brown built the Brown Palace Hotel and donated the Site of the State Capitol Building.
125 Isaac Dunkelburg, Blacksmith

★ First Bridge across Cherry Creek from which ceremonies were held Uniting Denver City and Auraria, Night of April 5, 1859.
★ Warren's Ferry, Located at 1st and Ferry Street
★ Fire Cistern, Located at 4th and Cherry Street
★ Hanging Tree, Located at 3rd and San Luis Street

MODEL of AURARIA and DENVER CITY in 1860

Constructed from data selected and supplied by Edgar C McMechen

AURARIA

A reputed "title" was acquired by the Auraria Town Company, from John S. Smith, Wm. McGaa, alias Jack Jones, and Nicholas Janassa, all old Indian traders who claimed "ranchas" on the site by nominal virture of marriage to Indian wives. They gave possession to the Auraria Town Company about Nov. 1, 1858.

Buildings and base by

Allan L. Evans
Stanley R Poole
Arthur E Hoyer
Arthur Jack
A.A.Boorman

James Slack.
Bennou Winkle
Andrew Willison
Myrlin Fallis
Bart Mosher

Harvey Gammill
Wagons by Eunice Welch, Arthur Hoyer, Stanley Poole.
Small Sculpture by Eunice Welch.

Scale 1/16" to the foot.

DENVER CITY

On September 24, 1858, the Lawrence Party from Kansas, organized the St Charles Town Company and claimed 640 acres on the east bank of Cherry Creek. This site was "jumped" November 17, 1858 by General William Larimer's Party from Leavenworth, and named Denver City.

The State Historical ▼▲▼▲▼▲ Society of Colorado.

Walter L. ▼▲▼▲▼▲ Maze 1936.

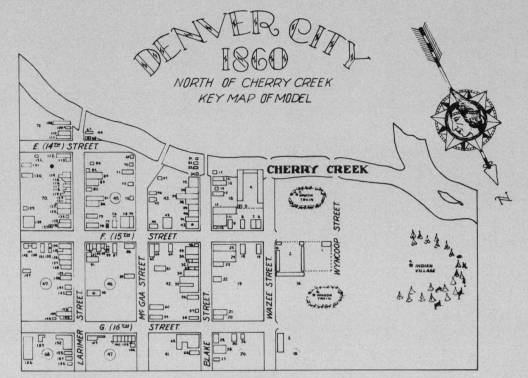

DENVER CITY 1860

NORTH OF CHERRY CREEK
KEY MAP OF MODEL

CHERRY CREEK

E. (14TH) STREET.
F. (15TH) STREET.
G. (16TH) STREET.

LARIMER STREET · McGAA STREET · BLAKE STREET · WAZEE STREET · WYNCOOP STREET

WAGON TRAIN · INDIAN VILLAGE

LEGEND

DENVER

*A. Cheyenne - Arapaho Village, windbreaks were typical of Arapaho tribe.
*B. and C. Wagon Trains in Corral.
1. Emigrant Corral, opened by Von Laun and Howard. Later owned by Taets and Post.
2. Mammoth Corral.
3. Al City Hospital, opened by Drs. J.F. Hamilton and U.D. Loss. Later Hotel for invalids; then the Buffalo House.
4. Elephant Corral, most famous emigrant corral in the Rocky Mountains.
5. Nichol's cabin only house erected by St. Charles Town Company. Home of John Postal and Squaw, Sister of Chief Left Hand of the Arapahoes, whose daughter married Thos. Fitzpatrick, famous Indian Agent. Later Hank Way's Blacksmith Shop.
6. A McCune and Company, Paint House.
7. Tritch Hardware, 2nd location.
8. Burton and Higgins, auction and storage.
9. Cooke and Sears, Later C.E. Cooke and Co., general auction.
10. Brandlinger's Cigar Store 1st Cigar Store in Denver 1st Cabin on Street.
11. Cooke and Company, commission and storage. Temporary home of the Overland Express.
12. Denver House, opened January 1859 by Blake and Williams. Horace Greeley spoke here May 7, 1859. Managed by Elbridge Gerry, noted trapper. Later a tough gambling hall, and site of the Palace Theatre.
13. Nye, Bradley and Company, hardware and miner's supplies 1st location.
14. Blanton and Company, general merchandise, 1st location.
15. Baldwin, Pegram and Co., provisions, hardware and clothing.
16. Pouvanski and Cunan, New York Clothing Store.
17. Louisiana Lunch Room. Most celebrated murder in Denver's early history (The Gordon Case) occurred here.
18. Simon Cort, Clothing Merchant.
19. Carr and Company, General Merchandise.
20. Hinkley's Express, early express line to the mountains.
21. Missouri House of P. O'Connor, 3rd location.
22. Unidentified cabin mentioned by Wm. N. Byers.
23. M.C. Fisher 1st Chemist.
24. Copeland, Townsend and Brezer, Commission Merchants.
25. Leavenworth and Pike's Peak Express, 1st permanent home.
26. Unidentified Lumber Yard.
27. Unidentified cabin, mentioned by Wm. N. Byers.
28. G.D. Bayaud and Co. Liquor stores of E.B. Waterbury and Geo. D. Boyd.
29. S. Reynolds, family apartment.
30. T.J. Bayaud's building. Occupant unidentified.
31. Stickney's House.
32. Unidentified house. Location established by Supreme Court records.
33. Edwards and Jacobs.
34. A.D. Steinberger and Wm. H. Bates, real estate.
35. B.H. Blanton and Company, merchandise, 2nd Location.
36. Gasnier Blacksmith Shop.
37. Mountain Boys Saloon and Ball Alley, front part 1st residence of H.P.A. Smith, 1st Probate Judge of Arapahoe County, K.T. Later the Empire House.
38. Tottam and Rogers Store.
39. Stag Hall Saloon.
40. Jos. Freeman's Indian Trading Post. Formerly owned a Trading Post near old Fort Laramie, mentioned in Parkman's "Oregon Trail".
41. City Bakery of Karczewsky. 1st location Auraria, Alden's Hotel.
42. Russell and Marshead's Wholesale House. Wm. H. Russell of Pony Express fame. Later became Cherokee House where the great fire of April, 1863, started.
43. B.F. Dalton and Company, Clothing Store.
44. Club House Saloon, where Pat Kelley killed Richard Doyle.
45. Melvin Hauser.
46. Primitive Log Cabin, mentioned by Wm. N. Byers.
47. Primitive Log Cabin, mentioned by Wm. N. Byers.
48. Shaw, Bailey and Co. Meat Market, Jos. E. Bailey. Later operated Bull's Head Corral, and helped organize Denver Union Stockyards. Corner later was Cheesman Drug Store, 3rd location of Mount's Bank.
49. Keith and Bond, auction-commission. Later Daniels and Brown Store, forerunner of Daniels and Fisher Stores Co. Site later covered by Cheesman's Drug Store.
50. Sutherland House, Later the Platte House, and then Hamaway's first Police Station where first Police (Night Police) had Headquarters here, John W. Schlagle, Supt.
51. Ford's Barber Shop. Barney L. Ford, negro proprietor. Later built fashionable restaurant here, and in the 70's erected Inter-Ocean Hotels in Denver and Cheyenne.

DENVER

52. Heatley and Chase's Progressive Club Original business venture most famous gambling firm in Denver's History.
53. Simon, Seamon and Company, tobacco merchants.
54. Empire Bakery of John J. Rothman, who became one of the leading real estate men in Denver.
55. Jones and Cartwright Building Famous Santa Fe Freighters. Left Store occupied by Sutherland Drug Co. Center by Jones and Cartwright; Right by Pioneer fur trader Thos. Boggs and Ceran St. Vrain.
56. Forrest Bros. and Company, Bankers, later the Miner's Bank.
57. Mud Render Cabin, mentioned by Wm. N. Byers.
58. Missouri Hotel, 2nd location.
59. Clark, Gruber and Co., private bank and mint, purchased by U.S. Treasury Dept, which established U.S. Mint here. Original Clark, Gruber minting machinery now in State Museum Bldg.
60. Stockton and Company, Furniture.
61. Charles A. Lawrence Livery Stable.
62. Garrish and Co., Grocery Store 2nd location. Denver City Council met here in November, 1860.
63. Karr and Soula, Grocery and Hardware.
64. Kinna and Nye, Stoves and Hardware.
65. Planters House, famous Pioneer Hotel, originally Bradford's Corner, home of the C.C.O. and P.P.Ex. and Stage Co. Post Office.
66. Rosenfield's Confectionary and Fruit Store, Later Mrs. Kern's Boarding House.
67. Collier and Clancy, Real Estate. D.C. Collier later founded and edited Miners Register, Central City.
68. C.P. Stout, 1858 Cabin 1st President of Denver Town Company. Present Police Building occupies this Site.
69. Denver and Auraria Reading Room and Library in log cabin of Sam Kinna. 1st Public Library and 1st Museum. 2nd location of Rocky Mountain News, 1st location of Lydia Maria Ring's School.
70. Residence of Jesus Abreu, old mountain man.
71. Tilton and Company's Store, once occupied as City Hall.
72. Primitive log cabin of Jose Marival, old mountain man.
73. Log Cabin of Henry Swaigart, later 1st store room of M.C. Fisher pioneer chemist.
74. J.F. Russell and Co., Paint Shop, 1st location Geo. Tritch's Hardware.
75. Tappan and Company, Commission Merchants.
76. Cook and Company, Commission Merchants.
77. Hickory Rogers, one of the 1st Six cabins in Denver in 1858.
78. Meyers and Co., Drug Store; later Graham's City Drug Store. 1st meeting of vigilantes on Second Floor July 28, 1860.
79. Denver Meat Market, later Stansbury's Old Tambem Saloon.
80. Metropolitan Billiard Saloon.
81. Greenleaf and Brower, Dry Goods. Greenleaf was pioneer poet, known as Potar Punsear. In spring of 1861, building occupied by David H. Moffat's Stationery Store and U.S. Post office.
82. Brown Brothers Bank 1st Bank in Denver.
83. Apollo Theatre 1st theatrical performance, Oct. 3, 1859, by C.R. Thorne and Co. Later, Jack Langrishe's Peoples' Theatre Erected by Gunnell and Barney, opened Aug. 1859 as Gunnell Hall. 1st convention of Provisional Government, Jefferson Territory held here Oct. 10, 1859.
84. Eldorado Hotel, Lower House of Provisional Assembly, J.T. met here. Legislature of Colorado Territory met 2nd floor in 1866.
85. District Clerk's Office.
86. Log Cabin, mentioned by Wm. N. Byers.
87. 1st location Missouri House.
88. Guiraud's French Store. 1st Catholic Service by Bishop J.B. Miege, of Leavenworth, Kansas. Later Site of Charpiot's Restaurant.
89. Buckley and Rice, store, 1st Episcopal Service by Rev. J.H. Kehler.
90. Wallingford and Murphy's Mercantile House. Confederate Flag raised here at outbreak of Civil War. Later, Military Prison.
91. Criterion Saloon, 1st proprietor, Ed. Jumps, 2nd Charles Harrison. 3rd Count Murat. Under Harrison's management Criterion became a resort of criminals.
92. Meyer and Company Drug Store, 1st location.
93. to 98. Lawrence and Dorset corner, six Frame buildings occupied by Saloons, grocery Stores, etc. These 2 Lots once offered for Yoke of Oxen and offer refused. Site of Pioneer Building.
99. C.A. Lawrence cabin 1858 one of 1st six cabins in Denver.
100-105. Beverly D. Williams Corner 6 buildings; Store adjoining alley. 2nd location of Lydia Maria Ring's School. Williams 1st Delegate from Jefferson Territory.

DENVER

106. Unidentified Log Cabin, mentioned by Wm. N. Byers.
107. Unidentified Saloon and Billiard Hall, mentioned in Hall's History.
108. Summers and Dorsell Livery Stable, 2nd location.
109. Geo. Wyncoop and Company, Real Estate. Claim Club's Office.
110. 1st Jefferson Legislature met here. Owner Unidentified.
111. St. James and 1st train Mercantile Store. 1st Store in Denver City, 1st Station of the Leavenworth and Pike's Peak Express. (Temporary)
112. J.H. Howard Jewelry Company.
113. 1st Federal Post Office in Denver City; Geo. McClure, Cabin built by Isador Bndolat, early squatter.
114. J.H. Dudley and Company, Real Estate.
115. Unidentified Store Building.
116. Henry Murat's Barber Shop.
117. Unidentified Cabin.
118. R.W. Roath, Pioneer Jewelry Store.
119. G. Wakely, Skylight Ambrotype Room.
120-121. Unidentified Buildings.
122. Nathan's Empire Clothing Store.
123. Unidentified Building.
124. 1st location in Denver City of Wm Graham's Drug Store and News Depot of H.F. Pierce and Company. Later, Schwenki Denver Vinegar Factory.
125. Variety Bazaar, L.N. Greenleaf and Company, Original Location.
126. Clayton, Lewis and Company, Merchants. Geo. W. Clayton Founded Clayton College for boys.
127. Wm. H. Larimer Cabin, 1st completed building in Denver City, finished November 25, 1858. (First glazed windows)
128. C.C.O. and P.P. Express Barns; also headquarters for Western Stage Company.
129. Fisher and Rogers Lumber Company.
130. Wyatt and Whitsitt, Real Estate and Law. 1st Office of Denver Town Company.
131. Kansas House of Samuel Dolman.
132. 1st Denver Residence of Henry Murat. Later site of old Chamber of Commerce Building.
133. Moyn and Rice, double cabin one of the 1st six in Denver 1858.
134. New York Store of Stuttcox Bros, Dry Goods. 2nd Floor Gov Gilpin's executive and military headquarters.
135. Arcade Saloon of Lawrence and Ely. Later, Salomon Schuline, Clothing.
136. Owned by Moyn and Rica, occupant unidentified.
137. St. Louis Clothing Store.
138. Garrish and Company 1st location, groceries and Hardware.
139. Ed Sanderline's Barber Shop. Popular negro barber for many years.
140. Fosdick and Cheever, Engineers and Real Estate 1st location.
141. Unidentified Log Cabin mentioned by Wm. N. Byers.
142. Unidentified Log Cabin mentioned by Wm. N. Byers.
143. Unidentified Log Cabin mentioned by Wm. N. Byers.
144. Scott U. Anthony and Frank Palmer, Land Agency and Real Estate.
145. Enos McLaughlin's Residence, 2nd floor. Miss A.E. Carpenter's Millinery Shop.
146. Clark and Recorder's Office. 2nd Office of the Denver Town Company (Chas. G. Cheever, Clerk, and R.E. Whitsitt).
147. Sanderline's Residence.
148. to 150. Jacob Gregory's Cabins.
151. Moyn and Rica Carpenter Shop and Furniture.
152. Broadwell House, most famous hotel in early Denver Owned by J.M. Broadwell January 25, 1860. Later the Pacific House, and still later, the Broadwell.
153. Unidentified Log Cabin mentioned by Wm. N. Byers.
154. Unidentified Log Cabin mentioned by Wm. N. Byers.
155. Unidentified Log Cabin mentioned by Wm. N. Byers.
156. The Denver Theatre, most famous of Denver's early theatres. Built as the Platte Valley Theatre, by Sam. G. Hunter and associates. Later bought by Geo Harrison, owner of the Montana Theatre in Central City, and still later, operated by Jack Langrishe and Pat Doherty.
157. Willoughby and Avary's Carpenter Shop.

● First Townsite Stake Driven Here

Walter L. Maze, 1936.

In the Summer of Sixty

1

In the summer of sixty, as you very well know,
The excitement at Pike's Peak was then all the go;
Many went there with fortunes and spent what they had
And came back flat-busted and looking quite sad.

2

'Twas then I heard farming was a very fine branch,
So I spent most of my money in buying a ranch;
And when I got to it, with sorrow and shame,
I found a big miner had jumped my fine claim.

3

So I bought a revolver and swore I'd lay low
The very next fellow that treated me so;
I then went to Denver and cut quite a dash
And took extra pains to show off my cash.

4

With a fine span of horses, my wife by my side,
I drove through the streets with my hat on one side;
As we were a-goin' past the old "Denver Hall,"
Sweet music came out that did charm us all.

5

Says I, "Let's go in and see what's the muss,
For I feel right now like having a fuss."
There were tables strung over the hall,
Some was a-whirling a wheel with a ball.

6

Some playin' cards and some shakin' dice
And lots of half dollars that looked very nice;
I finally strayed to a table at last
Where all the poor suckers did seem to stick fast.

7

And there stood a man with cards in his hand,
And these were the words which he did command,
"Now, gents, the winning card is the ace,
I guess you will know it if I show you its face."

8

One corner turned down, it's plain to be seen,
I looked at that fellow and thought he was green,
Yes I looked at that feller and thought he was green,
One corner turned down, 'twas so plain to be seen.

9

So I bet all my money and lo and behold
'Twas a trey spot of clubs and he took all my gold.
Then I went home and crawled into bed
And the devil a word to my wife ever said.

10

'Twas early next morning I felt for my purse
Biting my lips to keep down a curse;
Yes, 'twas early next morning as the sun did rise
You might have seen with your two blessed eyes,

11

In an ox wagon, 'twas me and my wife
Goin' down the Platte river for death or for life.

Louise Pound, *Folksongs of Nebraska and the Central West,* 1915.

BUILDING PIONEER: Libeus Barney (left), builder and proprietor of Apollo Hall, left a splendid account of early-day Denver in his Letters of the Pike's Peak Gold Rush. *The pioneer saloon (below), a white frame building constructed in 1859 on Larimer Street, served as the city's first theater, first city hall and was even used for early church services.*

BUT NO ELEPHANTS: Going West "to see the elephant" was the thing to do in the 1850s for "the elephant" often meant the California or Colorado gold regions. That popular expression led to the naming of Denver's first transportation hub (inset), the Elephant Corral, located between Fourteenth and Fifteenth and Wazee and Blake Streets. The pioneers bought, sold, swapped and rented horses, mules, oxen and cattle, but not elephants. Out of this livestock exchange evolved Denver's National Western Stock Show. The corral has survived as a lower downtown landmark, shown (left) in 1937 and was restored in 1980.

During Denver's early years, townsfolk built on the usually dry bed of Cherry Creek, despite warnings from the Indians. When the flood came in 1864, it carried away the Rocky Mountain News office and many other buildings. Also before the rains, inside the newspaper office (left), the staff stayed armed to repulse violent critics who tried to string up editor Byers. The fearless newspaperman continued to condemn Denver's lawless "bummers" as in the warning of July 18, 1860: "The rowdies, ruffians, shoulder-hitters and bullies generally that infest our city had better be warned in time, and at once desist from their outrages upon the people. Although our community has borne their lawless acts with fortitude, very nearly akin to indifference, we believe that forebearance has ceased to be a virtue....One more act of violence will at once precipitate the inevitable fate; and the terrors that swept over the fields of California at various times, and first purified its society, will be re-enacted here with terrible results to outlaws and villains, or else we are no judge of the determined countenances, compressed lips and flashing eyes that we have so frequently met in the last few days."

brilliant feats of arms in Indian warfare, the recent campaign of our Colorado Volunteers will stand in history with few rivals, and none to exceed it in final results," he wrote "All acquitted themselves well, and Colorado soldiers have again covered themselves with glory."

A few Denverites pointed out that the harsh punishment of peaceful Indians at Sand Creek might have been reserved for white troublemakers who were a greater threat to the stripling community. The need for law and order became apparent to editor Byers soon after he located his first office on the second floor of Uncle Dick Wootton's saloon. *News* editorials condemning the town's "bummers" sometimes came to the attention of gun slinging ruffians drinking below. They fired their responses through the ceiling and threatened to give Byers a necktie party.

Byers added extra planks to his floor, armed his staff and decorated the office with vigilante posters. He and other city fathers condoned vigilante justice and the election of "Judge Lynch." They deemed such measures necessary because the law enforcement officials of "Bleeding Kansas" were some 500 miles away and preoccupied with the Civil War.

Judge Lynch and the vigilantes often worked at night. In the morning, Denverites found corpses dangling from cottonwoods. Sometimes there was an explanation, such as the note found with former city councilman John Shear: "This man was hung. It was proved that he was a horse thief." According to North Denver folklore, the monstrous cottonwood at 1629 Platte Street was a hanging tree. Until it collapsed in 1980, the tree leaned over the street, supposedly from the weight of suspended criminals. The last legal Denver hanging came in 1886, twelve years after a chief of police was appointed and a uniformed, professional police department organized. As the harsh treatment of both red and white men suggests, townbuilding was often a violent process. Gentler refinements were left to a few pioneer women and preachers. Many men were preoccupied with dispossessing the Indians and bringing law and order to the frontier. But in their way, these gentler folk worked just as hard to civilize the would-be city.

CLEANING UP THE CITY: The first "rogue's gallery" of Denver was started by Sam Howe (upper right) in May 1885; the photo (top) was taken in 1900, with Chief of Police John F. Farley in the center. Judge Lynch quickly disposed of city malefactors such as Sam Dougan, shown here (above) in his final photo, taken in 1868.

*Wolfe Hall (above), an Episcopal school at
Seventeenth and Champa Streets, in 1870; it
was replaced in 1889 by the still-standing
Boston Building.*

CHAPTER 3

Sky-pilots & leading ladies

Sky pilots—as Denverites called their first clergymen—struggled to refine the frontier crossroads.

WOMEN'S TOUCH: Margaret Gray Evans (below), wife of Governor John Evans, was involved in many charitable activities. The Ladies Relief Home (bottom), founded in 1875 on West 38th Avenue, continues to be one of the best of many Queen City retirement homes.

While their husbands resorted to necktie justice, some pioneer women addressed the social problems often underlying crime. A few handed out food to every beggar who knocked on the door and tried to find yard or house work for every tramp. But as the number of destitute transients washed into Denver climbed into the hundreds, kind individuals could no longer handle the situation in such a manner. Concerned they banded together to organize charitable institutions.

Elizabeth Byers, wife of the newspaper editor, helped organize the Ladies Union Aid Society in 1860. This pioneer charity aided many hungry, sick, homeless and destitute people. In 1874, Margaret Gray Evans (wife of Colorado's second territorial governor), Elizabeth Byers and some of their friends, created the Ladies Relief Society. This group dispensed food, clothing and fuel, built homes for the poor and the aged and established a kindergarten, a day nursery, a free medical clinic and the Old Ladies Home (which still does saintly work on West 38th Avenue).

Various private and church charities worked in 1887 to create the Charity Organization Society, an umbrella group to coordinate and raise funds for all social services. (Ultimately, the Charity Organization Society became the Community Chest and then America's first United Way. This Denver idea of a consolidated eleemosynary fund raising has since been adopted by many other cities.)

Sky pilots—as Denverites called their first clergymen—also struggled to refine the frontier crossroads. General Larimer asked George W. Fisher, a member of his town company, to hold a service on November 21, 1858. Fisher, a carpenter and lay Methodist preacher, obliged with the first church service in the Cherry Creek hamlets. About a dozen men and two Indian squaws gathered at Russell's end of the double log cabin in Auraria for the prayer meeting while gambling went on in John Smith's half.

The next summer, two Methodist ministers were sent to Cherry Creek by the Kansas-Nebraska Conference. They held services in the cabin belonging to one of them, Reverend Jacob Adriance. Young Adriance, blessed with a fine voice, toured the streets singing hymns before the prayer meetings. Denverites left tents, cabins, saloons and gambling "hells" to follow the pied-piper preacher.

Southern Methodists built the first structure used solely as a church in the fall of 1860 at Fourteenth and Arapahoe streets. Shortly afterwards, the Southern Methodists went home to fight the Civil War, but Northern Methodists stayed to erect the Lawrence Street Methodist Church. Twenty-eight years after Reverend Adriance arrived, the Methodists moved into Trinity Church at Eighteenth and Broadway. (The church's shapely spire is now backdropped by boxy skyscrapers.)

To provide christian education, John Evans and other influential Methodists opened Colorado Seminary across Arapahoe Street from the Evans home in 1864. It closed after three years but was resurrected thirteen years later as the University of Denver. (Today, on the University's south Denver campus stands the Evans Chapel, a red sandstone that originally stood at Thirteenth and Bannock streets. The

RELIGION, EDUCATION: Dr. Henry A. Buchtel, later to become chancellor at the University of Denver and governor of Colorado, moved his flock into Trinity Methodist Church (top left), at Eighteenth and Broadway Streets, in 1887. The Lawrence Street Methodist Episcopal Church (top center) was built in 1864 for $21,000. Methodist Reverend Jacob Adriance (top right) used his fine singing voice to lure recalcitrant Denverites to Sunday services. University Hall (left), the pioneer building on the University of Denver's University Park campus, was completed in 1892 for $80,000.

CATHOLICS IN COLORADO: Father Joseph P. Machbeuf (right) was the first bishop of the Colorado Catholic Church. St. Mary's Catholic Church, the second church built in Denver, was at the southeast corner of Fifteenth and Stout Streets (1860–1900). By the 1870s, its name was changed to Immaculate Conception Cathedral.

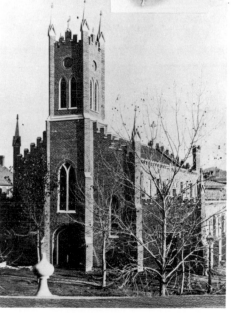

school which grew up around the chapel is now one of the largest private universities in the Rockies).

Father Joseph Machebeuf, Roman Catholic Vicar General of New Mexico Territory, arrived in Denver in the autumn of 1860. Father Machebeuf (who is Father Valliant in Willa Cather's historical novel *Death Comes for the Archbishop*) found Denverites possessed with gold fever. "Nobody in Colorado," according to Father Valliant, "would stick a shovel into the earth for anything less than gold." Among some 200 Catholics then in Denver, "there were men who owned mines and saw-mills and flourishing businesses, but they needed all their money to push these enterprises." Father Machebeuf raised money "down among the Mexicans, who owned nothing but a mud house and a burro.... If they had anything at all, they gave."

The Denver City Town Company also gave. They provided Father Machebeuf with the block between Fifteenth, Sixteenth, Champa and Stout streets where Saint Mary's Church was completed in time for Christmas Eve Mass in 1860. This—Denver's second church building—was used until the turn of the century. (In 1912, Catholics

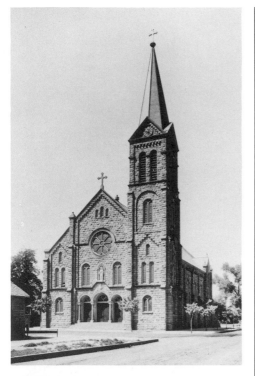

MORE CHURCHES: *St. Elizabeth's German Catholic Church (above) still stands at Tenth and Curtis Streets in Auraria where it now serves the Auraria Higher Education Center. St. Mary's Catholic Church (top right) opened for Christmas High Mass in 1860. Railroad Irish helped build the original St. Patrick's Church (center right) at 3233 Osage in the 1880s. When the new St. Patrick's was completed at 3325 Pecos Street, the old building was converted to the parish school. In 1961, it became the Original Mexican Cafe; the top half of the church was converted to a dance floor and the choir loft to a band stand. Inspired by the California missions, St. Patrick's parish built a new church in 1907 (bottom right) and marked it with a proper cornerstone (inset). It is now a designated Denver landmark.*

ENTER EPISCOPALIANS: St. John's in the Wilderness (left), Denver's first Episcopal Church, stood at Fourteenth and Arapahoe Streets. The architect kept the Norman Gothic church (above) to a modest height to accommodate the surrounding residential neighborhood of Capitol Hill.

completed the Cathedral of the Immaculate Conception. This twin-spired, gothic masterpiece on East Colfax Avenue was made a Minor Basilica in 1979 by Pope John Paul II.)

Father Machebeuf, appointed the first Bishop of Colorado in 1887, oversaw construction of Saint Elizabeth's Church in Auraria, Saint Patrick's in North Denver and Sacred Heart (the oldest church in Denver still using the original building) on Larimer Street. In 1873, five Sisters of Charity from Leavenworth, Kansas, founded Saint Joseph Hospital, Denver's oldest and largest private hospital. A few years later, the Sisters relocated on the present site at East Eighteenth Avenue and Franklin Street. The land there was a gift from Julia Gilpin, wife of the first governor of Colorado Territory. Sisters Beatrice Maes, Ignacia Mora and Joanna Walsh arrived from Santa Fe in 1864 to establish Saint Mary's Academy, the first step in a large Catholic school system that now includes Regis College, Loretto Heights College, Saint Thomas Seminary and many parochial schools.

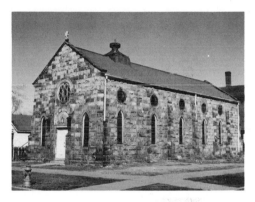

CHAPEL CHANGES: Episcopalians built Emanuel Chapel, the first church in Auraria, in 1876. Later, this stone structure at the corner of Tenth and Lawrence Streets (above) became the Jewish Sherith Israel Chapel; today, it is an art gallery.

The first Episcopalian service in Denver was held in a log cabin on Market Street where it crosses Cherry Creek. This cabin also housed a school, the Denver City and Auraria Reading Room and Library Association and a debating society. When debates over the Civil War became vociferous even on Sundays, the Episcopalians looked for another meeting place.

John H. Kehler—an Episcopal priest called father because he was 63 years old in a town of young men—moved his flock into the Criterion Saloon. "On the first Sunday the gambling was carried on on the first floor while preaching was proceeding on the second" wrote Sam Curtis (for whom Curtis Street is named). "The flooring was of rough boards with wide cracks between them, and every word uttered by the occupants of the saloon, including those at the gambling tables, was as plainly heard by the congregation as the sermon. On the next Sunday the gambling was suspended for an hour while preaching proceeded, which was considered quite a concession at that time."

Father Kehler's records indicate the uphill struggle of the pioneer churches in a community which had three dozen saloons before any churches appeared. Of Kehler's first dozen burials at Mount Prospect, there were five gunshot victims, two lynched murderers, a suicide and an alcoholic. Only three succumbed to "natural causes."

In 1862, Episcopalians finally graduated from groggeries. They acquired the pioneer Southern Methodist building and renamed their second-hand

STUDY HALL: Young ladies had to mind their studies at Wolfe Hall, the Episcopal school that stood at Seventeenth and Champa Streets.

PRESBYTERIAN ARCHITECTURE: The cornerstone of Central Presbyterian Church (below) was laid on July 7, 1891; however, the dedication service was not until Christmas 1892. Frank E. Edbrooke (left), architect for the church at Eighteenth Street and Sherman Avenue, also designed the Brown Palace Hotel, Oxford Hotel and Colorado State Museum.

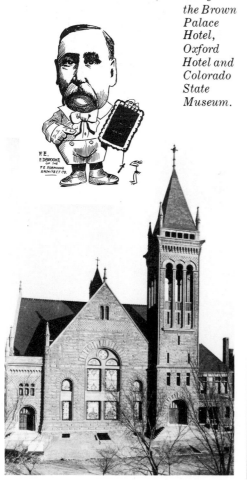

church Saint John's in the Wilderness. As the "wilderness" at Fourteenth and Arapahoe Street grew into a city, Saint John's evolved into the Norman Gothic cathedral now on East Fourteenth Avenue and Washington Street. Civilizing offshoots of the Episcopalian churches included Wolfe Hall (a prominent girls' school that stood at Seventeenth and Champa on the site now occupied by the Boston Building); a college in Golden that became the Colorado School of Mines ("World's Foremost College of Mineral Engineering"); and Denver's third oldest hospital (Saint Luke's).

Like other early congregations, pioneer Presbyterians also met in the only available public halls—saloons—until 1862 when they moved into a $6,000 brick structure. Thirty years later, Presbyterians resettled in the quarter-million-dollar landmark on East Seventeenth Avenue and Sherman Street—Central Presbyterian Church. In the same year, the denomination founded the "Princeton of the West"—Westminster University. (Although the school failed, its towers still dominate the suburb of Westminster that has grown up around it.)

Scarcity of members and money kept the Baptists churchless until 1866 when they moved into the "Holy Dug-Out." This basement with a temporary roof at Sixteenth and Curtis streets sufficed until 1873. After the railroads snorted into town, the Baptist fitted out a private car with a chapel and seats at one end and the minister's quarters at the other. From Denver, this church on rails traveled throughout Colorado Territory offering salvation. The first Baptist Church to look like a church opened in 1883 on Stout Street. Eight years later, the Baptist Ladies College opened on a 30-acre campus in East Denver (now Colorado Women's College).

Jewish pioneers organized Temple Emanuel in 1860 and built their first synagogue on Curtis Street in 1874. The Hebrews moved to the impressive structure at East Sixteenth Avenue and Pearl Street in 1899 and to the large, contemporary-style synagogue at East First Avenue and Grape Street a half century later. The National Jewish Hospital and the Jewish Consumptive Relief Society on West Colfax in present Lakewood facilitated Denver's emergence as a health spa and medical center. Rabbi William S. Friedman of Temple Emanuel, Rabbi Charles E. H. Kauvar of Beth Ha Medrosh Hagodol

In 1867, Baptists began a church on the northeast corner of Sixteenth and Curtis Streets; when building funds were exhausted, the basement was roofed and the structure (above) was used. The Baptist congregation never completed this church, sold the property and erected another church in 1873. Denver's first First Baptist Church opened in 1883 in the 1700 block of Stout Street.

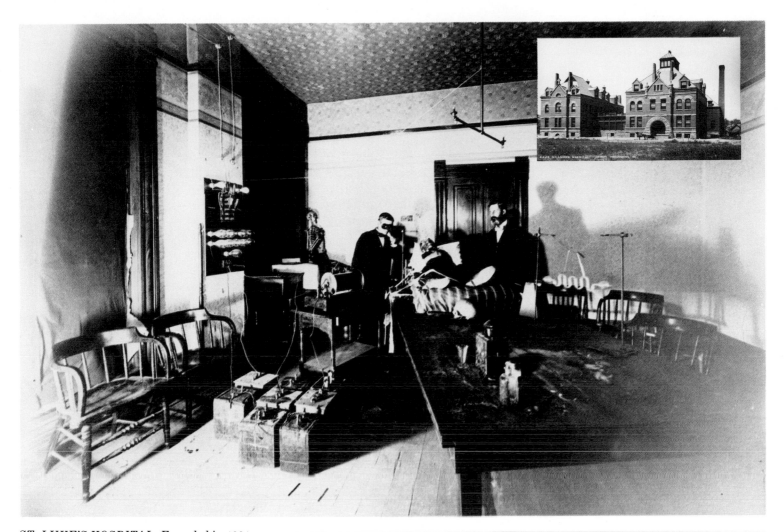

ST. LUKE'S HOSPITAL: Founded in 1881
at Seventeenth Avenue and Federal
Boulevard, the hospital moved to a new
building (above), complete with x-ray
facilities (inset), in 1891 at Nineteenth and
Pearl Streets.

ST. JOSEPH HOSPITAL: The hospital
moved to Eighteenth and Franklin Street
in the 1880s; interior of the hospital (left)
in the City Park West neighborhood which
operated one of the city's first ambulances
(above).

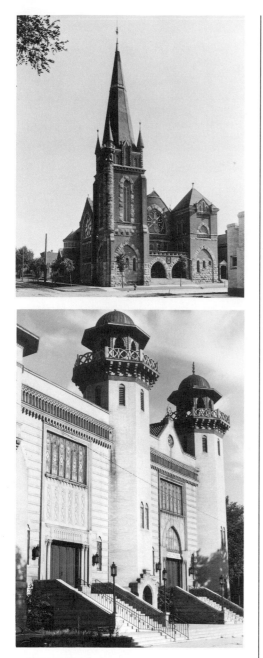

Congregation and Frances Wisebart Jacobs (whose philanthropy is commemorated by a stained glass window in the State Capitol) spearheaded many of the Jewish efforts to improve the quality of life in Denver.

Denver's small black community built most prodigiously considering their small and poor membership. The two dozen blacks living in Denver in the 1860s built a log cabin church on Seventeenth Street. By 1880, the Negro population had grown to a thousand. They completed a brick African Methodist Episcopal Church at Nineteenth and Stout, Antioch Baptist at 23rd and Wazee streets and Zion Baptist which thrives in the Five Points neighborhood to this day.

Numerous other denominations—Congregationalists, Disciples of Christ, Lutherans, Mormons, Quakers, Unitarians—all established themselves in Colorado during the territorial period. These churches promoted schools, hospitals and charities that did more than either the vigilantes or the early law enforcement agencies to mellow the community. By 1880, Denver had 27 churches. One British traveler found a chapel labeled "for rent," and reported that the market was "overstocked." Churchmen disagreed. They pointed out that Denver had 98 saloons in 1880 and claimed that houses of the Lord should outnumber the houses of demon rum. As late as the 1880s, Dean H. Martyn Hart of St. John's Episcopal Cathedral still thundered at his flock, "By your own admission, you left God on the Missouri River."

Yet early clergymen brought not only God but many other refinements to Denver. They circulated their libraries, gave lectures, promoted music and quiet Sundays and encouraged marriage and family life. Ministers also worked closely with the town's leading ladies, such as Elizabeth Byers, Margaret Gray Evans and Julia Gilpin, to improve education, health and welfare.

Churches and private citizens established various schools before the Denver public school system became solidly established in 1874. There was no permanent, free public library system until 1886. In the meantime, churches, temperance societies and other groups established lending libraries.

Not until 1870 did Dr. John Elsner, the city physician, collect "patients who were lying around in the hen houses and barns" and move them into the first hospital, ancestor of Denver General Hospital. While Dr. Elsner struggled with the city for funds, the churches and private charities cared for the indigent sick and dying who stumbled into Denver from health-destroying mines and from tuberculosis-ridden eastern cities.

Despite their good work, the struggling early houses of God were not spared the great fire of 1863. Flames burst upon the city from the Cherokee House, where early morning tipplers were reveling. Before sunrise on

DENVER'S DENOMINATIONS: The Swedish Lutheran Church (top), Temple Emanuel (above).

PIONEER BLACKS: Aunt Clara Brown (left), a former slave in Missouri, was one of the first of her race to join the 1859 gold rush. She charged 50 cents to wash a shirt and saved more than $1,000 to bring her family to Colorado. Denver's black community built the African Methodist Church (right) at Eighteenth and Stout Streets.

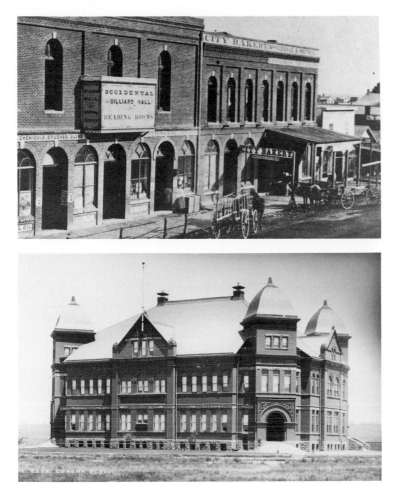

April 19, Denver City was a blackened waste. Seventy buildings went up in smoke and flames at a cost of $250,000. Afterwards, Denver rebuilt in brick.

Brick ordinances (and not Denver's dilatory early firemen) were the reason that the city never burned again. A volunteer hook-and-ladder company was formed after the fire, but they exhausted their funds on natty uniforms with red shirts, black trousers and leather hats rather than on fire-fighting equipment. Later the volunteer smoke-eaters acquired a second-hand steam fire engine, but someone carted it off to the mountains for hydraulic mining. Other volunteer fire companies emerged during the 1870s, but they were primarily social clubs, addicted to firemen's balls, hose races and parading in uniform. Not until 1881 did the stripling city establish a full-time, paid fire force.

Early photographs as well as *News* editorials reveal that Denver was dirty. Pigs, cattle and goats initially handled the trash pick-up, although they left their own messes behind. In 1878, Denver hired a city scavenger but abolished the job a few years later.

Real estate tycoon Henry M. Porter and four partners then contracted to establish daily rubbish removal. At first, they tried to recycle the city's offal, extracting grease for sale to soap manufacturers and fertilizer for farmers. "But it accumulated so fast (about thirty tons daily)," Porter recalled in his autobiography, that they were swamped. "We had to haul it into low places and dump it." Cherry Creek and the Platte were the "low places" and for decades served as dumps. Once pristine Denver waterways became open sewers.

Trout-filled waters of the South Platte had served the first settlers. But by 1859, thousands of miners were wading through the river with picks and pans, building rockers and sluices. The river turned murky and undrinkable. (Not until the 1970s would Denverites begin to clean up their river and anticipate the return of trout.)

HALLS OF LEARNING: Before the public library was established in 1886, many Denverites found newspapers and other reading material in saloons such as the Occidental Billiard Hall and Reading Rooms (top left). By 1872, the Denver High School (above) was built. Corona School (bottom left), later re-named Dora Moore School after an admired principal, was finished in 1890.

CITY DITCH: Called "the oldest working thing in Denver," City Ditch begins with this headgate (left) on the South Platte River just below Waterton Canyon. Carrying water to Denver since the 1860s, it ends in the big lake at City Park just after entering the park under a bridge (right) on Eighteenth Avenue. It is now covered over, to the despair of the neighborhood children and to the delight of their parents.

For irrigating water, townsfolk used the City Ditch constructed in 1865. It came from the Platte seven miles above Richard Little's flour mill (now downtown Littleton). Curving with the contour of the prairie, it carried river water to Capitol Hill. From there, laterals took the gurgling liquid to the city below. Ditch owner John W. Smith employed a natural depression and former buffalo wallow south of town as a reservoir. (Today Smith's Lake is the north lake of Washington Park and the ditch ends in the big lake at City Park.) With laterals honeycombing the town, City Ditch enabled Denverites to plant trees, lawns, gardens and vegetable patches. Its open canals bordering city streets were patrolled by water police who tried to keep people from drinking or illegally diverting ditch water.

In 1882, the city purchased the ditch. (In 1977 it was designated a Denver Landmark. Louisa Ward Arps, author of *Denver in Slices*, spoke at the dedication of the marker in Washington Park, where the ditch is still uncovered. She eulogized the waterway where she and many other children had waded and built mud castles as "the oldest working thing in Denver.")

For drinking water, the pioneers sank barrels into the river and creek beds where the sand acted as a filter. Many dug wells in their backyards, often next to outhouses. Such wells caused epidemics of typhoid, diphtheria, yellow fever and drove the water table deeper underground. By the early 1860s, bottled water and water wagons became a common—and expensive—necessity. A bucket of water cost 5 cents delivered to the first floor of a building and 10 cents to the second floor.

To provide more drinking water, James Archer's Denver City Water Company began operations in 1872. From this pioneer waterworks, wooden pipes carried drinkable water throughout the sun-baked city. Soon Denver outgrew this plant, and residents complained about opening taps for only a trickle of water and, sometimes, equally disappointed minnows.

Archer built a larger waterworks on West Twelfth Avenue on the east bank of the river. Nearby, he created Lake Archer reservoir. (It has since been filled in and is now the site of the Denver Water Board headquarters.) This plant also reached its capacity quickly. Relief came in 1883 with the discovery of artesian water, which spurted up from deep wells sunk into the Laramie formation of the Denver Basin. A few of these wells survive, permitting the Deep Rock Water Company to boast the nation's largest bottled water sales and the Brown Palace Hotel to serve Denver's best-tasting water and coffee.

The Arapaho and Cheyenne warned early Denverites not to build in or near dry gullies and creekbeds. The whites ignored this advice until the Cherry Creek flood of 1864 taught them to respect usually dry watercourses. (Subsequent Cherry Creek and/or South Platte floods of 1875, 1878, 1912, 1933, 1965 and 1973 reinforced the lesson.)

Although water was—and is—probably Denver's most crucial problem, stray dogs aroused the greatest number of citizen complaints (and over a century later Mayor William H. McNichols Jr., reported that this was still

the case). After editor Byers carped about wild dogs roaming the streets and terrifying horses and humans, the city hired a two-man wagon team. This dogcatching duo received a dollar for every canine shot and buried outside the city limits. Evidently, these pioneer dogcatchers were poor marksmen. Townsfolk soon began complaining about wounded mutts that both barked and bit.

Cats, on the other hand, were prized citizens of early Denver. City ordinances, which devoted an entire chapter to dogs, left cats completely unrestrained. Far less willing to immigrate than dogs, cats were scarce and in demand as the rodent population grew. Rodents, according to the *News*, infested downtown. One Larimer Street shoemaker awoke to his son's screams and found a fourteen-inch rat clinging to the child like a leech. After such scares, cats sold for as much as $25.

Dog catchers, water works, fire protection, hospitals, schools and other municipal services and utilities, of course, meant taxes. A few days after its founding, the Denver City Town Company began taxing members $1.50 per lot. The taxes were used for promotion, management and building the first bridge over the Platte at Fifteenth Street. Many foot-loose frontiersmen moved on rather than pay taxes. Others stayed and paid.

During the 1860s, more than three dozen saloons were annually taxed

FIRE PROTECTION: After the fire of 1863, Denver rebuilt in brick. Many of the solid brick homes (top) were decorated in carpenter Gothic trim. The old Denver Fire Department Station No. 1 (above) at 1326 Tremont Place is now the Fire Department Museum.

MOFFAT MANSION: By 1920, businesses had overtaken the old Fourteenth Street residential neighborhoods, although the Moffat Mansion (above) survived until it was replaced by the Mountain Bell Telephone building in 1929. Moffat had purchased his grand house and four lots for $18,000; it was sold to the telephone company for $110,000.

$400 each to help pay the city's bills. Gamblers and prostitutes—one way or another—were also forced to pay city officials. By taxing sin, the city made improvements demanded by respectable people who balked at paying taxes.

The town assessed property owners for improvements of the streets, sidewalks and alleys adjoining their land. Many improvements were made by private citizens such as David Moffat who dazzled the town of wooden sidewalks by installing a flagstone walk around his mansion at Curtis and Fourteenth Streets.

Tax-poor but in need of water, light, gas, communications and transportation, the city awarded franchises to private utility companies. These companies introduced streetcars in 1871, a water works and gas lights in 1872 and telephones in 1879. Many of these improvements were made at the suggestion of *News* editor William N. Byers, who also suggested that Denver develop its mining hinterland. As the first to write about many of the settlements, he not only promoted but named much of Colorado Territory. When Gregory found gold, Byers rushed up Clear Creek Canyon and pitched a tent on Main Street of what he called Central City. When Byers toured the broad valley base of Longs Peak, he named it Estes Park after its pioneer settler. He also named, promoted and invested in the resort of Hot Sulphur Springs.

Byers ballyhooed not only Denver but the entire Rocky Mountain region. Publicity, he believed, would bring the world to the Rockies. He was sure that the world was listening. The *News*, Byers crowed on April 25, 1860, "stands today the most widely known and universally quoted, of any newspaper of its age, ever before published in the United States."

Rival editors fumed that Byers—while serving as postmaster—held up mail headed for other gazettes. When the 1864 Cherry Creek flood washed the second *News* office from its stilts in the creek bed and almost drowned its editor, some barely disguised their glee. But it was a desperate woman with a pearl-handled revolver who brought Byers down in 1876.

As head of the Colorado Board of Immigration, Byers had written to encourage Mrs. Hattie Sancomb, a divorcee from Kansas, to join the thousands coming to the Promised Land. Mrs. Sancomb called personally at the *News* office on Larimer Street to thank him. She was smitten by the handsome, nobly-bearded editor and invited him out to her new home in Golden. Byers welcomed the affair at first.

Jefferson Randolph Smith, king of the frontier con men, earned the nickname Soapy Smith for the slippery soap sale routine he perfected on Larimer Street. Ultimately, Denverites washed Soapy out of town. He wound up in Skagway, Alaska, where a bullet put an end to his bunco games.

When he tried to end the relationship, Hattie accosted him outside his home and fired at him. Before rival papers could scoop the *News*, Byers came out with a full confession. Shortly afterwards, he sold his newspaper and abandoned hope of being elected governor when Colorado became a state in 1876.

Although out of a paper and out of office, Byers remained the settlement's number one booster. Denver and Colorado were booming, largely because Byers had focused attention on railroads during Denver's first decade. He knew that the fate of the infant town lay in the prairie farms and ranches and in the ores, lumber, stones and scenery of its mountains. If Denver were to become the area's market, its factory, its social, economic and political hub, transportation was the key. To catch the riches of the mountains and the plains, Denver needed a spiderwork of steel.

FOURTEENTH STREET: Denver's finest residential district of the 1870s was along the tree-lined Fourteenth Street (above). Along there were the residences of (top row inset, left to right) David H. Moffat, John L. Routt, John Evans and William Bradley Daniels. The Evans Chapel (second row, inset) is now part of the University of Denver campus. Colorado Seminary (left), founded in 1864 at Fourteenth and Arapahoe Streets, became the University of Denver.

An excursion train of the Colorado
Midland Railroad leaves Denver's Union
Station for mountain fishing and
wildflower gathering.

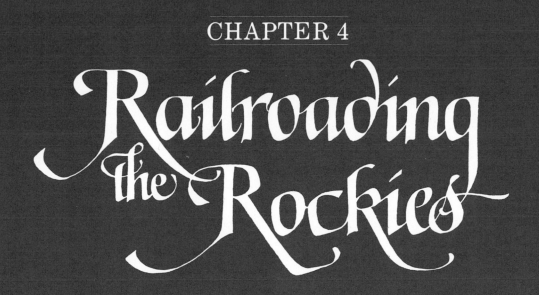

CHAPTER 4

Railroading the Rockies

In June 1860, the federal census taker found 4,749 Denverites. Ten years later, there were only ten more.

"**I**n Denver City they behold in the future another San Francisco," reported Libeus Barney, proprietor of Apollo Hall. Barney's saloon hall, where the pioneer city and territorial governments convened, rang with rosy political promises and predictions.

Provisional Governor Robert W. Steele of extra-legal Jefferson Territory told an 1859 Apollo audience that, within a year, the territory's population "will probably be swelled to 100,000." Perhaps Barney's well-stocked bar led politicians to such inebriated hopes. Barney's own letters of 1859 portray a small, stagnating crossroads:

Yours Truly
John Evans

John Evans came from Illinois to become a successful town developer, railroad builder and governor of Colorado.

The present stationary population of Denver is about 300, with some 200 log houses, of which not more than six can boast of a floor. There are three frame houses in course of erection, and every third building is a groggery, dealing out whiskey at from 10 to 20 cents a "nip," and warranted to kill at fifty yards.

There are but few *ladies* here yet there are many females of questionable morality about town, some in bloomer costume and some in gentlemen's attire throughout, while squaws are more than plenty....As I was passing one of their lodges a day or two since, I observed a squaw busily engaged picking vermin from her lord's head and eating them with marvelous gusto.

The 1859 population predictions and hopes for instant urbanity collapsed in the 1860s. In June 1860, the federal census taker found 4,749 Denverites. Ten years later, there were only ten more. Stagnation was attributed to the 1863 fire, the 1864 flood, the Civil War, Indian wars and the unsolved problems of extracting and processing mineral ores. In the self-proclaimed boomtown, townsfolk sold city lots for as little as 35 cents and entire blocks changed hands in poker games.

"Go-backers" left Cherry Creek as fast as the boomers arrived. "Because they cannot shovel out nuggets like they have been accustomed to dig potatoes," Byers editorialized, "they raise the cry that it is all a humbug...and take the back track for home where it is to be hoped that they will ever after remain."

The *News* editor knew that only railroads could carry Denver out of the doldrums. Hopes soared when John Evans replaced William Gilpin as governor in 1862. Evans was a medical doctor from Ohio. He had been a successful town promoter, city council member and railroad builder in Chicago. He had developed the fashionable northside neighborhood of Evanston and founded Northwestern University.

If anyone could bend the rails of the transcontinental into Denver, the new territorial governor could. On his first evening in town in May of 1862, Evans promised that the Pacific railroad would become Denver's "great commercial auxiliary."

Evans had been appointed a commissioner of the Pacific railroad as well as governor of Colorado Territory by President Abraham Lincoln, a fellow Illinois politician whom Evans had helped send to the White House. Some, including Mrs. Evans, wondered why this wealthy aristocrat (the 1870 census listed assets of $1.45 million) left Chicago comforts for the Colorado wilderness where he found Denver "really the only tolerable place." Perhaps

GOLDEN YEARS: Golden emerged as Denver's leading urban rival during the 1860s. After losing the railroad war to Denver, Golden remained a small country town as suggested by this view (top) looking north on Washington Avenue in the 1880s. Astor House (right) was Golden's finest hotel in the 1860s; it was saved more than 100 years later by a three-to-one vote of townspeople. Now known as the Astor House Museum, it offers exhibits, lectures and walking tours of the historic, early territorial capital.

GOLDEN CROWD: William Austin Hamilton Loveland (above) was the star promoter of Golden and its Colorado Central Railroad. Henry Moore Teller (top), who also promoted Golden's fortune and its railroad, became Colorado's best-known statesman. After serving as U.S. senator, he became secretary of the interior. Teller County and the Teller House in Central City are among the monuments to him.

he was motivated by the missionary idealism that led him to found Colorado Seminary, to give $100 toward establishing each church of any denomination and to promote arts and refinements of all kinds. Certainly economic motives did not prompt Evans to leave his profitable Chicago enterprises for a salary of $2,500 a year as governor of Colorado Territory.

Although Governor Evans assured Denverites he would capture the iron horse, the hamlet of Golden fifteen miles to the west at the mouth of Clear Creek Canyon organized Colorado's first railroad. Golden promoters W.A.H. Loveland and Henry M. Teller organized the Colorado Central in 1864. Working with Boston capitalists who had created Golden City in 1859, Loveland and Teller hoped to make their town the rail hub of Colorado.

Loveland and Teller's "Golden Crowd" also sought to politically railroad the "Denver Crowd" led by Governor Evans and editor Byers. After the first session of the territorial legislature found Colorado City uncomfortably crude in 1861, Golden seduced the legislature by offering free firewood and a meeting hall (the Mercantile Building still stands in Golden at Twelfth and Washington streets). In spite of Denver's efforts to also wine, dine and house the biennial legislative sessions, Golden remained the territorial capital until 1867.

While Golden City courted the lawmakers, backers of Golden's railroad courted the mining camps which shared the town's envy and mistrust of Denver. Many Coloradans considered Denver a parasitical supply-and-spree town that drained their wealth. The *Central City Colorado Times* applauded Golden's efforts to build the Colorado Central up Clear Creek Canyon as "good news for mining districts, for there is but little of the Denver egotism about the Golden folks. We can hope for advantages from Golden City that Denver in her exclusiveness would never grant. Denver is like the adder, which, perishing from the cold, was taken by the countryman out of pity into his bosom, but which on being revived by his warmth, as a return for his kindness, bit him. So Denver in her selfishness would have the mines of Colorado—the very bowels of her existence—shift for themselves."

Ignoring such criticism, Denver joined the race to get a railroad. Byers

MAKING TRACKS: Golden's Colorado Central (top) tapped the mines of Clear Creek Canyon and ran into Black Hawk (above) and Central City. With a pass (below), you could ride the Denver Pacific Railway which served Colorado and Wyoming in 1878.

had his eyes on the transcontinetal railroad that had started building west from Omaha in 1863. He began a barrage of editorial invitations. Making molehills out of the mountains, the *News* editor wrote that Colorado's Rockies are "fully described when we say *hilly*; but few elevations attaining the prominence of mountains, the valleys and slopes are rich in grasses, prolific in fruits, and abounding with inexhaustible forests of pine, fir and cedar timber, presenting a most vivid contrast to the barren and desert plains."

The directors of the Union Pacific Railway were more intimidated by the "hilly" land west of Denver. After an October blizzard almost buried chief engineer Grenville Dodge during his inspection of Berthoud Pass in 1866, the Union Pacific chose the South Pass route through the gentler hills of Wyoming.

Union Pacific construction crews worked across Nebraska, dipping into the northeast corner of Colorado at Julesburg. Then the railroad left the Platte River to cut across Wyoming. When the Union Pacific laid out Cheyenne, many Coloradans moved there, thinking the Wyoming town was destined to be the rail metropolis of the region. "Denver," gloated the *Cheyenne Daily Leader* for September 24, 1867, "was too near Cheyenne to ever amount to much."

Cheyenne quickly eclipsed Denver as the Rocky Mountain boomtown. Editor Byers and former Governor Evans were disturbed. They called a public meeting in the fall of 1867 to organize a Denver Board of Trade (predecessor of the Denver Chamber of Commerce). Immediately, the new Board organized the Denver Pacific Railway and Telegraph Company. If the railroads would not build to Denver, Denver would build to the railroads.

The Denver Pacific was incorporated on November 19, 1867. Within three days, Denverites invested $300,000 in their railroad, sometimes buying shares with promises to supply ties or work on the roadbed. Arapahoe County, of which Denver was then the county seat, voted for a $500,000 railroad bond in May 1868. That month, a general holiday was declared. About a thousand Denverites joined the celebration as grading began on the 106 miles to Cheyenne. John W. Smith, president of the Board of Trade, began shoveling dirt while others tapped beer kegs and a band struck up "The Railroad Gallop."

Two years later, Denverites celebrated the completion of the Denver Pacific, a standard gauge steam line that began regular freight and passenger service to Cheyenne in June 1870. A crowd of Indians, mountain men, miners, cowboys and others gathered to greet the whistling, smoke-belching engines that brought an end to Denver's frontier isolation. The first train carried one-day-old newspapers from Omaha, two-day-old papers from Chicago, champagne, oysters and other amenities of America's urban mainstream.

Two months later, the Kansas Pacific reached Denver from St. Louis and Kansas City. Still later in 1870, the Colorado Central completed the first stretch of its long-promised road—a short spur into Denver. Although the Golden line reached Black Hawk in 1872, it did not make direct connections with the Union Pacific and the transcontinental network until 1877. By then, Denver had a half dozen roads, and Golden had lost the soot-and-cinders competition.

For John Evans and his associates, the Denver Pacific was only the beginning. Before the end of 1870, Evans had put together the Denver and Boulder Valley Railroad to tap the Boulder County coal mines and fuel still more Colorado railroads. Even before the Denver Pacific was completed, Evans discussed plans for a mountain road with a confidant and fellow

BANKING ON THE RAILROADS:
Ground was broken (top) for the Denver Pacific Railway in May 1868 on the northern outskirts of the city. A pioneer steam locomotive of this railway was named the Walter S. Cheesman (inset) after one of the company's officers. Bankers who helped keep progress of the railroads on track were Jerome B. Chaffee (above left), the first president of the First National Bank of Denver, and David H. Moffat Jr. (above right). At the corner of Blake and Fifteenth Streets, the First National building (left) was under construction in 1865. This landmark, later called Constitution Hall because the state's constitution was written there, was destroyed by its owners in 1980.

The Kansas Pacific Railway reached Denver (below) from Kansas City in 1870.

officer of the pioneer road, David Halliday Moffat Jr. Moffat had left his poor upstate New York home at age twelve to become a messenger boy in a New York City bank. By the time he was sixteen, he was a bank clerk, and at seventeen he took a teller's position with a new bank in Des Moines, Iowa. In 1856, he became cashier of a bank in Omaha, where he met William N. Byers.

At the urging of Byers, Moffat came to Colorado. The lanky 20-year-old with large, luminous eyes and a walrus moustache opened a Denver book and stationery shop in 1859. Shortly afterwards, he returned to banking as cashier of the First National Bank of Denver where he made himself indispensable to bank president Jerome Chaffee. Chaffee became one of Colorado's first United States Senators in 1876 and resigned as bank president. Moffat succeeded him as president of First National. He remained president until his death in 1911 and used bank assets—as well as his own fortune—to help build various Denver railroads.

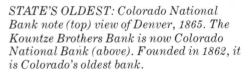

COLORADO NATIONAL BANK
DESIGNATED DEPOSITORY AND FINANCIAL AGENT OF THE UNITED STATES.

STATE'S OLDEST: Colorado National Bank note (top) view of Denver, 1865. The Kountze Brothers Bank is now Colorado National Bank (above). Founded in 1862, it is Colorado's oldest bank.

Moffat realized that railroads were the key to developing nineteenth-century Denver and Colorado. The fate of his own First National Bank was an example. After the railroads steamed into town, Denver emerged as the commercial center of the region. The First National had been chartered in 1865. It grew out of Clark, Gruber and Company's 1859 gold mint, assay office and bank after private mints were outlawed in 1863. Following the doldrums of the 1860s, the First boomed with the arrival of the Denver Pacific Railway, of which Moffat was the treasurer. A year after the railroad snorted into Denver in 1870, the First tripled its assets to over $1.5 million.

Colorado National Bank—the closest competitor to Moffat's bank—had been established in 1862 by the Kountze brothers. It became the city's second national bank in 1866. Colorado National also enjoyed the railroad prosperity, increasing its assets by almost $75,000 in the first three months after June 1870. Born in the gold rush and nourished by the railroad boom, these two pioneer banks remain bastions of Rocky Mountain finance. Their investments have shaped Denver's economic life.

David Moffat invested heavily in mining and worked with John Evans and other capitalists to construct a railroad from Denver to the mountain mines. They incorporated the Denver, South Park and Pacific. By 1874, they had completed 9.7 miles of track from Denver to the spectacular red sandstone formations in the foothills. There Evans created the Morrison

Stone, Lime and Townsite Company, named for George M. Morrison, a Scotsman who already had a home and a gypsum mill on the site.

In the mid-1870s, the Denver, South Park and Pacific slowly built up the canyon of the South Platte River. In 1879, the narrow gauge snorted over Kenosha Pass into the gold camps of South Park. From Como (where the Denver, South Park and Pacific depot and roundhouse still stand), the line climbed the 11,493-foot Boreas Pass in 1880 and then coasted into Breckenridge, Dillon, Keystone and Leadville. Another line of the D.S.P.&P. ran from Como through Fairplay and over Trout Creek Pass to Buena Vista and via Rio Grande tracks to Leadville. The third arm of the road burrowed through the Continental Divide at Alpine Tunnel in 1881. Like most of the ambitiously named Pacific roads, the Denver, South Park and Pacific never reached the Pacific. It wore out in the high country where Evans planted a town called Gunnison. Yet the D.S.P.&P. made Denver the entrepôt for Morrison sandstone and lime, South Park and Summit County gold, Leadville silver and Gunnison County marble and granite. Denverites favored the South Park line for fishing and wildflower excursions, while folks in the small towns created by the line saved their money for shopping sprees in the Queen City of the Plains.

Despite its heroic assault on the Rockies, the Denver South Park & Pacific was usually behind another mountain narrow gauge line, the Denver and Rio Grande. In 1870, General William Jackson Palmer incorporated the line that still carries Denverites to San Francisco Bay (with a little help from Amtrak). General Palmer was a handsome Civil War veteran who had come to Colorado as the managing director of the Kansas Pacific. His connections with eastern and British railroading and mining circles qualified Palmer for the job. Palmer named his Denver and Rio Grande Railroad for the Mexican border which he hoped to reach. In 1872, the line puffed into the evening shadows of Pikes Peak, where Palmer laid out the town of Colorado Springs.

From Pikes Peak, Palmer built south to Pueblo and to El Moro just east of Trinidad. His railroad only got as far as Santa Fe, although Palmer himself went south of the border to help construct the Mexican National Railway system. When fabulously large silver deposits were discovered at Leadville in the late 1870s, Palmer turned his road westward. After

IN THE FOOTHILLS: Strontia Springs station (top left) on the Denver, South Park and Pacific after the flood of May 1900. The foothills town of Morrison, as it looked in the nineteenth century (top right), supplied lime and sandstone to Denver industry via the railroad.

A bronze plaque in Denver's Union Station commemorates William Jackson Palmer, father of the Denver and Rio Grande Railroads. He introduced narrow gauge track and equipment able to negotiate the sharper curves and steeper grades into Colorado's mountain mining towns.

The Colorado Central, which at one point became the Union Pacific, Denver and Gulf, provided a spectacular trip through Clear Creek Canyon culminating with the Georgetown Loop.

winning a "war" with the Atchison, Topeka and Santa Fe for control of the Royal Gorge of the Arkansas, the Denver & Rio Grande chugged into Leadville in 1880. South of the Arkansas, the D.&R.G. crossed LaVeta Pass to reach the Rio Grande in the San Luis Valley, then climbed into the rugged San Juans where Silverton, Ouray, Telluride and other towns arose after the dispossession of the Ute Indians.

Ultimately Palmer's renamed Denver and Rio Grande Western honeycombed the Colorado mining districts and expanded Denver's economic empire to northern New Mexico and eastern Utah. The Rio Grande created dozens of towns, including Colorado Springs, Alamosa and Durango. (The road still maintains headquarters in Denver and remains an independent and profitable prodigy among rapidly disappearing American railroads.)

Once the iron horse reached the mines, Colorado's paydirt began to pay. During the 1860s, high ore freighting costs and primitive mining and smelting facilities undermined the golden promise of '59. Nathaniel C. Hill opened a successful smelter in Black Hawk, but few others could afford to do likewise. Only after railroads began to bring in more sophisticated equipment and ship ores cheaply to processing plants did Colorado mining production soar. Gold production climbed from $2 million in 1868 to $3.2 million in 1878. By the 1880s, annual production reached $4 million. By

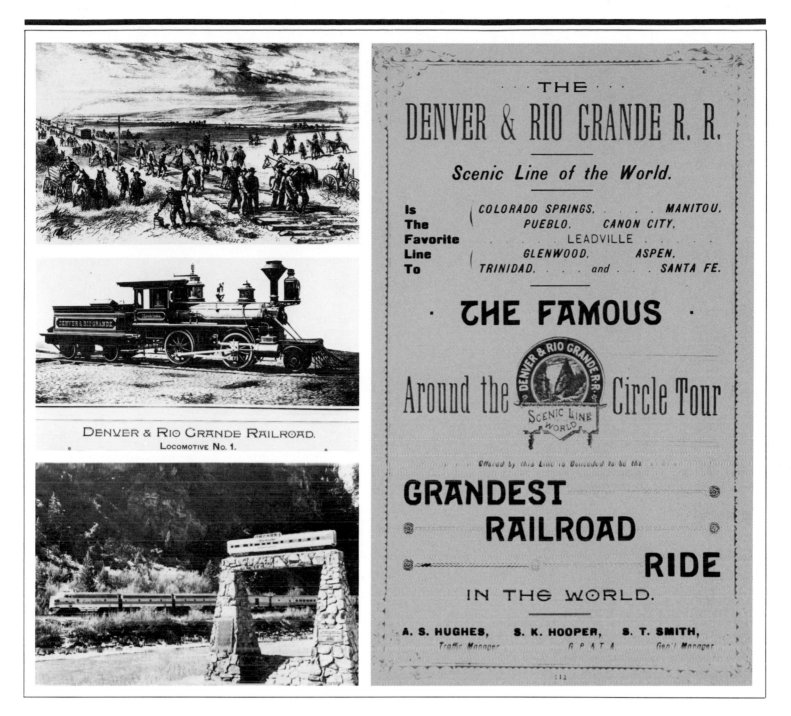

FAMOUS TRAINS: *The Denver and Rio Grande built its narrow gauge (top right) south from Denver along the Front Range in the 1870s, for such locomotives as the Montezuma (right center) to travel. An historic marker in Glenwood Canyon (right bottom) commemorates development of the famous Vista Dome passenger cars of the Denver-Rio Grande, offering "the grandest railroad ride in the world."*

1900, with the Cripple Creek strike, Colorado's annual gold crop reached an all-time peak of $28.7 million. Silver production went from $660,000 in 1870 to $3 million in 1874, reaching a peak of $20 million just before its demonetization in 1893.

Other riches of the Rockies also rolled into Denver by rail. By the turn of the century, Colorado copper became a million-dollar industry. Production peaked in 1938 at nearly $2.8 million. Marble, granite and sandstone quarries were opened to feed the building boom in Denver and Colorado and elsewhere. Yule marble from Marble, Colorado was used for the Washington Monument, Lincoln Memorial and Tomb of the Unknown Soldier in Washington. Oil—discovered near Canon City in 1862—became increasingly precious.

After the arrival of coal-burning and coal-carrying railroads, coal production soared from $16,000 in 1869 to $140,000 in 1873. Colorado coal—or black gold—became a $5 million industry by 1900 and peaked at $42.8 million in 1920. (Today, new records are being set by the coal trains rumbling through Denver daily.)

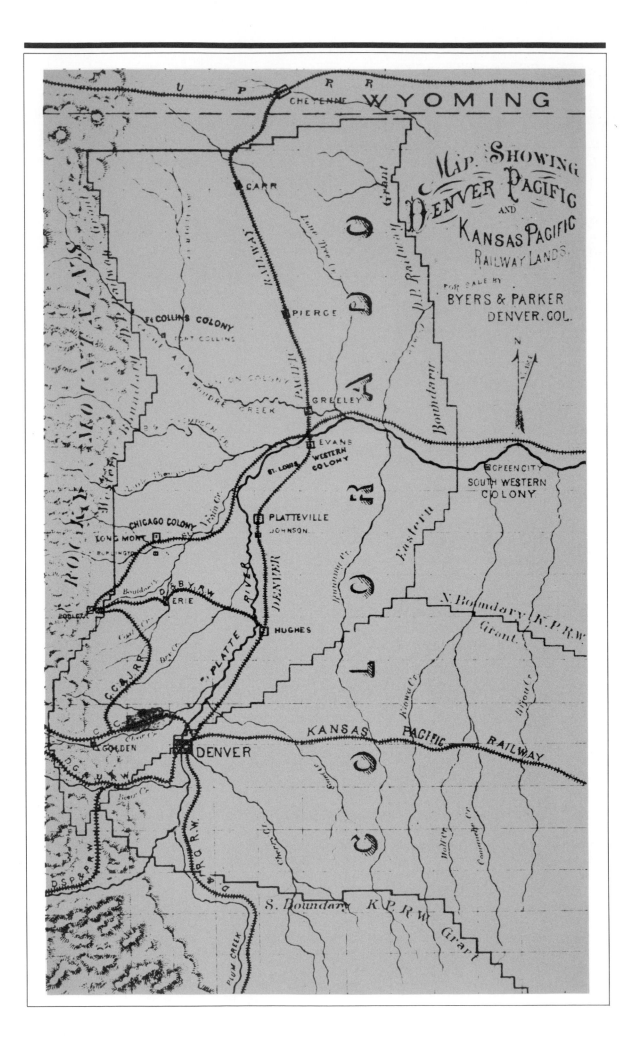

Railroad hegemony enabled the Queen City to attract not only mining profits but the mining barons themselves. From Central City, Georgetown, Leadville and other mining communities, they gravitated to Denver where they built office buildings downtown and mansions on Capitol Hill. Just as Golden and the mining towns had feared in the 1860s, much of the state's mineral wealth gravitated to Denver via the city's railroads.

After tapping the mountains, Denver railroad builders turned to securing a direct rail connection to a seaport. John Evans and some of his associates incorporated the Denver and New Orleans Railroad Company in 1881. Like the other three, this road never reached its original destination, although it finally did connect with other roads serving ports on the Gulf of Mexico.

During the 1880s, Evans and his associates sold the Denver Pacific, Kansas Pacific, Denver, South Park & Pacific and the Denver and New Orleans to Jay Gould and the Union Pacific Railroad. Evans, however, continued to talk and dream about building more Denver roads until his death in 1897.

David Moffat continued to dream and to build after Evans died. Moffat spent his later years building railroad track over the 14,000-foot barrier west of Denver. The Moffat Road finally surmounted the Rockies in 1904 at Rollins (Corona) Pass but Moffat exhausted his fortune keeping it open in winter. A tunnel was his dream. He died in New York City after failing to get more financing for his road which had never gone beyond the northwestern Colorado county named for him. At the time of his death, work had not begun on the tunnel under the Continental Divide at James Peak. Completion of the 6.21-mile-long bore in 1928 climaxed Denver's long and determined efforts to railroad the Rockies. The Queen City finally obtained a direct route through the Rockies to the Pacific when the Denver and Rio Grande acquired the Moffat Road and completed the Dotsero Cutoff.

In the six decades between the incorporation of the Denver Pacific and the completion of the Moffat Tunnel, a hundred different railroads built track in Colorado. Most of them fed into the steel spiderwork spun by the Queen City. Denver became the break-of-bulk point, the warehouse, the factory, the market and the main or branch office for many local, regional and national railroads.

Tracks ran north and south along the Front Range as well as east and west, enabling the city to expand its hinterland from Montana to New Mexico and dominate the Rocky Mountain region by the 1890s. Initially spurned by the transcontinentals, the Mile High City became a target for the Union Pacific; the Chicago, Burlington and Quincy; the Atchison, Topeka and Santa Fe; and Missouri Pacific—four roads that still served Colorado in 1980.

The other railroads have vanished—except for some scattered ties, occasional stone bridge foundations, a few rotting water tanks, ramshackle depots, fading roundhouses, crumbling shops and weedy rail yards. Denver's vast nineteenth-century rail network is largely gone today, the victim of automobiles, trucks and airplanes. But every once in a while, hikers, cross-country skiers or motorists discover some tell-tale sign that they are traveling on the gentle roadbeds that transformed Denver into the Rocky Mountain metropolis.

NEW HORIZONS: Denver stagnated during the 1860s gaining only 10 residents in that decade. Then, the Denver Pacific, Kansas Pacific and Colorado Central railroads steamed into the frontier crossroads and into Denver railroad stations (above), and the population soared to more than 35,000 by 1880. A map of the 1870s (far left) shows that many tracks led to Denver.

Stock show cowgirl, circa 1903.

CHAPTER 5

Sodbusters & civilization

From the beginning, Denver was a cowtown. Some of the '59ers brought cattle with them and left the travel-worn creatures outdoors to fend for themselves over the winter. In the spring, owners were surprised to find their cattle sleek after a winter of feasting on dried buffalo grass.

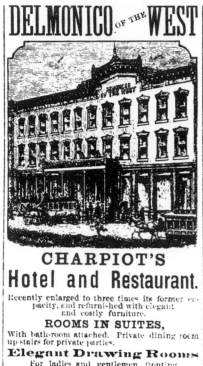

As railroads crossed the High Plains and pierced the Rocky Mountain barrier, they also reshaped the town at the confluence of the South Platte and Cherry Creek. Denver's population soared by over 700 percent between 1870 and 1880. The discovery of silver at Leadville and improved mining methods were part of the reason, but railroads were the main cause for the town's delayed boom. By 1890, Denver had become the third largest city in the West with a population of 106,713. Only San Francisco and Omaha were larger.

Travelers to Denver found the trip smoother after bone-shaking stagecoaches were replaced by cheaper, faster, more civilized railroad Pullman cars. Wide-eyed tourists chugged into the Colorado capital in search of Indians and buffalo, gold nuggets and trout. Businessmen found the city attractive as a market and a place to open branch offices and regional headquarters.

Denverites built hotels, restaurants, theaters, museums and other amenities to accommodate the growing number of tourists and commercial travelers. Railroad freight service enabled restaurants like Charpiot's "Delmonico of the West" on Larimer Street to serve fresh fruits, vegetables and fresh oysters as well as the Rocky Mountain variety. Exotic treats from all over the globe appeared in Denver shops, restaurants, cafes and delicatessens. After or before elegant dinners, guests and townspeople could choose from dozens of downtown theaters, although none of them rivaled Tabor's Grand Opera House that stood at Sixteenth and Curtis streets from 1880 to 1964. Dozens of theaters lined the "Great White Way" of Curtis Street until urban renewal destroyed them in the 1960s and 1970s. (The late 1970s opening of the Denver Center for the Performing Arts at the foot of Curtis Street culminated a long theater-going tradition.)

Few of the grand resorts of the railroad city survive. Two notable exceptions are the Brown Palace at Seventeenth and Tremont, and the Navarre across the street. Both are on the National Register of historic places. Tipplers and diners can also re-enter the nineteenth century at the Buckhorn Exchange at Tenth and Osage streets, another nationally

DENVER, COLO.

CURTIS STREET: Denver's glittering "Great White Way," the Curtis Street theater district (left) was shining brightly in the 1920s. Several score later, an old Vaudeville trouper, 80-year-old George B. Young (inset), bids farewell to the Tabor Grand Opera House on the eve of its destruction in 1964. In its grander days, the opera house, built in the 1880s at Sixteenth and Curtis Streets (below), was the city's finest theater. Meanwhile, over on Blake Street, St. Louis Hall and Bowling Alley blossomed with the city's population boom after 1870.

Denver's Hosteliers

HOUSES AND HOTELS: Barney Ford (above), a runaway slave who escaped via the Underground Railroad, became one of early-day Denver's finest innkeepers. In 1873, just 13 years after he arrived in Denver, he built the Inter Ocean Hotel (right), which was acclaimed by the Rocky Mountain News *as "the finest in the territory." By the 1960s, it had deteriorated to a skid row flop house and was destroyed.*

Thousands, perhaps millions, of dollars changed hands over the billiard tables (bottom right) in the Navarre (bottom left), 1725 Tremont Street, one of the most notorious sporting houses in turn-of-the-century Denver.

BALLAD OF BABY DOE: Horace Austin Warner Tabor (top right), king of Colorado's silver barons, moved from Leadville to Denver as the state's lieutenant governor in 1879. Elizabeth "Baby Doe" McCourt (bottom right), said to be the prettiest woman in Colorado, also moved to Denver to continue seeing Horace Tabor, the wealthiest man in the state, or so the legend goes. They shared a love nest in the Windsor Hotel (bottom), at Eighteenth and Larimer Streets, in the second floor room over the corner door. Their bedroom in the Windsor (far right) was preserved as a museum of extra-marital affairs until the hotel was demolished in 1960. Eventually, Baby Doe and Horace were married; however, after the death of her husband, she changed from one of the prettiest to one of the saddest sights (below) on the sidewalks of Denver.

73

PALATIAL SURROUNDINGS: The Brown Palace Hotel (right) has been one of the city's finest since its construction in 1892. Tipplers gather at the old stand-up bar (below) while well-heeled Denverites lounge in the lobby of the Brown Palace in 1911.

recognized landmark. Hidden on the wall of the Buckhorn amid hundreds of stuffed mammals and birds, frontier artifacts and Buffalo Bill memorabilia is Colorado liquor license number one.

Union Station, the gateway to nineteenth-century Denver, survives at the foot of Seventeenth Street. Most of the skyscraping banks and office buildings have been built uptown away from the depot that first made Seventeenth Street the Wall Street of the Rockies.

Many of the passengers disembarking at Union Depot came seeking better health in the dry, sunny Colorado climate. Denverites called them "lungers" or "chasers" or the "one-lunged army." These health seekers soon outnumbered gold and silver hunters. To accommodate them, Denverites built numerous hospitals, sanitariums, convalescent and old-age homes. "With the opening of the spring of 1871," Denver's *Inter-Ocean* magazine reported in 1880, "the consumptive stricken and threatened of the east, captivated by the promise of health in the pure air of the mountains, encouraged by the assurance of easy and luxurious modes of travel and charmed by the picture of railroad trains running through herds of buffalo were drawn in great numbers to Colorado. They came alike from bleak New England, from the breezy Northwest, and from the sultry South. They filled the hotels, crowded the boarding houses, and thickly invaded the private residences. In the cool mornings and evenings they moved in thronging, encumbering crowds through the streets, and in the heated mid-day, they blocked with their chairs, the shaded portions of the sidewalks."

The able-bodied came to Denver as well. For with the rail age, Denver became a booming, labor-hungry metropolis with many diverse industries. Agriculture became one of the most important employers in the Denver area.

From the beginning, Denver was a cowtown. Some of the '59ers brought cattle with them and left the travel-worn creatures outdoors to fend for themselves over the winter. In the spring, owners were surprised to find their cattle sleek after a winter of feasting on dried buffalo grass. Many, including Captain Jack Henderson (for whose ranch an Adams County town is named) took advantage of the generally mild winters, the vast open range and cheap Texas longhorns. Their pioneer ranches fed beef-hungry

Homes for the night

RISE AND FALL: The proud proprietor of the American House stands atop the hotel in its heydey (above left) when a drink would be served up with the flip of a bar token (below). By 1930, the American had fallen to a dollar-a-night skid row flophouse (top right); in 1933, a service station stood on the site (bottom right). The intersection is now the lower downtown terminal of the Sixteenth Street Transit Mall.

When the American House opened at 1601 Blake in 1869, Denver ballyhooed its first grand hotel. John W. Smith, a versatile entrepreneur and first president of the Board of Trade, equipped his hostelry with all the latest gadgets and conveniences.

In the largely unwashed frontier town, guests stewed blissfully in the metal bathtubs—a novelty which bellboys filled with pitchers of hot water. Afterwards, patrons, who included notable visitors such as Buffalo Bill, Generals Phil Sheridan and George Custer, Baby Doe Tabor and President Grant could collapse on feather beds.

Hotels, as Henry James suggested in *The American Scene*, became "the synonym for civilization" in a footloose, democratic society. As Denver's palace of the public, the American sported the finest billiard parlor in town. Crowds packed the place to see local hustlers take on visiting "hot shots."

Supremacy of the American House ended in 1879 with the opening of the Windsor Hotel. The Windsor boasted 176 marble mantels and a taproom floor covered with silver dollars. Subsequently, construction of the Albany, the Brown Palace and a dozen better uptown hotels left the American in the shadows of a fading lower downtown.

Today, American House and practically all of its nineteenth-century competitors have been demolished, robbing the city of its Victorian heritage.

Denver and the mountain mining camps. Ranches sprang up on the plains and in the mountain valleys, while dozens of dairies soon lined Cherry Creek.

Cattle had their run of early Denver. T.S. Sopris, night telegraph operator for the *Rocky Mountain News* in the 1860s, recalled, "Along about 10 o'clock p.m. Johnnie Murphys' cows would meander down from Curtis Street to forage along the fronts of the grocery shops for such stray cabbage leaves, potatoes and other vegetables as might have been left outside after closing time. Having made a clean-up, the blamed cows would lie down on the sidewalk, to await the coming of dawn."

John Wesley Iliff was the most famous and successful of the Colorado cattle barons. Iliff left his family's farm after supposedly spurning his father's offer of a $7,500 Ohio farm with the remark, "Just give me $500 and let me go West."

When he failed to find gold, Iliff settled in Denver, where he grew vegetables to sell or trade for cattle brought west by emigrants. Iliff also began buying up Texas longhorns to increase his herd. When the Union Pacific railroad construction team reached Wyoming, Iliff landed a fat contract to supply them beef.

He switched from Texas longhorns to English herefords and grabbed an expanse of open range on the northwest bank of the South Platte that stretched from Greeley to Julesburg. Iliff filed—or had his cowboys file—"dummy homesteads" along the river bank and any water holes to keep out "nesters" (as the cattlemen contemptuously called farmers). By monopolizing some 15,000 acres of riverbank, Iliff controlled an estimated 650,000 acres of public domain.

By 1878 (the year John Wesley Iliff died), more than 65,000 cattle carried the "LF" brand. Iliff's widow was a pioneer drummer—for the Singer Sewing Machine Company—who caught the cattle baron's eye while peddling her wares. She ran the ranch for ten years after his death. In his memory, she gave a tenth of the family fortune to establish the Iliff School of Theology at the University of Denver.

Railroad cattle cars made Denver a trail-end for the drives up from Texas along the Goodnight-Loving Trail. At first, the bawling longhorns were shipped to Kansas City and Chicago. Then, with the establishment of the Denver Union Stockyards in the 1880s, Denver became a major livestock center with acres of feedlots, slaughter houses, rendering plants and meat processing plants. Swift, Armour and Cudahy once operated major plants in the Mile High City. By 1890, hundreds of head of cattle and a greater number of sheep daily rode the rails into Denver slaughterhouses.

In 1898 the Chamber of Commerce, the Colorado Cattlemen's Association and other livestock interests planned a national stock show for Denver. They arranged for a public barbeque featuring the meat of five buffalo, four elk, two bears, fifteen antelope, ten beeves, 30 sheep and 200 opossums. Eighteen cooks worked all night to prepare the meat as well as 15,000 loaves of bread, 500 pounds of coffee, three barrels of loaf sugar, 10,000 pickles, 35 barrels of yams and 300 kegs of beer. January 27, 1898, dawned sunny. Throngs of Denverites rushed to Union Station for the shuttle trains to the stockyards coliseum. The ensuing riot was not caused by the several thousand visiting stockgrowers from throughout the United

COLORADO STOCK: *John Wesley Iliff (top) was the state's prime cattle baron and owned this Denver townhouse (above); he ran his livestock on the open range from Greeley to Julesberg. A jaunty stock show cowgirl (left) poses circa 1903.*

States and Canada but by some 25,000 unruly Denverites. Hobos, hoodlums, street urchins, winos and others crashed the ticket office and broke an iron fence protecting the tracks. They quickly filled the passenger cars, jammed into the locomotive and caboose and climbed on car roofs.

By noon, nearly 30,000 people had overrun the coliseum. The mob made a mad rush for the long food tables, breaking through lines and precipitating fisticuffs. Women and children were trampled, and one person was murdered. The 300 beer kegs were tapped, and a riotous feast began. After demolishing the food, the mob took care of the dirty dishes and silverware. Newspapers the next day reported the loss of 1,000 knives and forks, 2,000 tin cups, 50 china platters, 25 galvanized iron pails, 20 iron meat hooks, cleavers, hatchets and the beer glasses. No one held a national stock show in Denver for another eight years. The city still prefers to call the 1906 National Western Stock Show its first. By 1925, the annual festival eclipsed even Chicago's International Stock Show. That year, over $8 million in business was conducted during the one-week exhibition. The 1980 Stock Show broke all attendance records, with the rodeo, Beef Palace exhibits and Hall of Education attractions drawing over a quarter million spectators. "Houston's stock show may attract more people, but they're mostly Texans," observed Denver's National Western manager Chuck Sylvester. "Our show attracts folks from all all over North America and all over the world."

The National Western is Denver's biggest festival and a moneymaker as well. In 1980, 13,750 animals were sold. The top polled Hereford bull fetched over $99,000, and the average animal sold for $756. Despite Denver's efforts to outgrow cowtown status, even the most sophisticated newcomers seem to relish that one week in the middle of January—traditionally the coldest week of the year—when the live-stockers arrive. In honor of the stock show, Christmas lights are kept up until it is over, and many Coloradans revert to Stetson hats, bolo ties, pointed-toed boots and pearl-buttoned shirts for a week of reliving Denver's cowtown heritage. And every year, heroic efforts are made to surpass that first riotous show of 1898.

Railroads also made Denver a farm center. Many fortune seekers turned to agriculture after failing to find gold. Rufus "Potato" Clark cultivated acres of spuds and made a fortune. Clark donated some of his 4,500 pieces of property (which occupy 12 consecutive pages in the county assessor's books) to the University of Denver for their current campus. For farmers, as well as for miners and ranchers, the boom began with the blast of a locomotive whistle.

After building across the sparsely settled High Plains, the railroads began national and international recruitment campaigns to bring in settlers who would become railroad customers. To promote eastern Colorado, the Kansas Pacific set up an agricultural experiment station. They published prospectuses that claimed trees, shrubs, grains and vegetables could be grown "without resort to expensive processes of artificial watering."

Both the Denver Pacific and Kansas Pacific railroads received land grants and hired William N. Byers to help sell them. Byers promoted the Kansas Pacific towns of Deer Trail, Peoria, Strasburg and Byers in Arapahoe County as well as Bennett, Manila and Watkins in Adams County. Present-day Aurora has absorbed the old Kansas Pacific farm stops of Sable, Burnell and Schuyler.

Agricultural hamlets along the Denver Pacific railroad included Greeley, Evans, LaSalle and Platteville in Weld County and Brighton (formerly Hughes) and Commerce City (formerly Adams City) in Adams County. Arvada, Wheatridge and Lakewood were born on or near the Colorado Central tracks. These villages in the shadows of water tanks, windmills and grain elevators were the bread, beef and butter of Denver. After the gold and silver boom ended, they sustained the Mile High City.

Sod-busters were coaxed onto the Colorado plains during the wet

WESTERN STOCK: Denverites gathered at the 1907 National Western Stock Show (top left); before the amphitheater was completed and the coliseum opened, a monstrous tent (150 by 175 feet) housed the stock show at the corner of East 47th Avenue and Lafayette Street. The National Amphitheatre (bottom left) was completed just in time for the 1909 National Western Stock Show; it is still used for livestock judging events and continues to be a focal point of the exhibition. A 1973 aerial photo shows the barrel-roofed Denver Coliseum, south of Interstate 70, and the old amphitheatre, north of the freeway (top). The large square building on the north side of the amphitheatre is the $2½-million Hall of Education, Beef Palace and Horse Center on the site of the pioneer 1906 stock exhibit, auction and fair. From the beginning, cowgirls (above) as well as cowboys participated in Denver's National Western Stock Show.

Rufus "Potato" Clark's old farm house (right) stood on South Santa Fe near Evans Avenue, at least until 1956 when this photograph was taken.

decades of the 1870s and 1880s. They survived with the help of barbed wire, windmills, sod houses, dryland farming techniques and a rash of canal building. But many farms dried up and blew away in the droughts and dust storms of the 1890s, 1930s and 1970s. Abandoned farm houses, ranches and agricultural ghost towns dot the plains. In many cases, broken windmills and empty water tanks tombstone the heroic efforts to cultivate the Great American Desert.

Railroads made Denver the manufacturer and supplier as well as the market and food processor for High Plains horticulture. In the heart of the city, around Union Station, the old factories and warehouses of seed companies, farm machinery manufacturers and food processors can still be seen. One farm town relic still hides amid the downtown skyscrapers. Rocky Mountain Seed Company on Fifteenth Street remains a small, old-time farm store where clerks deal out garden goods and sound advice over the oak counter: "In Denver, spring can fool you. Here today and gone tomorrow. Don't dig up your vegetable patch until the soil is dry and loose enough to sift through your fingers. It's too early if you can make your dirt into a mudball....

And to grow taters in this area, just toss down the seed tater, stomp on it, and throw some straw on it."

The farmhouse museum, barnyard petting zoo and agricultural exhibits at the Littleton Historical Museum are skillfully reconstructed reminders that metropolitan Denver's history is rooted in prairie soil as well as mountain mines. Littleton, like most of the small towns swallowed by the mushrooming metropolis, began as a agricultural village.

Today the raw, high, dry plains may be experienced first-hand at the Plains Conservation Center in Arapahoe County. A three-square-mile tract contains native vegetation, jackrabbits, rattlesnakes, deer, antelope and prairie dogs. A sod school house, farm and museum help tell the story of the pioneer farms of the Denver region.

A 1,000-pound steer is quite an investment. After trimming to a 615-pound slaughterhouse carcass, it yields 165 pounds of chuck roast, 23 pounds of brisket beef, 19 pounds of shank steak, 51 pounds of short plate, 60 pounds of rib steak, 106 pounds of loin beef, 139 pounds of round steak, 32 pounds of flank steak and 20 pounds of kidney and suet. In addition, marshmallows, oleo, gelatin, candy, insulin, cholesterol, estrogen, leather, fertilizer, soap, cosmetics, prophylactics, buttons, explosives, china, camera film, sandpaper, violin strings and sporting equipment are made with slaughterhouse by-products.

FARM FOLK: A surviving nineteenth-century farm house (top) stands near Parker in Douglas County. To the north, east and south, metro Denver is surrounded by ranches and farms where folk work (above) to make the "Great American Desert" bloom.

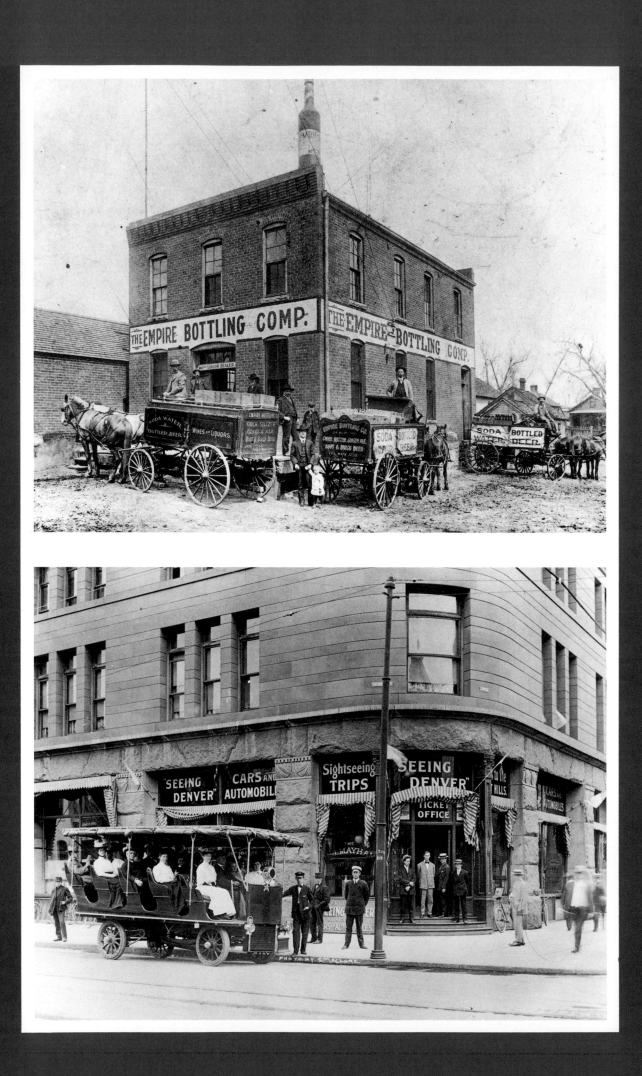

CHAPTER 6

Dreams & dollars

The Denver Chamber of Commerce, which replaced the Board
of Trade in 1884, was founded to
"promote general prosperity in
all the varied interests of Colorado and Denver."

EARLY CHAMBER: *General Roger Williams Woodbury (top), journalist and banker, was the first president of the Denver Chamber of Commerce. Promoting Denver during the Depression of 1893, Denver's business community tried to cheer up the town and perk up the economy with an annual carnival, the Festival of Mountain and Plain (below).*

From the beginning, Coloradans strove for economic independence. As early as 1859 they taxed all merchandise "not the growth, manufacture or product of the territory." Denver was hundreds of miles from the nearest industrial centers—Chicago, St. Louis, Omaha, New Orleans and San Francisco. Confronted by geographical isolation and high freight rates, Denverites aspired to manufacture every good and provide every service that Coloradans needed.

The Denver Chamber of Commerce, which replaced the Board of Trade in 1884, was founded to "promote general prosperity in all the varied interests of Colorado and Denver." John Evans, who had launched the Board of Trade to build the Denver Pacific, also sparked the new coalition of civic and commercial interests. So did mining millionaire Horace Tabor, William Byers and entrepreneur and *Denver Tribune* editor, Roger Woodbury, who was elected the Chamber's first president.

These captains of commerce set up committees to deal with finance, commerce, manufacturing, railroads, mines and smelting, stock growing, stockyards and packing, agriculture, architecture and arts, education and schools and membership. The Chamber built an elegant four-story building (the site is now a parking lot) at Fourteenth and Lawrence streets. The Chamber also maintained the city's first free library and the State Historical and Natural History Society in its building during the 1880s and 1890s.

Denver's businessmen helped stage an 1882 National Mining and Industrial Exposition which attracted international attention to Colorado's economic possibilities. The grandiose exhibition hall stood at the corner of Broadway and what is still called Exposition Avenue.

The Chamber also lobbied in Washington for an army base in Denver. After General Phil Sheridan selected a site on the southwestern outskirts of Denver, the Chamber purchased and donated the land. Construction began in 1887. Three years later, an expansive, well-landscaped fort with a hospital and burial grounds was completed. It was christened Fort Logan. The street leading to it was named Sheridan Boulevard in honor of the famous Civil War hero and Indian fighter. Nearby the town of Sheridan sprung up to service the fort. By 1900, the town boasted 117 families and seven saloons.

William Newton Byers presided over the Chamber of Commerce from 1892 to 1895. The greying but tireless booster involved the business community in economic and cultural activities ranging from courting industry to collecting Mesa Verde antiquities for the State Historical and Natural History Society. (The society moved into the Colorado State Museum Building in 1915 and became the State Historical Society of Colorado in 1927). The Chamber began ballyhooing Colorado as "The Switzerland of America" for tourists. They enticed cotton mills and clothing manufacturers to Denver and started tree-planting on the grounds of the unfinished State Capitol. The Chamber also distributed sugar beet seeds to farmers who were given cash prizes for the best results.

In 1893, Colorado was shaken to its financial roots by the depression of 1893. The national depression, coupled with a move to the gold

All that remains of Denver's old city hall at Fourteenth and Larimer Streets is the bell tower on a pedestal.

standard, crippled Colorado's leading industry—silver mining—and threw the city and state into a panic. Half of Denver's banks failed, many of them permanently. Construction froze, leaving unfinished building skeletons downtown and unfinished basement excavations on the surrounding prairie. Meadowlarks, prairie dogs and prickly pear cactus repossessed many unfinished, bankrupt subdivisions. The *Rocky Mountain News* and other newspapers bulged with dozens of pages of tax sale properties.

In Leadville, Aspen, Georgetown, the San Juans and other silver mining communities, the situation was even more desperate. As the mines closed, thousands of unemployed drifted to Denver where some joined Coxey's Army. Jacob S. Coxey, a former Republican mayor of Massilon, Ohio, was organizing a nationwide march on Washington to demand relief and jobs.

While out-of-work Coloradans squatted around campfires along the Denver river bottoms, city officials and Chamber leaders nervously sought a solution. After serving hundreds of meals a day to the bottomless pit of unemployed, the Chamber came up with a novel idea. They acquired lumber and hundreds of dollars worth of food and then propositioned the increasingly desperate army of homeless and jobless. Could the army become a navy and make riverboats from the lumber if the Chamber set up food stations on their route out of Colorado?

The unemployed agreed to channel their frustration and anger on to Washington. Although few flatboats of the "South Platte Armada" successfully navigated the sandbars, most of the "sailors" left Denver and joined the streams of protesters marching on Washington. In the national capital, an unsympathetic President Grover Cleveland and a frightened Congress had Coxey arrested for walking on government grass.

Economic hardships fostered social and political unrest. Numerous new political parties and embryonic labor unions began demanding that working people be given a larger slice of the shrinking pie. Many voters abandoned the Democratic and Republican parties and turned to the Populists. Coloradans elected Davis H. Waite, an Aspen newspaper editor, as their governor. Waite took office in 1893 and vigorously pushed a Populist reform platform that included 1) regulation, if not nationalization, of the railroads; 2)

WOMEN'S RIGHTS: in 1893 Colorado approved women's suffrage.

John Kernan Mullen, the flour king of Colorado, supposedly delighted in showing off his miller's hands, scarred and imbedded with millstone fragments from the time he went into flour milling as a small boy.

government assistance for farmers; 3) initiative, referendum and recall; 4) direct election of United States Senators; 5) women's suffrage; 6) a graduated income tax; 7) a return to the bi-metallic standard and unlimited coinage of silver; and 8) recognition of labor unions, safer working conditions and an eight-hour maximum work day with a minimum wage of $3 per day.

Governor Waite, an old man with a monstrous beard, looked and acted like an old testament prophet determined to purify the Sodom and Gomorrah called Denver. "It is infinitely better that blood should flow to our horses' bridles," he told supporters at Coliseum Hall in Denver in July 1893, "than our national liberties be destroyed."

"Bloody Bridles" Waite, as he was called thereafter, started his cleanup with Denver's police department. He fired two members of the Fire and Police Board, claiming they were in collusion with gamblers. The dismissed commissioners refused to surrender to the governor's appointees. Backed by a mob of police and gamblers, the dismissed officials barricaded themselves inside the old City Hall at Fourteenth and Larimer.

Governor Waite called in the state militia. With Gatling guns and field artillery they surrounded City Hall, whose windows and roof bristled with the guns of its defenders. Jefferson Randolph "Soapy" Smith, king of the city's con-men, stationed himself in the tower with sticks of dynamite. Governor Waite then requested federal troops from Fort Logan for "preserving the peace." Thousands of Denverites left their homes and jobs to watch "The City Hall War." After what the *Denver Republican* called "the greatest turmoil and excitement ever witnessed in Denver," Governor Waite withdrew the militia to prevent bloodshed. The sinful city was not ready for a moral cleansing or the economic reforms proposed by the governor. Waite had overseen the adoption of women's suffrage but this backfired when the women helped to vote Waite out of office by a large margin in 1894.

With silver mining and railroading in a slump, Coloradans turned to other occupations. Fortunately, many gifted individuals had been working to expand and diversify Denver's economic base. The Queen City's best known nineteenth-century entrepreneur was a serious-minded, clean-shaven immigrant whose name is still repeated a million times a day in taverns and liquor stores throughout the western United States. Orphaned as a teenager, Adolph Coors sailed to America with little except experience in German breweries. The young immigrant seemed less likely to survive than several dozen other nineteenth-century Denver brewers. John Good, the Zangs, Max Melsheimer and others outproduced Coors for decades after he opened his business in a Golden tannery in 1873. Coors (according to his early ads) also dealt in "ale, porter, cider, imported and domestic wines, seltzer water, etc." Early investment in bottled beer, diligent single-family ownership and rigid quality control were ingredients of the Coors' success story. At the 1893 Columbian Exposition in Chicago, Coors was the only beer from west of the Mississippi to win a prize.

Since Tivoli closed its landmark at Tenth and Larimer streets in 1969, Coors remains the only brewer in Colorado and the fifth largest in the United States. Adolph Coors Industries, which includes a porcelain plant and brewery on the original site in Golden, is the largest private employer in metropolitan Denver.

Bread, as well as beer, became important to the Queen City's livelihood. John Kernan Mullen, an Irish immigrant, spent a life of ten-hour days

making Denver the wheat, flour and milling capital of the Rockies. After emigrating from famine-stricken County Galway, the Mullens sent young John to work rather than to school. John applied at the Davis Flour Mill in Auraria and was told that there were no openings." I am not asking for pay," the fourteen-year-old boy told Mr. Davis, "I am only asking for a chance to work."

"If you want to work that badly," Davis replied, "you may begin tomorrow morning. If we get along all right, I will pay you board and room." Mullen impressed everyone by volunteering on winter days to wade through the mill ditch from the South Platte to break up the ice. He soon earned a line on the payroll and in a few years became head miller.

All the while, Mullen saved his money—first to rent and then to buy his own mill. In 1882, he built the Hungarian Flour Mill, named for a Hungarian milling process that produces fine, white flour. By the turn of the century, Mullen's Hungarian Flour Company was a multi-million-dollar, national operation with wheat fields, grain elevators, processing plants and offices from Oregon to Kansas.

Mullen proved to be one of Denver's more generous industrialists. He donated thousands to help build Immaculate Conception, Saint Leo's and Saint Cajetan's Catholic Churches. He founded the Mullen School, the Mullen Home for the Aged and the Mullen Home for Boys at Fort Logan. The Mullen family donated heavily to Saint Joseph Hospital, the University of Denver and other charities. After climbing from the bottom to the top of the industrial ladder, Mullen empathized with even the lowest-paid employee. Consequently, he instituted one of Colorado's first profit-sharing plans.

Another major industry—brick-making—was prompted by the abundance of clay and scarcity of lumber in early-day Denver. Thomas Warren, a

PHILIP ZANG,
MITGLIED DES BAU-COMITE'S.

BREWING IN DENVER: *Philip Zang worked for Denver's first beer makers—the Rocky Mountain Brewery on Seventh Street in north Denver. After years of hauling around Rocky Mountain lager, he bought the brewery, renamed it Zang's and made it the state's largest pre-prohibition suds maker. Only the brewmeister's mansion, a National Register Landmark (below), the stables and a hotel—converted into the Zang Brewing Company saloon in the 1970s—survive of the huge brewery complex.*

Kentuckian who also operated the first ferry over the South Platte, opened a brickyard in 1859. Warren found that iron oxide in the native clay gave Denver brick a warm, pinkish glow similar to that of the local sandstone. Others followed Warren's lead and soon bricks sold for as little as $6 a thousand while lumber cost $5 a hundred feet. Even before the fire of 1863 and the brick ordinances, Denver was maturing into a brick city.

With the building boom of the 1880s, dozens of brick companies sprung up. One of them, the Robinson Brick and Tile Company, still makes over 100,000 bricks a day. After a century of operation, board chairman Will W. Robinson, grandson of the founder, claimed brick would never go out of style although "it is as difficult and delicate as making fine china."

Charles C. Gates, a young mining engineer, founded the Colorado Tire & Leather Company in 1911. "You re-sole your shoes," Gates advertised, "why not your tires?" His retreads consisted of a leather band with steel studs strapped over the old wheel. The business started rolling in 1917 when Charles' brother John invented the world's first V-belt. After booming with the automobile age, the Gates Company entered the air age in 1967 when it acquired the high-flying Learjet Company.

By 1980, Charles C. Gates Jr. presided over an international empire that included 16,000 employees in 19 plants around the world with sales approaching a

SIGNS OF INDUSTRY: The Hungarian Flour Mill in Auraria (top) shortly before demolition; and the Gates Rubber Company's South Broadway plant.

billion dollars a year. Through the generosity of the Gates Foundation, Denver has received such amenities as the Gates Planetarium at City Park, the Gates Tennis Center and large grants to the Greenway Foundation which is converting Denver's long-abused waterways into a network of parks.

Of those who made Denver a manufacturing center, Charles Boettcher provides the best example of diversification. He epitomized the many mobile, imaginative and hard-working frontier entrepreneurs who conquered the West from behind roll-top desks.

At seventeen, Charles left Prussia in 1869 to visit his brother Herman, who had opened a hardware store in Cheyenne. Herman was swamped with business. He quickly put his little brother to work as a tinner, cutting, shaping and seaming tin cups, plates, coffee pots, roofs and cornices. Charles was paid a dollar or two a week and allowed to sleep under the counter. The youngster managed to compound his income with loans to fellow employees for their weekend sprees.

After the Denver Pacific Railway & Telegraph Company was completed between Cheyenne and Denver, the Boettchers opened stores in Greeley and Fort Collins. In all their stores, the family motto was "Hard goods, hardware and hard cash."

While operating the Greeley store, Charles met and married Fannie Augusta Cowan, daughter of a Kansas farmer. Soon after the nuptial, the couple moved to Boulder where Charles built a handsome, two-story brick store. It still stands at the junction of Broadway and the Pearl Street Mall with the doorway inscription in stone—"C. Boettcher A.D. 1878."

A year after opening shop in Boulder, Boettcher turned it over to an assistant and moved to Leadville, where a fabulous silver boom had astounded Colorado and the nation. Even the governor of Colorado, John L. Routt, donned overalls to dig a hole in Carbonate Hill. It sold a year later for $1 million as the Morning Star Mine.

By 1880, two-year-old Leadville was the second largest city in Colorado. The city fathers talked of moving the state capital up from Denver. In the two-mile-high "Cloud City," Boettcher managed to avoid the silver fever epidemic. "Axes and hammers," he told mine promoters, "don't go out of style."

Boettcher began investing his hardware profits in real estate, the Carbonate Bank of Leadville and the Leadville Light and Power Company (which the family traded to the Public Service Company of Colorado in 1924 for stock and a directorship). He also purchased the 180-square-mile Bighorn Ranch in North Park.

In 1890, the Boettchers moved to Denver's Capitol Hill area which had attracted many of his Leadville neighbors and business associates—Horace Tabor, Dennis Sheedy, John J. Campion, J.J. and Molly Brown. Boettcher purchased a large wholesale hardware company in Denver and began dealing in mining, milling, agricultural, railroad and construction supplies.

Fannie, his wife, finally talked the hard-working tycoon into a European vacation and visit with his relatives. Charles was particularly interested in the farms of the Saale River Valley which made Germany the world's largest producer of sugar beets. Although the Germans kept foreigners from snooping around their technologically advanced sugar beet factories, Charles learned what he could. Then he ordered Fannie to empty one of their suitcases. After cramming it full of choice sugar beet seed and directions for its cultivation and processing, the Boettchers abruptly returned to Denver. By the end of the year, he and some associates set up the Great Western Sugar Company.

During construction of the Loveland sugar beet factory, Boettcher noted that the cement was imported from Germany at an extremely high cost. He looked into the matter and found that limestone, silica, alumina and other materials for making cement were available in Colorado. Why was it imported? Engineers told him that American firms could not match the quality of the German cement.

Boettcher soon changed that. His Portland Cement Company (later a part of Ideal Basic Industries) began manufacturing quality cement and selling it across America. In 1908, Boettcher erected a pioneer all-concrete building as his new

Charles Boettcher, a German immigrant, created Colorado's greatest industrial empire.

Margaret "Molly" Tobin went to Leadville at the age of 15 and married James Joseph Brown when she was 16. Their Leadville silver mines made them millionaires and they moved to Denver, her rough mining-town edges were smoothed by European tutors. Molly's greater fame came when she sailed aboard the ill-fated Titanic. After the ship hit an iceberg and began to sink, she took command of a lifeboat and enforced the women-and-children-first rule with a pistol. She kept up passengers' spirits by singing hymns as they drifted in the ocean. She received a trophy for her heroism (below) and the name "Unsinkable Molly Brown."

Queen City manufacturers tried to produce every good needed in the Rocky Mountain hinterland, including "sheet metal of every description."

The Liebhardt Commission Company building, 1624-1630 Market Street, became a part of the Market Center restoration project in the 1970s.

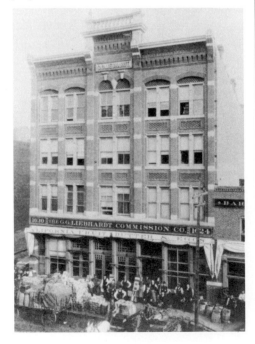

headquarters at Seventeenth and Champa streets (now the handsomely restored home of Colorado Federal Savings and Loan Association).

From his fifth floor office in the Ideal Building, Charles reigned over a rapidly growing industrial empire. He and associates founded the Western Packing Company, Capitol Life Insurance Company, the Denver National Bank, the National Fuse and Powder Company and many other ventures.

Boettcher became the president of the Moffat Road after David Moffat's death and oversaw completion of the long-awaited Moffat Tunnel. Although Colorado taxpayers in the counties served by the Moffat Road grumbled about paying for it, most welcomed the tunnel as a fast, year-round route through the snow-capped Rockies.

Fannie Boettcher saw little of her hard-working husband. As they grew further apart, she went on round-the-world shopping sprees but could not spend money nearly as fast as her husband made it. In the 1920s, Charles moved out of the home on Grant Street and into the Brown Palace Hotel. He quickly fell in love with the Brown and brought it. Shortly afterwards, his only son and close business associate, Claude, also moved to the Brown from his Capitol Hill home (which the Boettcher Foundation later gave to Colorado for the Governor's Mansion).

Claude moved his collection of bottled ships and nautical artifacts into the hotel—some of them may still be seen in the Ship Tavern. In the late 1950s, Claude converted the eighth-floor ballroom into two floors of rooms, including the presidential suite that Dwight Eisenhower used as his western headquarters.

In his 90s, Charles Boettcher continued to leave the Brown every day for his office five blocks down Seventeenth Street. Stories of his frugality delighted Coloradans. At night he left his hotel suite to buy soda pop across the street. Asked why he did not call room service, the multi-millionaire mumbled, "And pay the prices we charge here?"

The tycoon died in his sleep on July 2, 1948. He left a vast estate to the Boettcher Foundation, which he and Claude created for philanthropic and tax purposes. Since he had made his fortune in Colorado, Charles requested that all the foundation's funds be spent in-state. Since his death, the foundation has given away almost $50 million. Among the many results are the Boettcher School for Crippled Children, the Boettcher Wing of the Denver Museum of Natural History, the Boettcher Conservatory of the Denver Botanic Gardens and Boettcher halls in the Denver Center for the Performing Arts and the Colorado Heritage Center. Numerous schools, hospitals, public institutions and other causes have been blessed with Boettcher's millions.

In 1965, the Brown Palace Hotel became a part of the Boettcher Foundation, which ran the Brown in a traditional way, perpetuating the elegant comforts and services of a nineteenth-century grand hotel. There Denverites and visitors could find fresh-squeezed orange juice, artesian water, gentlemen in coats and ties and ladies in dresses.

Besides the Boettchers, hundreds of other hard-working business people also created diverse enterprises that enabled Denver to survive the nineteenth-century boom-and-bust cycle. The city had been founded on a gamble for gold and sustained by risky mining and railroad speculation. But by the turn of the century, Denver's business community had learned caution and diversity. Consequently, during the twentieth century, Denver has had a more stable, healthier economy than most American cities. Fluctuations in military spending, automobile sales, aviation, electronics, agriculture and other components of the economy have affected less diversified cities more critically.

When the energy boom of the 1980s plays out—as other mineral rushes have in the past—Denver's currently overheated economy should cool off and stabilize. For the city has a sound agricultural, industrial and commercial base.

METRO DENVER'S LEADING EMPLOYERS

1880s	1980
1. Smelting and refining	1. Wholesale and retail trade
2. Construction	2. Service industries
3. Meat packing	3. Federal, state and local government
4. Flour processing	4. Manufacturing
5. Lumbering	5. Self-employment
6. Metal working	6. Transportation and public utilities
7. Brewing	7. Finance, insurance and real estate
8. Textiles and clothing	8. Construction
9. Painting and paper-hanging	9. Mining and oil companies
10. Brick-making	10. Agriculture

—Statistics adapted from
Denver Chamber of Commerce

WOEBER BROS. CARRIAGE MANUFACTORY.

FOR, FROM FARMERS: *This 1920 scene on Blake Street (top) is a reminder that the Mile High City was the nucleus of a vast farming region. Denver stores sold everything from seeds and fertilizer to the final agricultural product. Whittmore and Company (above) was begun by a pioneer flour miller in 1864.*

NEW JOURNALISM: *The* Denver Post, *for years at 1544 Champa Street (left), was founded by bartender Harry Tammen and con-man Frederick G. Bonfils. Their sensation-seeking operation became one of the most notorious—and profitable—newspapers in America. Gene Fowler (inset), the best-known of many characters to work for the* Post, *wrote an uproarious book,* Timberline, *about the newspaper and the city it titillated. The* Post, *he wrote, launched "a blatantly new journalism, called by some a menace, a font of indecency, a nuptial flight of vulgarity and sensationalism...."*

CIVILIZATION? Despite the White River Massacre and Ute Scare of 1879, Indians (inset) were warily asked to help stage the 1882 National Mining and Industrial Exposition. Bustling markets in 1905 (left) gave Market Street its name, though the red light district's flesh markets four blocks away were better known. Faro tables (above) were one of many ways to lose money at Soapy Smith's Larimer Street gambling house. Confident that his customers could not read Latin, Soapy installed a doorway sign that warned, "Caveat Emptor."

WATER AND ICE: Walter Scott Cheesman (below) made a fortune supplying Denver with water. Fortunes could be spent in Sam Mayer's Diamond Palace (above) on Sixteenth Street. Seafood was kept cool during the winter of 1913 at 1642 Market Street (left), where the Seattle Fish Company still sells "anything that swims."

City Park Lake and Pavilion, 1906.

CHAPTER 7

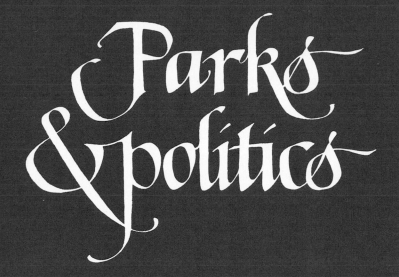

Parks & politics

> *"Why the hell does Denver need a Greek theatre?"* sniped one of many critics. *"We ain't got that many Greeks here."*

MILE HIGH GROWTH: Robert W. Speer (above), Denver's strongest mayor, came to Colorado dying of tuberculosis. After recovering in the high, dry climate, he beautified the Mile High City, which grew to be honeycombed with parkways and municipal attractions. As the city grew, annexations were added (below).

obert Walter Speer came to Denver from Pennsylvania in 1878 at the age of 23. Like thousands of others he came with lungs raw and bleeding from tuberculosis, under doctor's orders to seek out the salubrious Colorado climate.

Soon his friends marveled at what Colorado's sunshine and crisp air had done for the young man. Speer's color improved; he gained weight, a strong handshake and a broad grin. The only thing he seemed to be losing was hair.

He found a job at Denver's most elegant department store—Daniels & Fisher—selling carpets for $8 a week. But he left because the rug fibers irritated his lungs and switched to selling real estate. The ambitious Pennsylvanian thrived during the 1880s boom and began rubbing shoulders with the city's makers and shakers. He served as secretary of Horace Tabor's Lookout Mountain development company west of Denver.

On the other side of town, Speer became involved with the power elite in developing Denver's most prestigious neighborhood. He and some associates laid out Park Club Place (Downing to Franklin and First to Fourth streets). Industrialist Charles Boettcher and future United States Senators Charles Hughes and Lawrence C. Phipps converted the adjacent site into Country Club Place (Franklin to Race and First to Fourth streets). When Speer became mayor, he had Speer Boulevard end in front of these two havens for the wealthy. Critics charged that Speer Boulevard was a driveway to downtown for the Country Club set and Speer. Speer himself

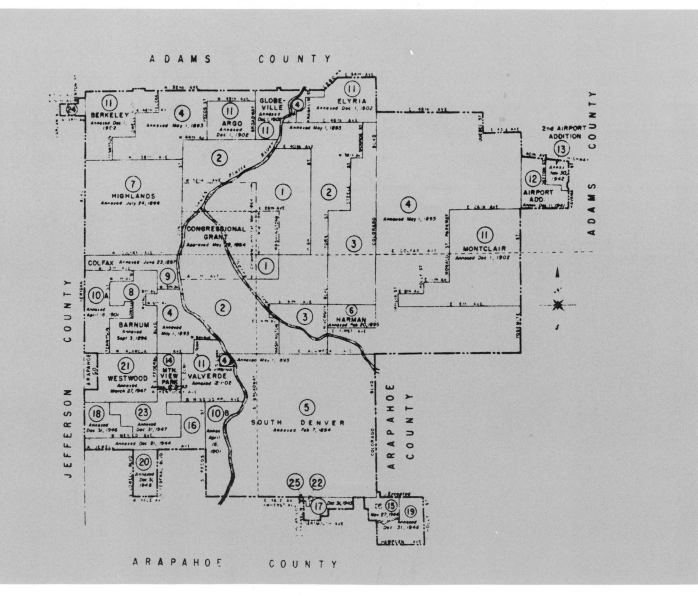

settled at 300 Humboldt Street. (In 1979, the National Register of Historic Places designated Park Club Place and Country Club Place as the Country Club Historic District. In this mansion-studded neighborhood and in the Denver Country Club just across Speer Boulevard, much of Denver's elite may be found to this day.)

Soon after his arrival in Denver, Speer went to work for the Democratic Party. After election in 1884 as city clerk, he moved through appointments as postmaster of Denver, fire and police board commissioner and president of the board of public works. Speer used the patronage jobs and city contracts he controlled to build the most powerful political machine ever seen in Denver. To insure their jobs, city employees joined Speer Democrat clubs and gave percentages of their paychecks to election campaigns. Underworld characters dealing with the police department and business people seeking city contracts and concessions found it wise to support the Speer coalition. Even without such shady underpinnings, Robert W. Speer was a crackerjack votegetter—a large, congenial, open-hearted man who seemed to be everyone's friend.

For several decades before 1902, the governor and state legislature had largely governed the capital city through the boards they controlled. After Governor Waite's "City Hall War," Denverites had begun campaigning for the right to elect their own leadership. In 1902 the city gained home rule under the 20th Amendment to the State Constitution.

The Home Rule Amendment also removed Denver from Arapahoe County and created the city and county of Denver. The outlying towns of Elyria, Globeville, Argo, Berkeley, Valverde and Montclair were then annexed to Denver.

Voters approved a new city charter in 1904 establishing a powerful chief executive and a relatively weak city council. The strong mayoral form of government seemed tailor-made for Robert W. Speer. In 1904, he was elected mayor in spite of all four daily newspapers. The *Rocky Mountain News*, *Denver Post*, *Denver Times* and *Denver Republican* for once all clamored in harmony, claiming that Speer's victory rested on 10,000 illegal votes.

Despite undeniably ugly electioneering, the chief concern of the new administration was to beautify Denver. Speer was inspired by a tour of European cities and determined to transform the dusty, drab, midwestern town into an urban oasis. The new mayor could be found in his office late in the evenings and on Sunday mornings poring over reports and plans for beautifying other cities, studying local revenues and expenses and scrutinizing blueprints for a better Denver.

In the heart of the city, Speer proposed a park-like civic center. Using the State Capitol and a projected new city and county building as the east-west axis, Speer had some of the nation's finest architects and landscapers lay out gardens, monuments, a library, fountains and an outdoor Greek theatre. "Why the hell does Denver need a Greek theatre?" sniped one of many critics. "We ain't got that many Greeks here."

The Queen City's worst eyesore was a sandy scar festering with dumps that cut through southeast Denver. Cherry Creek, according to Jerome

Buffalo Bill Cody was idolized by children during his last years in Denver, but adults tended to be more critical. They gossiped that his physician limited the great scout and showman to ten shots of whiskey which he took daily in quart steins.

Denver City and County Building was completed in 1932 at a cost of $4,730,547.

The original building of the Denver Museum of Natural History opened in 1908 in City Park. A half century later, this building had disappeared behind numerous additions, including the Phipps Auditorium and Gates Planetarium.

Smiley's 1901 *History of Denver* was a "blighting blemish" and a "miserable waste." Smiley suggested arresting the creek at Denver's eastern boundary and diverting it around the city via Sand Creek. Speer had more imagination. Working with the creek rather than against it, he walled it as a park-lined, landscaped median for Speer Boulevard. Speer had similar plans for a South Platte River drive and greenway—a dream realized 60 years later during the administration of Mayor William H. McNichols Jr.

Speer used his skill as a real estate developer to Denver's advantage. When the city attorney vetoed acquisition of land west of Sheridan Boulevard to enlarge Berkeley Park, Speer personally bought the land and sold the scenic plot with the million-dollar view to Denver for the price he paid for it—$8,000.

The idea of mountain parks outside the city limits evidently originated with John Brisben Walker. Walker was one of Denver's most incredible wheelers and dealers. He had attended West Point, served as a general in the Chinese army at the age of 20 and made $2 million in real estate by the time he was 26. He came to Denver in 1870 to supervise development of Highland Park (a Scottish development in north Denver, still remarkable for its tiny, twisting European streets with Scottish names). In order to experiment with the cultivation of alfalfa, Walker purchased a North Denver farm that was later platted as the Town of Berkeley. Walker gave 50 acres of his farm to the Jesuits for the establishment of Regis College. He also built now-demolished Riverside Park near the confluence of Cherry Creek and the South Platte, complete with a castle, steamboats and outdoor theatre. In 1890, Walker left Denver to purchase a struggling New York magazine called *Cosmopolitan*, which he transformed into one of the best-read, longest-lived American magazines.

He returned to Denver in 1905 and worked with Mayor Speer on many ambitious projects. He started a summer White House for American presidents atop Mount Falcon near Morrison and built his own mansion nearby. He was wrangling with Washington over who should pay for the never-constructed White House West when lightning struck his own home in 1918. Today the ghostly, charred remains of Walker's castle and the proposed site of the western White House are part of Mount Falcon Park. Although Walker died penniless in 1931, he and Mayor Speer started Denver's unique Mountain Parks system in neighboring Jefferson County. The mayor also began construction of the world's highest automobile road up 14,264-foot Mount Evans. Today these Denver Mountain Parks are particularly welcome as "No Trespassing" signs smother the Front Range.

Mayor Speer honeycombed Denver with parks and parkways. He made parks of vacant fields, dumps, even the foothills and mountains to the west. He doubled the city's park space from 573 to 1,184 acres. He believed that parks were to play in and one of his first acts after election in 1904 was to remove all "Keep Off The Grass" signs.

At City Park, where the zoo consisted of a few chained and caged animals, Speer installed zoological gardens where animals could cavort

DOWN WITH DEMON RUM: When Carrie Nation made several hatchet-swinging crusades through sinful, saloon-filled Denver, she wound up in the city jail for disturbing the peace. Before her arrest, she lectured the Little Temperance Union of the Denver Women's Christian Temperance Union on the evils of the demon rum. When she declared war on saloons and invaded Denver, this crowd at the St. Elmo Hotel Bar (above), Seventeenth and Blake Streets, had its defenses ready—when Carrie or any other anti-saloonists came to the door, boozers unified in a deafening roar of "Whore! Whore!" The rush for the back door of Jim Ryan's Monte Carlo Saloon (left), 1901 Market Street, shows what happened after prohibitionists closed the front doors. On January 1, 1916, statewide prohibition began in Colorado, moving tipplers to back rooms and cellars of numerous "soft drink parlors."

in spacious natural habitats. Behind protective moats—not iron bars—monkeys, sea lions, elephants and other beasts inhabited islands, mountains and other skillfully reconstructed environments. The old animal cages were put in the basement of the lakeside pavilion as drunk tanks for humans.

In City Park lake, an electric fountain was installed with nine color lights and 25 water jets to provide visual accompaniment for the free concerts of the Denver Municipal Band. Private donations solicited by the city and the Chamber of Commerce built the Museum of Natural History at the eastern end of City Park. (The original 1908 building is now hidden behind numerous additions—Phipps Auditorium, the Boettcher Wing and Gates Planetarium.)

Realizing the special charm of lakes in an arid climate, Mayor Speer built the south lake of Washington Park and Sunken Gardens Lake (now grassed over) and added Berkeley, Sloans and Rocky Mountain Lakes to the park system. The city provided bath houses and bathing beaches at City Park, Washington Park, Sloans Lake and Berkeley Park. Visitors found plenty of fish in the well-stocked waters as well as sail boats, canoes and paddle boats. In winter, these ponds were converted to ice skating rinks.

Robert and Kate Speer never had children of their own but made all Denver's children their special cause. Mayor Speer's favorite statues were the Children's Fountain in City Park and Wynken, Blynken and Nod in Washington Park. Working with Anna Louise Johnson, the Speers had

Temperance Chorus

C-O-L-O-R-A-D-O yell
Who are we? The L.T.U.
Ho! Ho! Ho! Watch us grow!
When we vote the saloons will go.

PARK PLAY: The turn-of-the-century view from atop the roller coaster in Lakeside Amusement Park (left) looked out on open prairie. Boating (center left) and bathers (center right) at Berkeley Park Lake in the 1920s. Ladies enjoyed the links at Overland Park (bottom left), Denver's first golf course. Lawn bowling was the sport (bottom right) at Washington Park.

playgrounds set up throughout the city. "Three years ago," reported the *American City Magazine* for May 1910, "Denver did not know that a good playground for children was ... something else than a vacant space where children, unsupervised, had the opportunity to fight it out. Today Denver is one of the leading cities in the playground movement."

Adults also found plenty to do in the parks. Horseshoe pits, tennis courts, swimming pools, lawn tennis courts, athletic fields, race tracks, exercise programs and a variety of concerts, shows and special programs were available. For senior citizens, there were plenty of benches from which to enjoy floral plantings, landscaped vistas and people-watching.

While president of the Board of Public Works, Speer began laying out Denver's parkway system. He used landscaped medians and extensive setbacks that still give Denver a spacious, tree-shaded charm. Speer's never-completed masterplan called for parkways to connect the city parks and enable strollers and bicyclists to pedal all around the town on greenways. (In the 1970s, Denverites partially revived the Speer dream when they began construction of what is now one of America's most extensive off-street bike path systems.)

Boss Speer changed the color of Denver from brown to green. In 1905, he inaugurated a tree-planting program. The city gave saplings to Denverites who agreed to plant and care for them. By 1918, the city had given away over 110,000 trees and doubled the number of shade trees.

In the interest of a clean as well as a green Denver, the city spent millions installing and repairing storm and sanitary sewers during the Speer era. The city began cleaning sidewalks—including the 400 miles of pink flagstone installed by Mayor Speer. To make life smoother for bicyclists and pioneer automobile owners, Speer ordered the paving of over 150 miles of streets. He installed granite curbs that survive to this day. The "No parking 2:15 a.m. to 6 a.m" signs sometimes puzzle newcomers and tourists. The nightly streetsweepers often startle early-morning revelers but they are part of the Speer legacy. As a result of such efforts, Keep America Beautiful judged Denver "The Cleanest Big City in America" in the 1970s.

Denver's greatest asset, Speer realized, was the view of the snow-capped Front Range of the Rocky Mountains. Even lifelong Denverites still round a corner or reach the top of a hill and thrill at the panorama framed between Pikes Peak and Longs Peak. While the mountains had not been growing any higher, buildings and billboards had. Realizing the threat, Mayor Speer had telegraph and telephone cables buried underground, worked out a compromise 12-story height ordinance and tried to ban billboards.

In 1916, the Denver Chamber of Commerce recognized another threat to the mountain view. They introduced a smoke abatement ordinance to reduce black smoke caused by "wasted" factory fuels. (Despite these early efforts by concerned citizens, mountain viewing in the 1980s is chancy. Smog, billboards and numerous highrises have made an old tradition obsolete: no longer can Denverites always give lost travelers directions to turn toward or away from the mountains.)

Partly to boost Denver as a convention city, the mayor in 1908 dedicated the $500,000 municipal auditorium—then the largest in America except for Madison Square Garden. (The handsome auditorium at Fourteenth and Curtis is now the anchor structure for the Denver Center for the Performing Arts.) Speer, the Chamber of Commerce and the business community raised $100,000 to celebrate the opening of the auditorium by bringing Denver its first and only national political convention. The Democratic Party lovefeast focused national attention on the Queen City of the Plains.

"Whiskers are in evidence everywhere," snickered the *New York Times* on July 7, 1908, "homespun suits are to be seen, also the 'biled' shirt." It was a "hayseed" convention according to the *Times*, and journalist William Allen White agreed. He compared "this gathering of the 'peepul' ... this

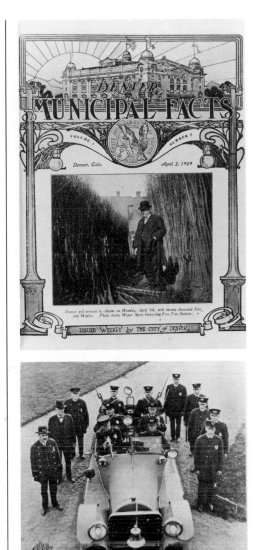

GIFTS TO THE CITY: On April 5, 1909, Mayor Speer presented Denver citizens with 20,000 elm and maple trees; he is shown (top) inspecting Free Tree Station. With their new motor-bandit chaser (above), acquired in 1921, the Denver Police were prepared for even the worst 1920s gangsters.

CITY BEAUTIFUL: Denver street cleaners, circa 1916 (top), with the old Chamber of Commerce building at Fourteenth and Lawrence Streets in the background. Henry H. Tammen, former Windsor Hotel bartender (above left) and Frederick G. Bonfils, moustached con man from Kansas City (above), founded the Denver Post in 1894 and subsequently attacked Mayor Speer's city beautification programs as being too expensive.

uprising of the oppressed," to "the great barbaric yap of which Walt Whitman speaks." Populists and Democrats combined forces to write a pro-farmer, pro-miner, pro-labor party platform reminiscent of Governor Waite's proposals back in 1893.

Denverites draped downtown with a heavy foliage of red, white and blue bunting. Brass bands greeted each state delegation arriving at Union Station. Thousands donned "I Live in Denver—Ask Me" buttons and showed delegates around town. Others brought carloads of snow down from the mountains and dumped it in front of the auditorium so delegates could cool off with a snowball fight. A band of Apache Indians circled downtown on a streetcar and let out war whoops whenever they spotted a delegate.

"Why yes," the *Denver Post* reassured conventioneers, "we can read and write, lots of us, and we don't know a woman in Denver who carries more than one revolver when she comes downtown shopping." Damon Runyan, ace reporter for the *Rocky Mountain News*, summarized: "Miss Denver, in a sassy creation of red, white and blue, appliqued with green and edged in purple mountains, stood waiting to receive all visitors and conventioneers with open arms before they went bustling up Seventeenth Street in search of a room, with bath."

The *Chicago Tribune* noted that many delegates tended to caucus in Mile High City saloons and wondered "what effect altitude has on alcohol and just what effect altitude and alcohol together have on Democrats." The result was the nomination of William Jennings Bryan, a lemonade man. Despite support from Colorado and other western states, the aging "boy orator" from Nebraska was defeated that fall in his third and last presidential race.

After the convention, Coloradans began enjoying the auditorium. Speer established America's first municipal theater there and brought in

Denver Municipal Auditorium, under construction at Fourteenth and Curtis Streets, circa 1907.

When completed in 1908, the Denver Municipal Auditorium was second in size only to Madison Square Garden.

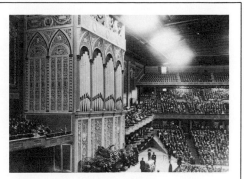

Thousands of Denverites flooded the auditorium for Mayor Speer's funeral in 1918.

Broadway plays, bands, dancers, lecturers, travelogues, movies and exhibitions. The hand-shaking, back-slapping mayor often stood by the Fourteenth Street door with free tickets for the handicapped and elderly whom he personally escorted to front-row seats. Free Sunday afternoon concerts were begun so that all citizens—even the poorest—could enjoy culture.

Railroads, businessmen, city hall and the Chamber of Commerce promoted tourism as well as conventioneering. Tourists demanded a minimal amount of urban services while spending money and paying sales taxes. "Cool, Colorful Colorado" and "Denver, The City Beautiful," became stops on the national tourist circuit. Several passenger trains a day unloaded thousands of tourists at Union Station.

Although the mayor and the Chamber did not advertise them, Denver's 500 saloons, 2,000 "brides of the multitude" and dozens of gambling houses also attracted many visitors. Old timers recall that Market Street glowed scarlet at night. Ladies of all ages, colors, sizes and proclivities posed under illuminated signs reading "Men taken in and done for" and "Friendliest house in town." Window shoppers browsed through a wide selection ranging from the parlor house niceties of Jennie Rogers and Mattie Silks to tiny cribs offering bargain-basement sex.

If the mayor and business community kept quiet about the city's demimonde along Larimer and Market streets, a growing chorus of reformers did not. Judge Benjamin Barr Lindsey was Colorado's best known Progressive and the founder of Denver's world famous juvenile court system. He exposed the city's seamy side in his best-selling book, *The Beast.* Lindsey worked with *Rocky Mountain News* editor Thomas M. Patterson, future United States Senator Edward Costigan, social worker Josephine Roche and others to bring Progressive ideas to the Mile High City.

In a sage political move, Mayor Speer declined to run in 1912 and let the reformers have their turn at city hall. The city-cleansers supported a successful state-wide vote for prohibition effective January 1, 1916, cleaned out the red light district on Market Street and closed down many of the gambling resorts. They installed the commission form of city government and began dismantling the Speer machine.

Although they did give Denver a moral bath, the reformers could not match the smooth administration of urban services and city-building abilities of Robert W. Speer. After four years of bickering among "city cleansers" and three different "reform" mayors, Denverites reinstated Speer in 1916. In this last campaign, he carried every ward in the city.

Lavish and long as his list of accomplishments was, Mayor Speer kept the city on a firm financial footing. He worked closely with corporate kingpins, trying to persuade them to return a portion of their wealth to the community. "Give while you live," the mayor told well-heeled audiences in

Thomas M. Patterson, longtime publisher and editor of the Rocky Mountain News *was a liberal reformer and constant critic of his Democratic party rival Mayor Speer.*

BRIDES OF THE MULTITUDES: On Market Street, between Nineteenth and 21st Streets, prostitutes plied their trade (above) until reformers routed them in 1912. Market Street had been Holladay Street, but the name was changed at the request of the Holladay family. Four of these some 2,000 ladies of easy virtue (lower left) on Market Street, shown here in their leisure. Belle Bernard's brothel (lower right) was one of dozens that made Market Street one of the most infamous flesh markets of the Rockies.

one of his favorite speeches. "What a man does for himself fades with him—what he does for his community lives long after he is gone."

Many responded. They gave millions for parks, playgrounds, swimming pools, statues, gardens, museums and other amenities. The marble colonnade in Civic Center carved with the names of civic benefactors is but one reminder of the love, money and effort that past Denverites have invested in their city.

Judge Benjamin Lindsey and other critics called Speer a "Corporation Democrat." Undoubtedly, Speer did protect corporations and privately-owned utilities, but he got them to give to the city in return. The Denver Tramway Company, for instance, contributed to park-building and upkeep in exchange for a monopolistic franchise.

Speer's arm-twisting of corporations became legendary. For decades, city fathers had realized the need for viaducts over the railyards. As people crossing the tracks were killed or injured regularly by trains, the city sued the railroads, asking that they construct safe crossings. Railroad attorneys resorted to expensive and prolonged litigation that forestalled any solution.

Soon after Speer became mayor, he ordered all litigation against the railroads dropped. Then he requested that the presidents of all railroads involved meet with him in his office. Speer arrived bright and early but waited a long time only to have lawyers and other lackeys come in lieu of the chief executives. "We have been delegated," they informed the mayor, "to negotiate with you in regard to the 20th Street Viaduct."

"I invited the presidents of your roads to attend a meeting for that purpose," Speer replied with a poker face. "I have nothing to take up with you gentlemen. This meeting will be adjourned now."

The next day an ordinance was introduced in city council requiring that the railroads post watchmen at their 20th Street crossings. All trains would have to make a full stop to allow pedestrians and other traffic to cross the tracks. Despite intensive lobbying from the railroads, the ordinance passed. Railroad officials screamed that the proposal would tie up rail traffic hopelessly and dared Speer to enforce the measure.

Speer requested another meeting. This time, every railroad president arrived promptly. "That ordinance," Speer said, banging his fist on the table, "will be enforced unless you gentlemen agree to construct that viaduct and stop the menace to the lives of Denver citizens."

The 20th Street viaduct was completed in 1911 with $66,730 in city funds and $546,848 from the four major Denver railroads. Subsequently, Speer built Alameda Avenue underpass and other safe track crossings with help from the railroads and the Denver Tramway Company.

Under "Boss Bob," as the newspapers called him, the city and county of

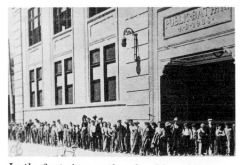

In the first six months after Mayor Speer opened a Municipal Bath House at 20th and Curtis Streets, it attracted 62,688 bathers.

Denver County clerk and recorder's office, early 1900s.

Denver undertook some novel activities. Because the local papers concentrated on the scandals rather than the achievements of the Speer administration, the city began publishing *Municipal Facts*. Although something of a whitewash, this heavily illustrated journal remains a valuable before-and-after record of Denver's metamorphosis.

During the Speer era, the city built its own asphalt factory, greenhouse and even a municipal bakery, which hired and fed the unemployed poor. During the World War I coal shortage, Denver opened a coal company to provide cheap coal for needy citizens (and to force private companies to lower their rates). To recruit new employers, Speer worked with the Chamber of Commerce to establish an Industrial Bureau. To supervise the greening of Denver, Speer established the office of City Forester. It is a unique position that still exists to promote tree-planting, care for living trees and remove dead and diseased ones. Denver is a city of lawns and gardens. Because the city would be a desert without careful gardening, it has been suggested that a garden hose and sprinkler belong on the city seal.

During the World War I "Victory Garden" days, Mayor Speer inaugurated a program of neighborhood gardening by plowing up 1,134 vacant lots for cultivation. The water department provided free water for the communal vegetable patches. Some subsequent mayors have continued the practice.

Health and education also concerned Mayor Speer. He determined to make Denver General Hospital one of the finest municipal hospitals in the United States. To financially strengthen the hospital, he launched a statewide campaign to make the legislature provide adequate funds for the

State Mental Hospital in Pueblo. Denver General's ward for the insane was then closed and patients transferred to Pueblo (a step specified for years by state law but made impossible by a legislature unwilling to accept financial responsibilities).

Such administrative and financial reforms enabled the city to bring health care into the neighborhoods and homes of citizens. (One outstanding example is the Denver Visiting Nurse Service which makes visits to administer skilled health care.)

Several new schools were built during the first two decades of the twentieth century, but national attention focused on the one started in 1916 by Emily Griffith. This spunky school marm realized that poor working people and foreign-speaking immigrants desperately needed free adult education. She founded Denver's unique Opportunity School. (Renamed the Emily Griffith Opportunity School, it now occupies an entire block of downtown Denver and offers hundreds of courses on evenings and weekends as well as weekdays. A part of the Denver Public Schools, it has provided thousands with a second chance at learning to read and write English, to pursue hobbies and crafts and to study job skills from typing to aviation mechanics.)

Although Mayor Speer and progressive reformers such as Emily Griffith rarely saw eye to eye, they all bettered Denver.

On July 4, 1906, Denverites turned out en masse for dedication of the Welcome Arch at Union Station. The 70-ton arch with 1,600 light bulbs supported a huge "Welcome" sign to greet disembarking passengers. The opposite side of the arch bore the Hebrew word "Mizpah" (May God be with you until we meet again).

After the band finished "My Country Tis of Thee," Mayor Speer declared that the arch "is to stand here for ages as an expression of love, good wishes and kind feelings of our citizens to the stranger who enters our gates." Denver later forgot Mayor Speer's hope that the Welcome Arch would stand for ages to greet newcomers and tourists. It was torn down in the early 1930s as "an impediment to the automobile," and the surrounding greenway was removed for a car park.

Robert W. Speer died in office in 1918. Over 10,000 Denverites jammed the city auditorium to say goodbye to the city's most loved, most controversial and most effective mayor. His wife Kate donated much of her husband's small estate of $40,000 for the gold eagle and chiming clock tower that still crown her husband's dying dream—the City and County Building in Civic Center.

Denver is a city of lawns and gardens. Because the city would be a desert without careful gardening, it has been suggested that a garden hose and sprinkler belong on the city seal.

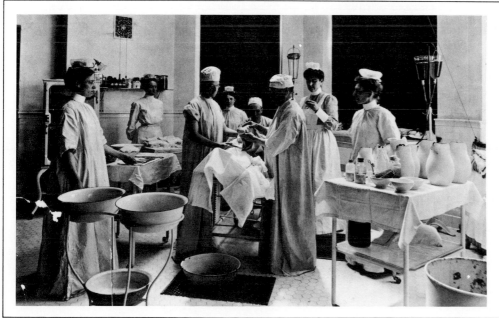

HOSPITAL CARE: Mayor Speer, who came to Colorado a sick tubercular, endeavored to make Denver a healthy city and Denver General Hospital (above), circa 1900, the best in the country. The hospital was equipped with an operating room (left), circa 1900.

BUILDING DENVER: Colonnade of civic benefactors in Civic Center (above), as Mayor Speer wanted it. The building that housed the Denver Public Library (below) from 1910 to 1955.

NEW JOURNALISM: An elephant named "Little Hip" joined the Newsboys' Union waiting in front of the Denver Post for the 5:30 edition (above), seated comfortably in an Apperson Jack Rabbit driven by Fred Tobin of the Tobin Motor Car Company. Meanwhile, the journalism class at the University of Denver (below) checks proofs in 1919.

Fountain Flyers' air circus over Park Hill and Montclair in the 1920s. Colorado Women's College is seen at left, St. Luke's Church and Stanley School at right center; main streets are Oneida and Montview.

CHAPTER 8

Homes on the range

Suburbanization began with a contraption called the street railway...passenger coaches pulled along railroad tracks by horses.

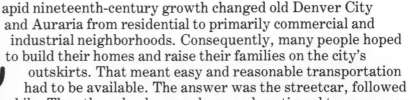

Rapid nineteenth-century growth changed old Denver City and Auraria from residential to primarily commercial and industrial neighborhoods. Consequently, many people hoped to build their homes and raise their families on the city's outskirts. That meant easy and reasonable transportation had to be available. The answer was the streetcar, followed by the automobile. Thus the suburbs were born and continued to grow over the next century.

Beginning in the 1870s, thousands moved out to new streetcar suburbs. They found the streetcar cheap, fast transportation between jobs, markets and amusements and new suburban homes where they could raise their families amid spacious lawns, rose gardens, vegetable patches and open countryside.

CURTIS PARK: Denver's first streetcar (below) ran from Twelfth and Larimer Streets to Sixteenth Street and then out Champa Street to 27th Street where the first streetcar suburb, Curtis Park, sprung up in the 1870s.

Suburbanization began with a contraption called the street railway. Street railways were passenger coaches pulled along railroad tracks by horses. (Actually mules did much of the work but their name did not lend itself to corporate titles). The Denver Horse Railroad was the first of several dozen companies to serve the Mile High City. It was a $100,000 corporation enfranchised by the legislature of Colorado Territory with the proviso that its fares not exceed 10 cents. After initially relying on horsepower (and mulepower), the Denver Horse Railroad and a growing number of competitors began experimenting with various other means of locomotion. A variety of steam engines, cable systems and trolleys were used in the nineteenth century.

Late in 1871, the Denver Horse Railroad Company opened the city's first streetcar line. It ran along Larimer from Seventh to Sixteenth streets, out Sixteenth to Champa and out Champa to the open countryside, ending at a prairie dog town on what became 27th Street.

Developers hastily subdivided the land around Curtis Park—Denver's first city park—which graces the block between Curtis, Champa, 31st and 32nd streets. The park subsequently gave its name to the surrounding neighborhood. After Mayor Wolfe Londoner, storekeeper J. Jay Joslin and other prominent citizens moved to Curtis Park, the pioneer suburb blossomed. More streetcar lines and hundreds of homes were built during the 1870s and 1880s on upper Larimer, Curtis, Stout and Welton streets.

In the 1870s, many expected Denver to expand to the northeast. Speculators, home buyers and merchants all began moving that direction. However, the railroad tracks were one detriment that bordered Curtis Park on the northwest. On the proverbial wrong side of the tracks, the factory towns of Argo, Swansea and Globeville arose around smelters of the same names. These immigrant-filled, industrial neighborhoods exuded smoke, noise and smells that threatened the bourgeois tranquility of Curtis Park. Shrewd developers and home buyers became convinced that Denver's fashionable suburbs would be to the south and east. By the 1880s, other streetcar lines and other developers steered growth elsewhere and undermined the preeminence of the Curtis Park area.

Starting in the 1890s, a succession of poor whites, blacks, Orientals and Mexican-Americans displaced many of the well-to-do in Curtis Park. It became part of the larger neighborhood of Five Points (named for its central intersection of Welton, Washington, 26th Avenue and 26th and 27th streets). Although some favored the area for its cultural diversity—Jewish shops, Japanese stores, black jazz clubs and Mexican-American

One of the oldest homes in Curtis Park—the frame cottage of David Crowell built around 1873 at 2816 Curtis Street—has been restored by Brian Congleton (below), a Denver architect.

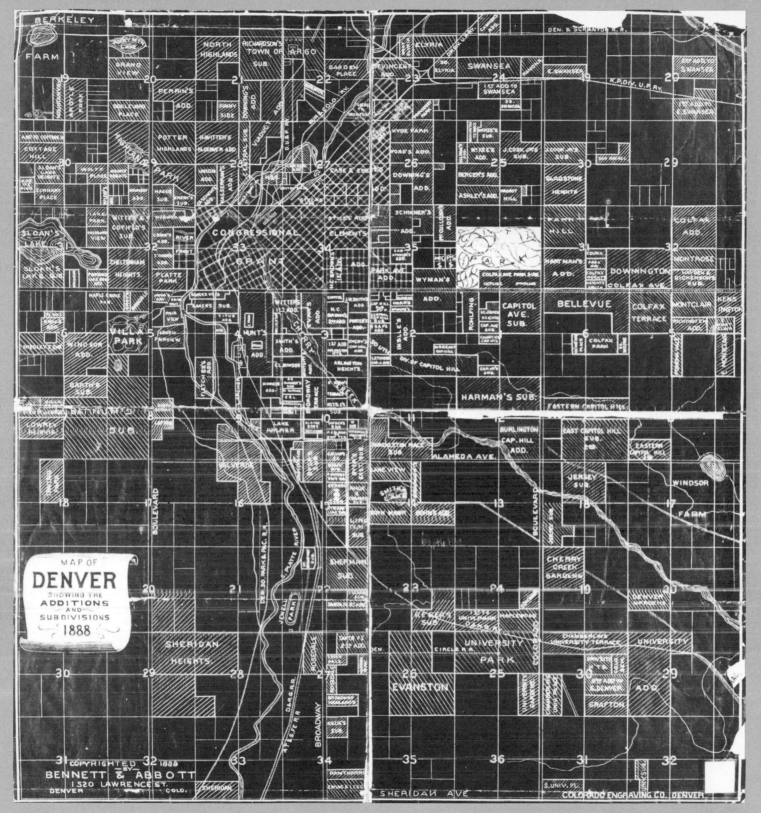

cantinas—many Denverites thought of Five Points as off-limits.

A century after its birth, Curtis Park underwent a rebirth after city lovers made a happy discovery—Curtis Park had remained a fairly intact Victorian neighborhood with almost half the homes owner-occupied. Astonishingly, no large-scale industry, freeway, urban renewal project or other major change had shattered the old neighborhood. There were entire blocks of cottages from the 1870s and two- and three-story houses from the 1880s. They survived behind storefront additions, subdivided apartments and tacked-on rental rooms.

An assortment of urban pioneers began massive restoration, working

Map of Denver showing additions and subdivisions, 1888.

E 267. 16TH ST. VIADUCT

STREETCARS, SUBURBS: The Sixteenth Street Viaduct (above) carried streetcar passengers over the South Platte River and the rail yards to north Denver. After the streetcar line reached 27th and Champa in 1871, the streetcar suburb of Curtis Park grew up along the tracks. This view of Denver's oldest suburb (left inset) was taken in the 1880s from the top of Gilpin School at California and 29th Streets. The Fifteenth Street streetcar line ended at Federal Boulevard in front of the Grand View Hotel (right inset); tracks such as those in the foreground still lie under many major Denver streets.

house by house, block by block. They have been supported by Historic Denver, Incorporated, a preservation group founded in 1970 to fight demolition of the city's architectural heritage. With the cooperation of individuals, realtors, bankers, public officials, minority groups and longtime Five Points residents, Curtis Park began to shine as no new suburb ever could. Ornate iron fences and roof cresting, brick corbelling, metal cornices, carpenter Gothic porches, front and back parlors were lovingly restored and foundations and structures stabilized. Although wiring, plumbing, bathrooms and kitchens had to be replaced, much of the woodwork, stained glass windows, brass fixtures and decorative fireplaces had survived a century of neglect.

In 1980, Historic Denver moved its annual house tour out of upper-class neighborhoods and had socialites, developers and many amazed Denverites inspect the reborn slum. Inspired by the Curtis Park renaissance, other inner-city neighborhoods began the long-postponed and difficult process of renovation and restoration. Numerous middle- and upper-class Denverites returned to the walk-to-work, close-in neighborhoods of Five Points, Highland, Jefferson Park, Auraria, Baker and Capitol Hill.

All of these neighborhoods originally sprouted along streetcar lines. In 1872, the Denver Horse Railroad Company changed its name to the Denver City Rail Way Company and constructed the still-standing office building and car barn at Seventeenth and Wynkoop opposite Union Station. Soon it had dozens of competitors. To develop their properties on Fifteenth Street and elsewhere, ex-governor John Evans, William Byers and other capitalists formed the Denver Tramway Company in 1886. They first experimented with electric cars invented by Sidney Short, professor of physics at the University of Denver and constructed by the Colorado Iron

114

Works of Denver. Townsfolk found these horseless contraptions on Fifteenth Street shocking. The ground-level electric wire slots and tracks jolted any creature who happened to step on them—particularly in wet and icy weather. Mercifully, the Denver Tramway Company switched to overhead electric trolleys.

In 1888, the Denver City Cable Rail Way Company incorporated, with its main office in New York City. It also entered the people-moving business. The powerhouse and car barn at Eighteenth and Lawrence streets (now recycled as a restaurant and offices) and the old viaducts at Sixteenth and Larimer streets are vestiges of Denver's once extensive cable car system. At one time, the Denver City Cable Railway Company claimed that its Welton Street line was the longest cable car route in the world.

Dozens of smaller streetcar companies also facilitated the expansion of the nineteenth-century city and its suburbs. Real estate promoters either started their own streetcar lines or tried to coax an existing company to build in their direction. Most of these smaller companies were shattered by the panic of '93. This enabled the Denver Tramway Company to seize control of all lines except the Denver, Lakewood & Golden Railroad Company by 1900.

The Evans family, principal officers and stockholders of the Denver Tramway Company, tore down the governor's old house at Fourteenth and Arapahoe streets in 1911 to construct the Tramway Building. The handsome red brick and white terra-cotta tile landmark now houses the University of Colorado at Denver.

Along Fifteenth Street, tracks of the city's second streetcar line still occasionally pop through the pavement. This line, launched in 1873, started at Larimer and ran out Fifteenth across the South Platte River bridge to north Denver where it ended in a turn-around at West Seventeenth Avenue and Federal Boulevard. Although General Larimer had mapped out the town of Highland fifteen years earlier, development did not arrive until the streetcar. By the late 1870s, flush times came to Highland and the rest of northwest Denver. (Oldtimers still call it north Denver—and they are correct by the compass.)

The north Denver subdivisions of Highlands, Highland Park and Berkeley aspired to be the fashionable residential areas. They prided themselves on their moral and geographical elevation above smoky, smelly, sinful Denver. "Highlands," crowed that town's first annual report after its incorporation in 1875, "has good streets, electric lights, sewer system, rapid transit and water—but no saloons."

Despite numerous churches and a temperate and prayerful citizenry, Highlands was bankrupted by the crash of 1893. Unable to maintain water, sewers and other services, Highlands (Zuni Street to Lowell Boulevard and West Colfax to 38th avenues) accepted annexation to the neighboring Queen City whose evils it had long denounced.

Waves of different immigrants moved into north Denver during its first 100 years. "Chubby" Aiello of Patsy's Italian Inn—family-owned since its birth as a restaurant and speakeasy in 1922—recalled the changes over his long life in north Denver: "On our corner—Navajo and 37th—there were four different businessmen—a Jew, a German, an Irishman and us. Now the Mexicans are moving in. Some Italians don't like it, but they don't remember that this neighborhood was not always Little Italy. When we Italians began moving in, the Irish didn't want us any more than the English and Scottish had liked the railroad Irish moving in during the 1870s and 1880s.

"And I saw what happened to the Germans during the first world war. When the second war came with Mussolini and all that, I changed our name from the Italian Inn to Patsy's. Patsy was my kid brother, Patsy O'Brien Aiello."

In the 1980s, north Denver continues to be a melting pot. Italian residences may be distinguished by the grapes and tomatoes shading

Old streetcar track occasionally pops through the pavement of Denver streets, shown here at West 34th Avenue and Navajo Street in front of the historic Notary House.

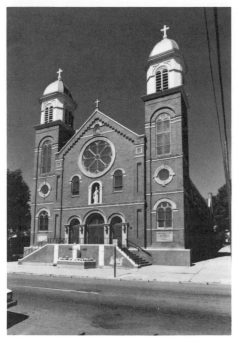

LITTLE ISRAEL: In west Denver, Morris Eber was proprietor of a grocery store (left) at 1463 Platte Street, 1912. The Katz Bakery (above) stands abandoned on old West Colfax under the viaduct.

LITTLE ITALY: Our Lady of Mount Carmel Catholic Church (above) has been the spiritual and social center of Denver's Italian community. It was built with the help and prayers of Mother Frances Cabrini, the first United States citizen to be canonized a saint. Carbone's Sausage House (right) on West 38th Avenue in north Denver is owned by one of the city's pioneer Italian clans; Carbone Bakery and Carbone Restaurant nearby also offer tasty treats.

backyard statues of the Blessed Virgin while Mexican-Americans may surround backyard statues of Our Lady of Guadalupe with peppers and chili. Jews, Germans, Irish, Slavs and other ethnic groups also flavor the neighborhood with their taverns, churches and shops. Five of the churches are designated Denver landmarks—the chapel at St. Elizabeth Center, the Chapel of Our Merciful Savior, (Episcopal), Asbury Methodist, Saint Patrick's (Irish Catholic) and Mount Carmel (Italian Catholic). The newer churches of Our Lady of Guadalupe (Hispanic Catholic), Highland Presbyterian, Berkeley Baptist, First Foursquare Spanish Gospel, the Hebrew Educational Alliance and Transfiguration of Our Lord Ukranian Catholic church all attest to the rich cultural diversity of north Denver.

Across the railroad tracks and across town, construction of the Broadway streetcar line in 1874 resulted in the development of a more homogeneous

neighborhood—Capitol Hill. Henry C. Brown was an orphan from Ohio who came to Denver during the original gold rush. He platted Capitol Hill on the east side of Broadway between 20th and Tenth avenues to the alley between Grant and Logan streets. In order to facilitate subdivision, Brown straightened the diagonal street pattern of the central business district into an east-west, north-south checkerboard grid on the east side of Broadway.

To enhance his land, he built the Brown Palace Hotel and gave two blocks for the State Capitol. He kept bragging that "Brown's Bluff" would one day be Denver's millionaire row and chased squatters off with his hatchet. After streetcars reached Capitol Hill, Brown's once remote bluff became the elite addition to Denver, but Brown lost his hotel, his bluff and his fortune in the crash of '93.

In the 1880s, Capitol Hill mansions began piling up in crenelated parapets, Gothic revival towers, Queen Anne gables, Romanesque arches and neo-classical columns and porticos. Heavy sandstone and granite walls and wrought iron fences guarded these bastions of the mining, ranching and business tycoons. Millionaire's row on Grant and Sherman, Pearl, Logan and Pennsylvania streets became the city's "good addresses." (John W. Smith, the versatile pioneer businessman, named these streets for his home state, his daughter and Civil War generals he admired.)

The Denver Tramway Company extended its Broadway line south to Alameda Avenue in the late 1880s after a $200,000 enticement from developers. A neighborhood called Broadway Terrace sprouted on the west side of the tree-lined Broadway between West First and Sixth avenues. After a long history of decline, Broadway Terrace began a revival in the 1970s similar to the rebirth of Curtis Park. In some meticulously restored residences, aficionados of Queen Victoria have even reinstated antimacassars and aspidistras.

South of Broadway Terrace on the Broadway streetcar line lay the large incorporated suburb of South Denver. Bounded by Colorado Boulevard on the east, roughly the Platte River on the west and by Alameda and Yale avenues, South Denver attracted many middle-class families. After James Fleming was elected the first mayor of South Denver, he converted his mansion at 1520 South Grant into the town hall. South Denver was annexed to Denver in 1894, and the Fleming mansion is now a community and senior citizens center. Today South Denver is noted for its fashionable University Park and Washington Park neighborhoods. The shortage of carriage houses for the pre-1893 two-story homes and of driveways for the post-1893 bungalows is a reminder that the area began as a streetcar suburb.

By the 1880s, Broadway had emerged as the north-south thoroughfare of Denver and as the dividing line between east and west street addresses.

A turn-of-the-century view captures the tree-shaded tranquility of the Capitol Hill neighborhood.

J.E. BATES & CO. OWNERS.
1609 & 1611 CURTIS ST. DENVER. COLO.

LOGANDALE

ENGLEWOOD

BROADWAY

ENGLEWOOD PLACE

SOUTH BROADWAY CABLE AND ELECTRIC ROAD

BROADWAY TO ENGLEWOOD

ON BROADWAY: The South Broadway streetcar line, in the foreground (above), spawned many surburban developments. The Cherrelyn Horse Car (right), which ran from Englewood to Cherrelyn District, proceeds south past the house at 3689 South Broadway, which is still standing in Englewood.

Broadway streetcar lines reached as far south as the rural hamlet of Englewood before the depression of the 1890s froze streetcar suburbanization.

Englewood remains an unannexed suburb to this day. It began near the site of William G. Russell's 1858 gold discovery. Incorporated in 1903,

Englewood consisted of several scattered settlements, including Fiske Gardens and the Tuilleries (two spacious beer gardens), Orchard Place (where apple trees were planted by Jacob Calvin Jones who became Englewood's first mayor) and Skerritt's farm, named after the first settler whose house still stands at 3560 South Bannock Street.

After Thomas Skerritt used his horses and plow to extend Broadway south from Cherry Creek to Little Dry Creek, various streetcars built into Englewood, including the fabled Cherrelyn horsecar now preserved on the grounds of Englewood City Hall. A single horse pulled the wooden Cherrelyn passenger coach up South Broadway and then was allowed to rest on the front platform as the vehicle coasted back downtown.

Streetcar commuters changed Englewood from a rustic village to a suburb of 4,356 by 1920. Between 1940 and 1960, the population climbed from 9,680 to 33,398 and then stabilized as the early Arapahoe County suburb became hemmed in by other incorporated towns.

In the 1960s, Englewood sold its city park for what was then hailed as the world's largest shopping center—Cinderella City. Afterwards, as Englewood evolved from a suburb to a highly developed urban area, some citizens began to miss the city park and once-open spaces. Many moved to greener pastures elsewhere in Arapahoe County or further south to Douglas County.

Immediately south of Englewood lies Littleton, the seat of Arapahoe County. When the first Broadway trolley passengers reached Littleton in 1907, they found a country town wrapped around a quaint Main Street that continues to be a focal point for the community. Relics of the early days include many small shops and the tiny Oasis Saloon. The town hall and public library have been recycled respectively as a theater and a restaurant.

DEVELOPING LITTLETON: The town of Littleton developed around a flour mill (below) which burned in 1959. Richard Sullivan Little (bottom), who was born in New Hampshire in 1829, developed the town which bears his name; he died in Littleton in 1899.

Littleton began as the home of Richard Little in 1860. A civil engineer from New Hampshire, he established a farm and the Rough and Ready Flour Mill. A village sprang up around the mill, encouraging Little to plat his town in 1872. Little's mill became noted as one of the best in the state, despite several fires. (The last blaze destroyed it in 1959.) In 1890, some 400 Littletonians decided to incorporate. Richard Little died in 1899. His town, as Jerome Smiley wrote two years later, exuded "the air and quaintness of a New England village." The community consisted of many balloon frame (early day pre-fab) homes shipped in on the Denver & Rio Grande and Atchison, Topeka & Santa Fe lines, both of whose depots have been preserved by the Littleton Historical Museum.

Littleton, which fancied itself the milling, bee-keeping and pickle capitol of Colorado at various times during the nineteenth century, was rated one of the ten most desirable suburbs in America during the 1970s by the *Ladies' Home Journal*. The *Journal* based its award on Littleton's well preserved Main Street, its progressive, civic-minded and prize-winning *Littleton Independent* newspaper, its fine library and historical museum, good parks, Arapahoe Community College and an affluent, active and community-conscious citizenry. There were about 30,000 Littletonians by 1980 with three times that many living in the greater Littleton area.

While Capitol Hill, Broadway Terrace, South Denver, Englewood and Littleton mushroomed along the Broadway line, other settlements arose on East Colfax. Four miles east of Broadway, a burly, bearded German baron platted what he called "the suburb" of Denver. Baron Walter von Richthofen was the uncle of the famous "Red Baron" of World War I fame. Walter von Richthofen was a most flamboyant and compulsive town builder. He had flubbed North and South Denver developments before trying his hand on the east side. Unwilling to wait for the East Colfax

LITTLETON CHANGES: Main Street in Littleton (above) looking west from Littleton Boulevard in 1973, shows the change from a streetcar to an automobile suburb. On Main Street stood the Carnegie Library (inset), built in 1916.

streetcar to reach his projected paradise, Richthofen operated a tally-ho coach drawn by four splendid horses. Potential lot buyers boarded the coach in front of the Tabor Opera House on Sixteenth Street. Richthofen then dashed ahead with his Russian wolfhounds nipping at the feet of his stead, leading land hunters out to the patch of prairie he called Montclair.

After the tally-ho trip across bleak, dusty land broken by a few farmhouses, Richthofen's prospective buyers were shown his showcase home—the prickly Prussian castle that still stands at Twelfth and Olive. Few bought Montclair property before the streetcar line pushed out East Colfax to Pontiac Street. Despite the Baron's promotions, the Montclair area between Montview Boulevard and Sixth Avenue Parkway, Syracuse and Colorado Boulevard, had less than one house per block until automobile suburbanization began in the 1920s.

Baron von Richthofen interested a fellow German nobleman, Baron Eugene von Winckler, in the tract north of Montclair and east of City Park known as Park Hill. Baron von Winckler was a Prussian Army officer supposedly dismissed for falling off his horse while delivering a message to the German emperor. He hid this disgrace by emigrating to America.

Some said Baron von Winckler never recovered from his horse fall. After buying the chunk of northeast Denver, he frittered his time away, trying to install a race track instead of pushing land sales. He failed at both horses and houses and committed suicide, evidently to the relief of all concerned. His land went to more skillful developers who turned Park Hill into one of Denver's finest neighborhoods.

When Denver's black community began moving into Park Hill in the 1960s, many whites left. But others stayed and with the help of neighborhood churches established the Greater Park Hill Community Association to promote smooth integration. Whites and blacks learned to share the same blocks and work together to preserve their elegant neighborhood. After the racial woes and real estate block-busting of the 1960s, the *Greater Park Hill Community Inc., News Letter* of the 1970s boasted of serving one of best integrated communities in America.

At the Pontiac Street terminal of the East Colfax streetcar line, nineteenth-century passengers could see a ranch miles to the southeast. The homestead had been there since the early 1860s when it was established by the Gully family of Tipperary, Ireland. Out on Tollgate Creek (named for a tollgate on the Smoky Hill Trail), the Gullys were by themselves—and liked it that way.

Once in a while, John, the youngest son of Thomas and Temperance Gully, drove steers and dairy cows into Denver's Wazee Street corrals. He sold them, hit a few Larimer Street saloons, bought supplies with the remaining cash and headed back out to the plains. Perhaps only the

BARON IN MONTCLAIR: Richthofen Castle (left) is largely hidden behind huge trees at East Twelfth Avenue and Olive Street. Built by Baron Walter von Richthofen, uncle of the famous World War I "Red Baron" Manfred von Richthofen, the castle is still standing in the quiet east Denver area. Richthofen's "molkerei" (right), which originally housed lung disease patients.

Arapahoe County tax assessor who tried to keep tabs on the land they were acquiring suspected that the Gullys were prospering.

In 1892, John Gully came into Sacred Heart Church on Larimer Street to get married. He told the priest that some other Irish Catholics—the Kennedys, Delaneys, Slaterlys and O'Briens—had settled around the Gully place. As children proliferated, John Gully set up a school on the homestead where his wife and sister did their best to educate the youngsters. At the insistence of their womenfolk, the men persuaded a priest to come out to hear confessions, say masses and administer the sacraments at one of their favorite East Colfax roadhouses.

The Gullys watched Denver grow eastward toward their ranch with apprehension. In 1891, Donald Fletcher, a Capitol Hill real estate tycoon, planted the town of Fletcher around Galena Street and East Colfax. A few years later—after Fletcher absconded leaving townspeople with debts he had incurred for a water project—they renamed the town Aurora.

Irishman John Gully and his family built this pioneer structure in the 1860s and for decades, it was the social and civic center of Aurora, Denver's fastest growing suburb and Colorado's third largest city.

Aurorans wanted little to do with the Gullys and their friends. In venerable East Colfax bars, oldtimers still talk about the Gully boys—the three sons of John who never married and mostly raised hell. After John died in 1915, his sons took to making moonshine and holding rodeos. The ranching business suffered but revelers enjoyed getting smashed at those crazy Sunday afternoon rodeos. The last of the brothers, Edward, died in 1962, just as suburbia was about to swallow the homestead his grandfather had established a century earlier.

The Gullys left little but Thomas Gully's diary and the family home with several decades of unpaid bills and collection agency threats tucked under the floorboards. The Aurora History Center and Aurora Historical Society (both founded in the 1970s) moved the homestead from the intersection of Buckley Road and East Mississippi Avenue with the help of Medema homes, subdivider of the Gully property. It was relocated in an Aurora city park for restoration while heritage-hungry Aurorans scrutinized the Gully diary, papers and unpaid bills for insight into early Aurora and its pioneer settlers.

After World War II and the expansion of Fitzsimmons Army Hospital, Lowry Air Force Base and Stapleton International Airport, Aurora became the fastest-growing major suburban area in Colorado and one of the fastest growing in the United States. In 1920, Aurora's population was 983. By 1960, it had burgeoned to 48,548. Today, it is above 200,000, making it the third largest city in Colorado.

Aurorans began in the 1970s to support a library system, historical society and history center to enrich and unify the community.

The streetcars, suburbs and stories of Denver's decentralization are endless. Lines constructed along East 23rd, Seventeenth, Eighth and Evans avenues resulted in the development of the neighborhoods of City Park, Cheesman Park, University Park and the incorporated town of Harman whose town hall still sits at East Fourth Avenue and St. Paul Street. "Rapid transit lines," reported the *Denver Republican*, October 20, 1890, "have been the making of the East Side. Since its advent, the whole suburb of Denver has been built up with houses."

In 1927, the Frog Hollow section of Barnum contained Clark's Brick Yard (upper center), Western Pottery (lower center) and a sprinkling of homes and truck gardens. Circus owner Phineas T. Barnum, who developed the Barnum neighborhood in west Denver, claimed the location was so favorable and the climate so benign that no one would ever die. Frog Hollow is bounded by Federal Boulevard at top, Barberry Place on the left, Tenth Avenue in the upper right and Bryant Street in the lower right.

West of Sheridan Boulevard (Denver's western boundary), the town of Lakewood was platted in 1889 by W. A. H. Loveland, the Golden pioneer and railroad builder. Lakewood—which did not incorporate until 1969—grew up as a hodge-podge of neighborhoods. They ranged from chicken coop houses on West Colfax to the "millionaire's row" of Lakeridge Road; from tent-city tuberculosis sanitariums to the 1920s model suburb called "The Glens;" from trailer parks to Green Mountain's $200,000 solar homes on curvi-linear streets.

The Lakewood Historical Society published the community's first history for the 1976 centennial-bicentennial celebration and began the struggle to preserve the few surviving landmarks. The Loveland home at 1435 Harlan Street, Molly Brown's "Avoca Lodge" at South Wadsworth Boulevard and Yale Avenue, the Old Stone House on South Estes Street, Kendelview (with its *allé* of trees) at 3001 South Kipling Street and the the Verner Z. Reed estate which became the Jewish Green Gables country club are among the surviving reminders that Lakewood has an intriguing but still largely buried history.

Lakewood's greatest treasure—May Bonfils Stanton's Belmar Estate—was sacrificed to suburban growth as land values soared in the 1960s. Ostracized by her sister Helen and Denver society, May built Belmar to outshine any estate in Denver. It was modeled after the Petit Trianon at Versailles with several lakes and formal landscapes of trees, shrubs and flowers. On the site today are the Irongate Office Complex (named for the still standing Belmar gateway) and Villa Italia Shopping Center. Villa Italia with its neo-Roman grandeur became a "downtown" for Lakewood although Westland Shopping Center and smaller "shoppettes" compete as nuclei.

The stables of Belmar now house the Belmar Museum, headquarters of the Lakewood Historical Society. Small remnants of the vast grounds have been preserved as the Belmar Park.

Students of suburbia may find Lakewood particularly fascinating. Among the many motor courts is the White Swan at 6060 West Colfax with a huge plaster swan in front. The Lakewood Grill and Bar, Taylor's Supper Club, Lane's Tavern, the Lariat and the Rock Rest are the most venerable among a maze of watering holes. Lakewood lost perhaps its best example of suburban fantasy architecture when the fast-food palace built as a huge hot dog (complete with relish) was moved up to the mountain town of Conifer.

Construction of West Sixth Avenue freeway and the Federal Center transformed the small, rural communities strung out along the West Thirteenth Avenue route of the Denver, Lakewood and Golden Railroad. This pioneer automobile expressway was begun during World War II to link Lowry Air Force Base with the Denver Ordinance Plant (now the Federal Center) which made Remington arms and K-rations. The freeway prompted thousands to settle between Sheridan Boulevard and Simms-Union Boulevard between West 26th and Jewell avenues.

Lakewood's population approximately doubled during the 1950s, 1960s and 1970s, reaching almost 140,000 by 1980 to make it Colorado's fourth largest city.

Lakewood, Aurora, Littleton, Englewood and dozens of smaller communities within metropolitan Denver began as agricultural centers, gained recognition as railroad stops and then attracted streetcar lines and suburban settlers by the hundreds. They really began to boom in the twentieth century after the invention of the locomobile.

The first one in Denver was David W. Brunton's shiny electric Columbia runabout. Brunton, a mining engineer, attended the 1898 auto show in Boston, tested several cars and had a runabout shipped out to Denver. He spent May 9, 1899, assembling the vehicle in his front yard. The next day, he astounded pedestrians, drivers of horsedrawn vehicles and trolley-car traffic by cruising the streets of Denver.

What did he feed it? How could he stop it? What kind of waste did it drop? Newspaper reporters followed Brunton around town making daily

Although Monaco Parkway became a fashionable address after the development of Park Hill, the corner of Monaco and 26th Streets accommodated squatter Joseph Germain until his death in 1934.

reports on the meanderings of his horseless carriage. A year later, newspapers began carrying ads such as this one in the *Denver Post*, May 1, 1900,

---

$750   LOCOMOBILE $750

The famous Steam Wagon. Cheap to buy. Cheap to run. No noise, odor or vibration. Ready for immediate delivery. Lightest and easiest running automobile on earth. Any person can run it from one to 40 miles per hour. Call on us and be convinced. Write for free Catalogue. Felker Bicycle Company. State Agents. 417 16th Street.

Few found these horseless carriages practical, but they became fashionable toys for the rich, a must to park in the carriage house along with other fancy buggies.

Many considered automobiles to be expensive, noisy, smoky nuisances. A suspicious public balked at buying cars for years, but several factors expedited the motorization of America. Bicycle clubs—the Denver Wheelmen alone had 25,000 members in 1900—agitated successfully for construction of smooth, paved roads. Ironically, bicyclists pushed for better roads only to be driven off them by the growing number of motorists.

Automobile owners organized the Colorado Automobile Club to lobby for government subsidy of their hobby. They coaxed the Colorado Legislature to establish a state highway commission in 1909 and to appropriate state funds for road building. In 1916, the Federal Road Act initiated matching federal funds for state road building. The program culminated with the

OLD ELEGANCE. The Obrecht house (top), 5238 East Seventeenth Avenue, is one of the oldest in Park Hill. Mr. and Mrs. Robert Ewalt (above) in front of their meticulously tended Park Hill bungalow.

Denver, the Mile High City, in the 1950s.

Interstate Highway Act of 1956 which provided nine federal dollars for every state dollar spent to build a national network of freeways.

After Interstates 25 and 70 cut through the city and construction of a belt freeway began in the 1950s, Denver's suburbanization accelerated. As early as 1940, the metropolitan area contained more residents (445,000) living outside the city and county than inside (415,000). By 1960, almost a million persons resided in the suburban counties while the city's population remained around 500,000. By 1980, three out of every four residents of the metropolitan area lived in Arapahoe, Douglas, Jefferson, Park, Adams, Boulder and Gilpin counties.

Before 1974, Denver annexed portions of the surrounding counties with the consent of the owners. Using water and other urban services as an inducement, the city doubled its area between 1941 and 1973—from 59 to 118 square miles. The most notable holdout was the Arapahoe County enclave of Glendale, which is now surrounded by southeast Denver.

In 1974, suburban counties convinced voters across the state to approve an amendment to the constitution. It required the approval of all voters in the county involved—not just owners of the area to be annexed—before Denver could annex its neighbors. Named the Poundstone amendment (after the Englewood lobbyist who spearheaded its drafting and passage), this act has limited expansion of the city and county of Denver.

Twentieth-century suburbanization was largely determined by the automobile, just as the streetcar had shaped nineteenth-century

TRAMS AND TROLLEYS: The Denver City Cable Rail Way Company building (top left)—a brick mason's tour de force—was saved from demolition and restored in the 1970s. The Denver Tramway Building (center left) at Fourteenth and Arapahoe Streets initially housed the offices, car barns and shops of the Denver Tramway Company. After trolleys disappeared in 1950, the building was acquired by the University of Colorado for its Denver campus. A June 1950 photograph (lower left) shows the oldest trolley in service (#319), a trackless rubber tire trolley (#654) with a brand new bus (#262); also, the oldest operator, Amiel J. Singer (Badge #1), and the newest, Bob Lynch (Badge #993). Streetcar #72 on Curtis Street (above), in front of the Telephone Building, May 1936.

DRAWN TO DENVER: The University of Colorado at Denver (above) at Fourteenth and Arapahoe Streets graduated from an Extension Center to an independent campus in the 1970s; by 1980, some 8,700 students enrolled in the fast-growing school, one of the university's four campuses in the state. Attracted to Denver in 1912 were many thousands who came to Agnes Phipps Sanitarium (lower right), now the site of Lowry Air Force Base.

decentralization. As American families began acquiring one or more automobiles, streetcar ridership declined sharply. Faced with growing competition from automobiles, the Denver Tramway Company began switching from streetcars to trackless, rubber-tired buses in the 1920s. The little yellow trolleys made their final runs on June 3, 1950 and were retired. It was the end of the streetcar era.

The Tramway company's buses fared only a little better than their streetcars. As Denverites came to own almost one car for every man, woman and child in the 1970s, the Denver Tramway faced bankruptcy. In 1971, it sold out to the city and county of Denver for $6.2 million. City ownership was only a temporary bail-out as the Colorado legislature had already authorized the creation of a Regional Transportation District for metropolitan Denver. On September 7, 1973, voters throughout the region approved a one-half percent sales tax to finance the regional transit system. Shortly afterwards, the Regional Transportation District (quickly dubbed *RTD* and *The Ride*) began an ambitious program for expanding bus service. They also initiated long-range planning for a light rail system.

As Denver's per capita car ownership and smog levels rose to among the highest in the nation, city planners and concerned citizens began looking for alternate transportation systems. Denver constructed one of the best bikeway systems in America but placed its greatest hopes in *The Ride*, which doubled bus ridership during the 1970s.

The Regional Transportation District initiated a difficult courtship of motorists as far away as Boulder, Pine Junction, Longmont and Castle Rock. Express buses, park-and-ride stations and a massive publicity campaign helped, but the soaring price of gasoline and automobiles also led many to reconsider their long, costly love affair with the automobile.

Denverites have increasingly returned to mass transportation, just as they once boarded suburb-bound streetcars pulled by reluctant horses and mules.

As automobiles and buses increasingly snarl metro traffic, the planners are contemplating a light rail system. The tracks may follow freeway medians and little used existing railroad corridors. Denverites may well ride out of the twentieth century on vehicles similar to the street railways that carried their grandparents into it.

HAPPY DAYS ARE HERE AGAIN: *At the New Deal Inn (left), 3759 Lipan Street, "wets" drink to the repeal of prohibition—the end of America's "Noble Experiment," as it was known. Repeal brought smiles to many faces, including the waitresses at Paul's Place (above), 2376 Fifteenth Street; Katie and Alvena Leubke (inset), wife and daughter of the proprietor of Paul's Place, await parched customers after the long dry spell, 1916-1934. In the 1960s, Paul's Place became My Brother's Bar where artists, musicians and actors gathered; owners Jim and Angelo junked a jukebox for classical music tapes. The Arabian Bar on Navajo Street (token at left) still has a basement wine press used during prohibition. During the 1977 football season, the old speakeasy gained new notoriety when a customer who dared to play the jukebox during a televised Denver Bronco game was shot and killed.*

129

Depression-stricken Denverites panned the
South Platte during the 1930s and
sometimes found a dollar a day in gold.

CHAPTER 9

Drowsy Denver

With the mining booms, the bust
of 1893 and Mayor Speer's fit of
city building behind them, Denverites aspired to quiet,
secure existences.

After a rough birth in the gold rush and an explosive adolescence, Denver entered the twentieth century cautiously. Although sons and daughters of the pioneers sometimes dressed up in old-time costumes to relive the past, they had little interest in making earth-shaking history of their own.

Rather than risk everything to build a railroad or dig a mine, second- and third-generation capitalists held on to their stocks and dividends, their bank accounts and interest. They never forgot the crash of '93. Over highballs at the Denver Club, financiers recalled with horror how David Moffat had almost bankrupted the First National Bank of Denver to build his railroad. Moffat's death in New York City, they whispered to one another, may have been by his own hand.

For years, Colorado General Hospital dominated the sagebrush along Colorado Boulevard that now bristles with high-rises.

Mayor Stapleton, left, brought dignity and decorum to city hall and other events.

The bankers toasted to a gentlemen's agreement—no Denver bank would lend out more than 18 percent of its assets. Gerald Hughes, who had helped pick up the pieces at the First National after Moffatt's death, swore that if the First ever loaned out over a third of its assets, he would liquidate it.

With the mining booms, the bust of 1893 and Mayor Speer's fit of city-building behind them, Denverites aspired to quiet, secure existences. They sipped hot toddies around winter fireplaces and dozed in tree-shaded summer backyards. Only a good view of the mountains seemed important.

To swat the flies and keep their rocking chairs steady, the power elite turned to Benjamin Franklin Stapleton. "Interminable Ben" was repeatedly re-elected mayor with the exception of one term between 1923 and 1947. The Stapleton years were a period of relative tranquility, slow growth and satisfaction with the status quo. The city grew from 213,381 in 1910 to 322,412 in 1940. Nineteenth-century boomers hell-bent to double growth each year rolled over in their graves and rattled their coffins.

Benjamin F. Stapleton was born in modest circumstances in Paintsville, Kentucky, in 1873. After graduation from the National Normal University in Lebanon, Ohio, he studied law and was admitted to the Ohio Bar in 1896. Shortly afterwards, he moved to Denver—just in time to join the Colorado Volunteers for the Spanish-American War.

During that "Splendid Little War" (as Secretary of State John Hay called it), Stapleton served in the Philippines. Sergeant Stapleton returned to Denver and became commander of America's first Veterans of Foreign

Mayor Benjamin Franklin Stapleton governed the Mile High City from 1923 until 1947, when a man half his age was elected.

Overland Park Auto Tourist Camp, maintained by the City of Denver, was popular with vacationers in the 1920s and Okies in the 1930s.

Wars Post—the John F. Stewart Post # 1 organized in 1899.

Using the VFW as a political base, Stapleton became a cog in the machine of Mayor Robert W. Speer. He was rewarded with positions in the offices of the city treasurer and the clerk and recorder. From 1904 to 1915, the dapper, hard-working attorney and party loyalist served as police magistrate and afterwards as postmaster of Denver.

Stapleton was a lean man with thin hair, wire-rimmed spectacles and a tight-lipped seriousness. He revived the moribund Speer machine in 1923 for the first of his many mayoral races. Stapleton reassembled the old Speer coalition of Seventeenth Street's power elite and the blue collar class. He also found support among military veterans and a para military group called the Ku Klux Klan. The Klan had been founded after the Civil War in the South but enjoyed national prominence and popularity during the mid-1920s.

These white-sheeted goblins interrupted Denver's drowsy decades with a nightmare of bigotry and misguided patriotism. The majority of Denverites—the two-thirds of the population that was neither Catholic, Jewish, black, brown, yellow or foreign-born—quickly awoke from the bad dream and rejected the Klan. But from 1923 to 1926, the goblins maintained an invisible and powerful empire in the Centennial State.

One Denverite in every ten joined—or was pressured into pledging allegiance and dues to the Ku Klux Klan. With almost 25,000 members in the capital city and about that same number in other Kolorado Klaverns, the Klan became important to politicians. At the peak of its short-lived ascendancy, the Kolorado Klan claimed to control over 100,000 votes and the clout to swing any Colorado election.

In the mid-1920s they did precisely that. Elections were fought mostly along Klan and anti-Klan lines. The hooded empire helped to elect Benjamin Stapleton mayor of Denver in 1923 and to defeat a recall vote. The Klan also supported the election of Governor Clarence Morley and both of Colorado's United States senators. In exchange for Klan support, candidates either joined the Invisible Empire or signed statements of support.

After afficionados of "100-percent Americanism" swept city and state elections, even the anti-Klan *Denver Post* acknowledged in 1924 that

Grand Dragon John Galen Locke presided over Kolorado's Ku Klux Klan in the 1920s.

"beyond any doubt the Ku Klux Klan is the largest, most cohesive and most efficiently organized political force in Colorado today." National attention was drawn to the Kolorado Klan by *Nation* magazine. *Nation* reported that Governor Morley hired a full-time messenger to bring him instructions from the state's Grand Dragon, who spoke for a hooded army that ranked second only to the Indiana Klan in per capita membership.

The clout of the Kolorado Klavern was due largely to one man—Dr. John Galen Locke, a physician denied membership in the Denver Medical Society for failure to meet the standards of modern medicine. He was a short, plump Napoleon, extremely proud of his Van Dyke beard and meticulously trimmed moustache, which he daintily stroked with ring-bejeweled fingers.

Locke remains an enigmatic figure. After helping found the Denver Doers Club in 1921, he transformed that organization into the nucleus of his empire. Since his medical patients were primarily Italian Catholics and some of his attorneys and secretaries were Catholic and Jewish, some suspect that the Grand Dragon was motivated by money and power rather than by patriotism or bigotry.

Klan klambakes, karavans, klanklaves and kross burnings on South Table Mountain and Ruby Hill gave some bored, identity-hungry white Denverites something to do. But it gave already poor and troubled minority groups a great deal to worry about. Wherever they turned in Denver during the 1920s, members of ethnic groups found signs of intolerance—"We serve fish everyday—except Fridays;" "Doing business with *jews* is bad business;" "No lice, No rats, No Greeks." Denver's 35,000 Catholics, 11,000 Jews, 25,000 foreign-born and 7,000 blacks primarily experienced insults and economic boycotts, but sometimes there were beatings, forced expulsions and death threats.

Locke allegedly enriched himself from sheet sales and membership fees and by dipping into donations to his spooky outfit. When rumors surfaced that Locke had accumulated close to $500,000, even the Internal Revenue Service became suspicious. When Locke told federal agents that he had lost his records, government sleuths tried to break into the bank-like private mausoleum he had built at Fairmount Cemetery before his death. But the G-men failed to find them there.

Locke also got into financial tussles with the national Klan. He and his followers then left the national organization and founded a similar group, the Minutemen of America. But after William Adams defeated Governor Morley in the 1926 election and Mayor Stapleton denounced Locke, his army of white righteousness fizzled into insignificance.

The Grand Dragon carried the Klan's financial secrets to the grave after a coronary killed him on April Fool's Day in 1931. His faithful followers sneaked into Fairmount Cemetery at night for a final cross burning before the crypt of their discredited leader.

Despite Klan harrassment, various members of Denver's black community fought for the rights guaranteed their people by federal laws, state statutes and city ordinances. One of them—Dr. Clarence Holmes, a dentist—founded the Colorado unit of the National Association for the Advancement of Colored People in 1915. Benjamin F. Hooper, a tavernkeeper, operated just a few doors down Welton Street from Dr. Holmes, his lifelong friend.

Clarence Holmes graduated from Manual High School and applied to the University of Colorado. They told him they "did not accept colored applicants." Holmes went to Howard University in the national capital and graduated from the dental school in 1920. He practiced dentistry at 2602 Welton Street for over half a century before retiring in 1976. "I've yet to have any tense moments from mixing the different races in my office," Holmes once told the *Denver Post* "and there's nothing more personal than a person's mouth." Holmes was active in a wide variety of civic as well as civil rights groups.

In the 1920s, 90 percent of Denver's blacks were confined to the crowded,

dilapidated Five Points neighborhood. Those who tried to move elsewhere met threats, cross-burnings and bombings. In 1921, Mr. and Mrs. Walter B. Chapman were blown out of their front porch chairs at 2112 Gilpin Street. Chapman, a mailman, sold the house to another Negro family, the Starrs. Despite another bombing, the Starrs stayed. Holmes got the NAACP to offer a $200 reward and the city put up $250. Yet the bomb throwers were never found.

Dr. Florence Sabin labored to give Denver the finest public health care in America.

Some whites resorted to restrictive covenants forbidding that property ever be leased or sold to "colored persons." For years, the alley between Race Street and High Street north of Colfax was one of the unofficial color lines. Having the boundary in the alley enabled people to sit on their front porches without seeing members of the other race. This sharply defined ghetto did not disappear until after 1957 when the Colorado Supreme Court outlawed racially restrictive covenants.

Even within their ghetto, blacks were treated as second-class citizens. For example, in the early twentieth century, Benny Hooper tried to find a place to swim on sweltering summer afternoons. The Curtis Park pool and Mayor Speer's bathhouse at 20th and Curtis streets were open to blacks only one day a week—and that was the day before they changed the water so white children would not be "contaminated."

"We'd just swim in the river down around 23rd Street," Hooper recollected, "but even there the cops would fish us out. They said we were polluting the Platte!"

After reaching the sixth grade at Ebert School, Benny dropped out to shine shoes and bell-hop downtown. When World War I came, he was the first Negro to go.

Hooper came back in 1919. He and other black veterans found themselves in a community seething with racism and KKK activity. "Seemed like every place in town was off limits to us," he recalled. "I

started a little club up on Arapahoe. Blacks came in wondering where they could stay, ready to make trouble. I cooled them off with a couple of drinks and let them sleep on my floor. Then Mayor Stapleton dropped by one day, put his arm on my shoulder and said, 'Benny, folks are complaining. Why don't you get a new location?' " At the mayor's suggestion, Hooper found a place in a largely Jewish neighborhood—2627 Welton Street.

Hooper recalled how unwelcome returning black servicemen had been. He named his new place the Ex-Service Men's Club. He spent his lifetime expanding his resort to include a hotel, the Casino ballroom, the Deluxe Pool Hall and Recreation Center and the club room which boasts the backbar from Senator Lawrence C. Phipps' old East Colfax mansion.

In the 1920s, Hooper and his hotel full of doughboys decided to join the annual Veterans Day parade. "We shined hell out of our shoes, and I got some brand new uniforms. Every man looked great. When we got downtown, I said we were the best looking outfit and should march first. But this sloppy looking white told us we had to march last. And we couldn't carry weapons."

UNION STATION: *The original Union Station (facing page, top right) was completed in 1881 and survived until 1894 when the center section and south wing were gutted by fire. The second Union Station (facing page, lower right), with remodeled tower, was fronted by an attractive park which later gave way to parking space. The Welcome Arch at Union Station (facing page, top left) was dedicated on July 4, 1906, and torn down in 1931. On the city side of the Welcome Arch (facing page, center left) was the Hebrew word "Mizpah" meaning "God be with you until we meet again." For decades, a Christmas tree in Union Station (facing page, lower left) welcomed holiday visitors to Denver. Today, the train station is dwarfed (top left) by the downtown skyline of skyscrapers. Monthly, model train operators work a large layout (lower left) in the basement of Union Station.*

Hooper called on Mayor Stapleton. A bargain was struck. "Benny's men" were allowed to march in the middle of the parade with inoperable rifles carved from wood and painted to look like real ones. And later in the fall, Hooper organized the Five Points vote for Stapleton.

"I even started working on Doc Holmes," Hooper remembered. "He was a real strong Republican, said Negroes should never leave the party of Lincoln." Hooper finally talked Holmes into letting him put up a big Stapleton sign in his front yard. Hooper felt that a live Mayor Stapleton could do more for blacks than a dead President Lincoln.

"The Ku Klux Klan didn't like us," Hooper began with a grin. "They burned some crosses up here in the Points but I put a counterman up front who looked just like he was white. They'd see him and they wouldn't do nothing."

Hooper's place became the hottest club in Five Points. "Benny Hooper's De Luxe Recreation Parlor and Ex-Service Men's Club," according to a *Rocky Mountain News* feature story, "is a swell place, and the business is good. The noisy black-and-tan crowd around his door is the sporting, fun-loving, easy-going element.... You find Benny at the front counter," the *News* continued. "He gives you a shrewd once-over before he opens up. If he likes you, he'll talk about his patrons, and introduce you to favored customers." Benny's long list of favored customers included once-celebrated, now-forgotten boxers, musicians, ball players, gamblers and politicians.

When the Great Depression reached Denver, Hooper's place became a less jubilant community center. Five Points was hit harder than any other neighborhood in the city. Whites may have lost money and jobs, but blacks faced starvation.

Hooper, according to old-timers, did as much as anyone to get his people through the Great Depression. Ever since he has been known as "the unofficial mayor of Five Points." Brass inscriptions on his backbar trophies commemorate Hooper's philanthropy. Working with bandleader George Morrison, Hooper approached Frederick G. Bonfils of the *Denver Post* with a proposal.

In those days, the *Post* sponsored huge jackrabbit hunts on the plains east of town. Hooper pointed out that rabbit stew would taste mighty good up in Five Points and persuaded the *Post* and white gun clubs to dump truckloads off at his club. As savory aromas drifted out of Hooper's kitchen, hundreds lined up for free dinners. He also got wealthy whites to donate gallons of milk which he served to the children of Five Points.

Hooper still worked a 2 p.m. to 2 a.m. shift at his fading Ex-Service Men's Club in the 1970s, a slight, light-complexioned man in an old-time suit. Yet he realized Five Points was dying as the center of the black community. "We used to have all the colored balls, charities and events right here in the casino, but now they have them all over town, even out in Arapahoe County."

As blacks moved out to City Park and Park Hill—"Struggle Hill" to those who finally got into that elegant old neighborhood in the 1960s—Chicanos and whites moved into the Points.

The move out of Five Points symbolized better times for blacks. According to one black leader, Denver's black community is one of the most prosperous and well integrated in America. Census projections in 1980 estimated that the 91,185 blacks in the Denver metropolitan area had an average education of 13.2 years compared with the national average of 10.9 years. The estimated 1980 average income for Denver black families was slightly higher than the average for all Americans. Sixty-eight percent of Denver's black families owned their homes and forty-four percent had two cars. Black gardeners toiling in front of substantial homes on Monaco Parkway, 26th Avenue and Martin Luther King Boulevard often own the estates they tend.

In the 1920s and 1930s, it was a different story for blacks and for the city's even poorer Spanish and Japanese people. Few had houses of their own and when public housing was proposed, Mayor Stapleton snapped, "If those people would only go back to where they came from, we wouldn't have a housing shortage."

Housing also became a problem for many white Denverites during the 1930s depression. At first, Coloradans thought they might escape aftershocks of the 1929 stock market crash in distant New York City. After all, Colorado's relatively stable, diversified economy was less overheated than that of many states. Yet Colorado's fate was intertwined with the nation's fortunes. Collapse was inevitable, although it came later and was less devastating than elsewhere.

Cautious, relatively sound Denver banks found themselves having to do business with others that were not. As rumors and news of collapsing banks reached Colorado, long lines queued up outside the fortresses of Seventeenth Street. Tellers at the savings account windows of the First National started the day with $100,000 and saw it disappear by mid-afternoon. After President Franklin D. Roosevelt moved into the

White House in 1933, he declared a bank holiday. The news did not reach Denver until 9:40 in the morning. Crowds were already lined up outside such banks as the First National, Colorado National, American National and Central Bank. Inside, officials appointed courageous spokesmen to slip out the side doors and tell the crowds that the banks had been closed indefinitely.

Federal auditors soon found most Colorado firms sound and allowed them to reopen with the backing of the Federal Deposit Insurance Corporation. But 66 of Colorado's 237 banks never re-opened, including many smaller, rural ones.

Even when the banks did re-open, few people had anything to deposit. By 1932, a third of Denver's 85,000 working people were unemployed. On one day—June 5, 1932—four Denverites committed suicide. Colorado industry, agriculture and commerce declined drastically. Iron and steel production fell by 1932 to 12 percent of its 1929 figures. Coal production declined by half, throwing thousands of miners out of work. New passenger car registrations in 1932 dropped to half the number of registrations in 1929. Department store sales plummeted by a third.

Farmers were hit especially hard. The price of a bushel of wheat dropped from 96 cents in 1929 to 37 cents in 1932. Sugar beets fell from $6.93 to $4.92 a ton. Apples brought 42 cents a bushel instead of $1.45, and livestock prices collapsed to a third of their pre-depression worth.

While Seventeenth Street finance and Sixteenth Street shopping

The Emily Griffith Opportunity School taught gold panning on the South Platte River during the Great Depression.

declined, skid row on Larimer Street thrived. Pawnshops, secondhand stores, missions and soup kitchens proliferated. Hundreds of vagrants camped out in hobo jungles that lined the South Platte River and the tracks.

Thousands of Denverites unable to meet rent or mortgage or tax payments moved into squatter housing of cardboard, scrap lumber and adobe. These "Hoovervilles" popped up in depressed suburban areas as well as in the core city. Residents of Denver's Hoovervilles wasted their days looking for jobs that a prostrate private sector could not provide. To create jobs, architect Charles D. Young and others formed the Unemployed Citizens' League of Denver in 1932. It was modeled after a coalition of the same name in Seattle that also sought to help the unemployed help themselves. Within a year, the Denver league had 34,000 members in 25 locals, including Mexican-American and Negro units.

The league operated a wide variety of programs. Members worked two days a week. They were paid in food, supplies, coal or anything but money. Leaguers operated their own school where they taught a wide variety of courses, including language skills, job skills and economics. They ran a bakery that turned out 500 loaves of bread a day. They cut timber, picked produce and mined coal for a percentage of the harvest. They repaired and recycled old clothing and shoes and took turns giving each other haircuts. They published a newspaper called *Dawn*.

Both Denver's Unemployed Citizens' League and Colorado's nationally prominent old age pension plan were effective anti-depression projects eclipsed by the battery of federal programs inaugurated by New Dealers in Washington. These lavish federal relief and recovery measures interested Ben Stapleton, who returned to office in 1935 after George D. Begole's one term at City Hall.

Stapleton made his comeback with the help of his campaign chairman, George E. Cranmer. After the election, Stapleton offered Cranmer any position he wanted. Cranmer chose manager of parks and improvements. Scion of a prominent Colorado family, Cranmer hoped to make his mark by reviving Speer's green dreams of a city beautiful. A small, eccentric man given to bat-wing collars and bow ties long after they were out of style, Cranmer became the administration's sparkplug.

To complete many parks and improvements, Cranmer used city land, Works Progress Administration (WPA) and Public Works Administration (PWA) funds and materials and Civilian Conservation Corps (CCC) labor. Tax-delinquent property seized by the city gave Cranmer plenty of land with which to work.

Cranmer and Stapleton used or traded tax lands to acquire the right-of-way for the Valley Highway (the stretch of Interstate 25 paralleling the South Platte valley in Denver), West Sixth Avenue freeway and West Alameda Avenue Parkway. These expressways expedited tourism and the weekend mountain excursions to which Denverites had always been addicted.

To the delight of Denverites ever since, Cranmer added an outdoor theater and a ski resort to Denver's Mountain Park System. After Cranmer's cajoling, various individuals donated acreage to the park system. For example, Martin O'Fallon of Crane-O'Fallon plumbing supplies, gave the mountain park now named for him.

In Red Rocks Park, Denver's flamboyant manager of parks and improvements orchestrated construction of an outdoor amphitheater. Denver donated only the land and a token fee for architect Burnham Hoyt. WPA funds and materials and CCC labor were used, as well as some dynamite, but Cranmer—according to his tape-recorded memoirs—tried to keep that quiet in order not to disturb the mayor who thought of Red Rocks as "a nice rock garden."

One of Cranmer's proposals was the development of the Winter Park Ski Area at the west portal of the Moffat Tunnel. After touring several

MEXICO'S CHILDREN: In 1939, in Denver's Mexican-American barrio, children (top) lived inside this eight-by-nine foot room lined with brown wrapping paper on Mariposa Street. The worst part of the barrio was torn down to construct the Lincoln Park Housing Project (above) in 1940, bounded by West Colfax Avenue, Mariposa Street, West Thirteenth Avenue and Osage Street.

ROOF LINES: The golden capitol dome (facing page) is reflected in one of downtown Denver's glass skyscrapers. In 1950, however, the Daniels and Fisher Tower (facing page, inset) still dominated a city that had changed surprisingly little since the nineteenth-century boom. The city would change drastically beginning in the 1960s as hundreds of old landmarks gave way to office and residential towers. In the Clements historic district, Victorian gingerbread houses (below) have been given a colorful face-lifting.

"HOOVERVILLES": Denver's depression housing was concentrated along the South Platte River bottoms, in the Five Points, Highland, Globeville, Swansea and Jefferson Park neighborhoods. The two photos at right were taken in May 1939 at Nineteenth and Clay Streets; the photos above were shot along the 3000 block of Inca Street.

European resorts, Cranmer discussed the idea of a municipal ski area with friends, sportsmen, ski clubs and anyone who would listen and possibly donate to the cause. With a $14,700 donation raised by the Denver Chamber of Commerce, a $38,000 Public Works Administration grant and land ultimately obtained by Denver from the United States Forest Service, Cranmer created Colorado's first major ski area. The Denver and Rio Grande scheduled a still-operating ski train to Winter Park, and Denver began promoting itself as the capital of winter sports for all America.

The Stapleton administration and the Denver Water Board (whose commissioners are appointed by the mayor) inaugurated the present process of diverting western slope water to the much more populous and developed eastern slope. In 1936, Denver Water Board engineers completed the first transmontane diversion by funneling Fraser River water through the pioneer bore of the Moffat Tunnel into Boulder Creek. From a series of reservoirs, the water was then conveyed to the farms, factories, kitchens, bathrooms and gardens of the eastern slope.

Completion of the Jones Pass Tunnel (1939), Roberts Tunnel (1946) and the Colorado Big-Thompson Project (1947) further facilitated growth. With these water diversions, the Stapleton administration watered the seeds of Denver's post-World-War-II boom. Ironically, these projects of the sleepy, slow-growth Stapleton era made future growth possible.

Because a third of Colorado is federal government land, the Civilian Conservation Corps (CCC) became especially active in Colorado. By 1936, over 5,000 poor youths (including many Denverites) worked in 41 CCC camps in Colorado. The CCC spent $50 million in Colorado before the enterprise was discontinued in 1943. The projects in the Denver area included construction of roads, hiking trails, camp grounds, bridges and other accessways that encouraged use of the municipal mountain parks and Rocky Mountain National Park.

Under the supervision of Dr. LeRoy Hafen, the State Historical Society of Colorado made excellent use of Federal Writers and Federal Artists Project funds. A massive survey, compilation and exhibition program systematically documented the state's history. Thousands of old-timers were interviewed, newspapers were collected and indexed, and a wealth of raw material gathered and preserved.

George Cranmer, in suspenders and bow tie, surveys his dream-come-true, the outdoor amphitheater at Red Rocks Park west of Denver.

Dr. Hafen, the state historian and longtime editor of *The Colorado Magazine*, publicized the state's heritage in the magazine and numerous books. From the Federal Writers' project came the unsurpassed, *Colorado: A Guide to the Highest State*. Historians and artists collaborated in the 1930s and 1940s to build the minutely-detailed, fascinating dioramas that still are the most popular exhibits in the Historical Society's new building at 1300 Broadway. Artists also constructed life-size dioramas at the Denver Museum of Natural History in City Park.

The Works Progress Administration spent $111 million in Colorado to build roads, bridges, culverts, sidewalks, schools, libraries, parks, airports, sewage disposal plants, sewers, dams, tunnels and other public facilities. WPA employed approximately 150,000 Coloradans at everything from preparing hot school lunches to riprapping Cherry Creek and the South Platte River. The WPA theatrical project hired local talent, including Denver playwright Mary Chase, who later wrote the Pulitzer-prize winning play, "Harvey."

Federal dollars were used also to improve and expand Stapleton Air Field at the eastern end of 32nd Avenue (now Martin Luther King Boulevard). When dedicated in 1929, Stapleton Field consisted of two dusty runways, one hangar, a tiny terminal and a wind sock. While a few foresaw that Stapleton Field would become Denver's transportation hub, others scoffed at "Stapleton's Folly" or "Simpleton's Sand Dunes."

Probably no one foresaw that within 50 years, Stapleton Field would become the seventh busiest airport in America in terms of passengers and the tenth busiest in the world. (By 1980 a plane arrived or departed every minute. Denver became a flight of several hours rather than a rail or automobile trip of several days from cities all over North America.) The tourist and commercial tempo increased tremendously. Jet planes changed Denver from an isolated regional capital to a major American metropolis. Denver inaugurated direct flights to Europe via huge planes that bore little resemblance to the United Airlines DC-3s that first brought air passengers to Denver in 1937. These tiny, twin-propeller planes offered "Skylounge" service, sleeping berths and three seats per aisle.

After the United States entered World War II, Uncle Sam began spending much more money in Colorado. The Denver Chamber of Commerce bought the land for Fitzsimmons Army Medical Center and raised money to purchase the old Phipps Sanitarium site for Lowry Air Field. Both sites were transferred to the military before World War II but were not fully developed until the war.

Lowry had been founded in 1937 and named for a Denverite killed in

UP, UP AND AWAY: A modern-day hot air balloon race (facing page) offers a bright contrast to the champagne christening of an early air ship (facing page, inset) at the Denver Union Airport. Inflation keeps the U.S. Mint in Denver (top) busy, as prices soar skyward; the mint is also a popular tourist attraction (above) of the Mile High City.

World War I. The base became America's chief technical air training center. A few miles east of Lowry, another air field was established in 1942. It was on 2,210 acres, with an initial appropriation of $20 million. It was named Buckley Field in honor of John Harold Buckley, a Longmont lieutenant killed in France during World War I.

To meet the wartime challenge, the Army expanded Fort Logan and converted it to an induction center. Fitzsimons Army Hospital, founded in Aurora in 1918 and named for the first American medical officer to die in World War I, grew during World War II into one of the largest military hospitals in the world.

Through the efforts of the Stapleton administration and the Chamber of Commerce, Denver also attracted a huge weapons plant. The plant was owned by the federal government and operated by Remington Arms Company which hired 20,000 employees. After the war, the plant site bounded by West Alameda and Sixth avenues and Kipling and Simms streets was converted to the Denver Federal Center.

The multi-million dollar New Deal and World War II programs exceeded the wildest hopes of the Denver Chamber of Commerce, which had launched a promotional venture during the 1930s to make Denver the "Little Capital of the United States."

Numerous federal agencies, many contracts and thousands of federal jobs transformed the Denver area. Relatively high-paying, secure, white-collar government employment added stability and diversity to the local economy. By the end of World War II, the federal government was the largest employer in metropolitan Denver.

Thousands of new jobs attracted many newcomers to Denver during and after the war. Military personnel stationed in the drowsy, tree-shaded town with its enviably mild, dry, sunny climate and spectacular mountain backdrop, settled there after the war. Between 1940 and 1950, Denver's population grew from 322,412 to 415,789 while the suburban counties climbed from 445,000 to 612,000. Most of the new arrivals came to agree with the *Denver Post*'s motto—"tis a privilege to live in Colorado."

Hordes of bustling newcomers settled primarily in the Denver area and awoke the Mile High City from its long nap. The drowsy decades of relatively slow growth, streetcar and railroad transportation, a low profile downtown, and cautious conservative leadership ended in the 1940s. After the relatively slow pace of the 1893-1945 era, Denver began a growth spurt reminiscent of the original gold rush. The instant city created by nineteenth-century mineral bonanzas became a major American metropolis. It offered many occupational and recreational advantages and a relaxed, outdoor western lifestyle. Soon it became a rarity to find a native among the hundreds of thousands who called themselves Denverites.

Although Denverites dissented, an out-state vote margin brought state-wide prohibition to Colorado on January 1, 1916. Determined dry crusaders such as these WCTU demonstrators in the 1928 presidential election sought to keep Colorado dry to the bitter end.

*Early promotion of electrical appliances by
the Colorado Public Service Company.*

CHAPTER 10

Post-war awakening

"The remarkable thing about Denver is its ineffable closedness...it is probably the most self-sufficient, isolated, self-contained and complacent city in the world."

Gene Amole, whose long career includes stints with numerous newspapers and radio stations in Denver, has made the city's classical musical station, KVOD, one of America's most successful challenges to rock and pop air waves.

Marvin Davis, son of an English sailor, came to Denver in the 1950s to run a struggling oil company; he quickly transformed Davis Oil Company into a multi-million dollar business. Sometimes called Denver's 500-million-dollar man, he watches construction (above) of one of his downtown structures, the 410 Building on Seventeenth Street. "They call Denver the Mile High City because it's sitting on Marvin's wallet," comedian Bob Hope once quipped at the Davis' annual Carousel Celebrity Ball for the Children's Diabetes Foundation of Denver.

The end of World War II began the boom for Denver. Thousands moved to the Mile High City and found a sleepy, provincial town.

John Gunther's 1947 best-seller, *Inside U.S.A.*, claimed that, "The remarkable thing about Denver is its ineffable closedness.... It is probably the most self-sufficient, isolated, self-contained and complacent city in the world."

Robert L. Perkin, a leading Denver journalist, reached a similar conclusion in the chapter on Denver he co-authored for the 1949 book, *Rocky Mountain Cities*: "Today Denver is the reluctant capital of a region larger than most nations. It is big and beautiful, and the climate is still superb. It is also smug, sleek and satisfied. It is contentedly disinterested in its own continuing growth, abhorrent of risk-taking, chary of progress."

The March 10, 1947, issue of *Time* magazine attributed Denver's drowsiness to a mossback mayor: "To newcomers, Benjamin Franklin Stapleton seems one of the most ineffectual old men in the rambling, shady city of Denver. He dreads change. He falls asleep at public meetings, mumbles in monosyllables, and exudes a little less social warmth than Marley's ghost."

Partly to disprove such pundits, Mayor Stapleton literally went to bat on a warm May 1, 1947, during pre-game antics as the Denver Bears opened their Western Baseball League season. The 77-year-old city executive stepped up to home plate to promote the hometown team and demonstrate his own fitness. The pitch came from a young California congressman, Richard Milhous Nixon.

Nixon may have thrown a curve. Mayor Stapleton swung bravely, missed and fell flat on his face. Floyd McCall, a photographer for the *Denver Post*, captured the aging Democrat sprawling in the dust before the future Republican president.

McCall rushed his photograph to the editor of the *Denver Post*, Palmer Hoyt, who was spearheading the drive to oust Stapleton. Hoyt was former editor of the *Portland Oregonian*, and had been selected to head the *Post* only a year earlier. But Hoyt declined to run the embarrasing photo of his political enemy. *Life magazine*, however, ran it full page with the caption, "Mayor Strikes Out." This proved to be the case at the polls.

Stapleton lost to a 35-year-old political newcomer, James Quigg Newton, scion of a prominent Denver family who were Grant Street neighbors and Seventeenth Street investment house partners of Charles Boettcher. Quigg was a graduate of Yale Law School, former legal secretary of William O. Douglas (when Douglas headed the Securities Exchange Commission before his appointment to the Supreme Court) and a World War II naval officer.

Douglas suggested to *Post* editor Hoyt that Quigg Newton might make a good mayor. With the enthusiastic support of both the *Post* and the *Rocky Mountain News*, Newton challenged "Interminable Ben."

"Denver," Newton told audiences, "must throw out the machine gang." He promised to revitalize City Hall and bring Denver into the twentieth century. Newton claimed that he, unlike Stapleton, would promote growth. "If industry is not persuaded to locate here," Newton declared, "this city may be eclipsed by other cities in the region."

Capital city voters trooped to the polls in 1947 in record numbers to give Quigg Newton a landslide victory. The retiring mayor graciously showed his successor around the City and County Building and laid a fatherly hand on Newton and said, "Young man, I've left you a beautiful city."

Mayor Newton, however, found that much housecleaning and yardwork was needed. Working 12 to 14 hours a day for a salary that had remained at $6,000 a year since 1919, Newton began by cleaning out the deadwood at City Hall. He also repaired Speer's decrepit auditorium and added a new wing.

The new mayor hired an eastern architect to re-design the garish

James Quigg Newton became Denver's 36th mayor in 1947 at 36 years of age.

Christmas lighting of the City and County Building with a more subdued, sophisticated display. This change raised the ire of townspeople who forced Newton to re-instate the traditional lighting, ornaments and nativity scene. (Attempts to change the Christmas decorations and remove the mountains from Colorado car license plates have been among the hottest postwar political potatoes.)

Mayor Newton enjoyed a love affair with the news media. Scarcely a day passed that Newton and Hoyt of the *Post* did not confer. The *Post* had pilloried Stapleton unmercifully. But it began a daily feature, "Good News Today," that often contained inside reports from City Hall. Newton also inaugurated a weekly radio show, "The Mayor's Mailbag."

Probably no other mayor had such strong support, such an opportunity to get things done. During his two terms, Newton renovated and reformed municipal government. He replaced the Speer-Stapleton political patronage system with municipal civil service—the Career Service Authority. City contracts and purchases were opened to competitive bidding, property taxes were re-assessed along more equitable lines, and the city charter and ordinances were recodified, updated and clarified. Newton beefed up the Denver Planning Office and established the Intercounty Regional Planning Commission, predecessor of the Denver Regional Council of Governments.

The old Health and Charities Department was remodeled into two new departments—Welfare and Health and Hospitals. Newton tapped Dr. Solomon Kauvar, son of the prominent, progressive Rabbi Charles E.H. Kauvar, to head health and hospitals. Solomon's brother Abraham later took his turn at the helm of the city's largest department. Both doctors Kauvar advanced May Speer's old dream of first-rate health care for all. They oversaw construction of a new Denver General Hospital building, establishment of neighborhood health clinics and a greater emphasis on disease prevention and home health care. Close co-operation between the city and the University of Colorado's medical center—an arrangement originally worked out by Mayor Newton—further enhanced Denver's national reputation for health care.

The city's numerous public and private health care facilities, as well as its residents' love of the outdoors and exercise, has led various magazines and national city watchers to call Denver "the healthiest big city in America." For this blessing, Denverites do not deserve all the credit. The Colorado climate is invigorating. Cool nights follow the hottest summer days and 300 days of sunshine a year melt most winter snows quickly, often bringing out bicyclists, joggers, golfers and tennis players while skiers head for the powder-snow mountains.

The dry sunny air has long earned thanksgivings from senior citizens, the ailing and the poet in many people, including a nineteenth-century scribbler for Denver's *Great Divide* magazine:

> *Sunshine for the pale and palsied,*
> *Sunshine for the chilled and weak,*
> *Giving pallid lips the rubies*
> *And the rose to Pallor's cheek.*

Thomas Hornsby Ferrill, Colorado's poet laureate, shows his love for his native Denver in books and public poetry readings. His friend poet Robert Frost once described Ferrill in verse: "A man is as tall as his height/Plus the height of his hometown./I know a Denverite who, measured from sea to crown,/Is one mile five-foot-ten."

Bill Hosokowa wrote many books on the Japanese, following his release from a World War II relocation camp. He has risen through the ranks to become a top editor at the Denver Post.

Sunshine does not solve all problems, however. In 1947, Mayor Newton began investigating poverty, discrimination, pollution and overcrowding. They were issues many of his predecessors ignored or glossed over. During Newton's first year in office, his Committee on Human Relations published the *Report of Minorities in Denver.* The report pinpointed an on-going problem—the poverty compounded by discrimination that has stalked Denver's largest ethnic group—the Spanish-surnamed people.

A few Spanish-speaking people lived in Denver from the beginning, coming up from the Rio Grande Valley where they began to settle in 1598. They were the first Europeans to explore, write about and name the Colorado terrain but they became second-class citizens after the Treaty of Guadalupe Hidalgo when Mexico surrendered the Southwest, including much of Colorado.

This 1848 treaty ended the Mexican War and guaranteed the property and cultural rights of thousands of newly annexed Mexican-Americans. These new Americans had only a little more luck than the Indians in defending their government-guaranteed rights against the advancing Anglo-American frontier.

Mexican-Americans helped to build Colorado's railroads and dig coal. In the twentieth century, agri-business and industry began recruiting them in large numbers. The Great Western Sugar Beet Company imported car loads of stoop labor from Old and New Mexico. After the harvests, many flocked to Denver's river bottoms and poor neighborhoods.

The Capital city's miniscule Mexican-American population began to grow rapidly after 1900. This group introduced a conservative, tradition-rich, Catholic heritage that sometimes clashed with the prevalent culture. The newcomers ate unusual foods, relied on folk medicine administered by *curanderas*, seemed to prefer nocturnal hours for work and play, celebrated different festivals and clung to their older, less materialistic, more family-oriented culture.

Denver's Spanish-surnamed population climbed from 1,390 in 1920 to 12,345 in 1940. This increase alarmed some people, particularly during the job, food and housing shortages prevalent in the depression years. In April 1936, Governor "Big Ed" Johnson catered to popular prejudice and declared martial law on the Colorado-New Mexico border. For a brief period, Johnson tried to keep out indigent, job-hunting Mexicans. (Johnson

Pikes Peak rises above the plains, still snow-capped though the tender green of spring breaks through. Mountain recreation offers a fast swoosh on skis in the winter or a more leisurely ride in the summer.

National Western Stock Show in Denver.

CHICANO PRIDE: Manuel Silva outside his restaurant on Larimer Street (top). Mexi-Dan's Bakery down a block.

and many Coloradans, did not always distinguish between Mexican aliens and Spanish-speaking Colorado citizens.)

While Denver blacks had an average family income that was two-thirds that of whites, many Spanish-American families subsisted on a third of what the average white family had. Whereas almost half of the whites and a third of the blacks owned their homes, only eleven percent of the brown families did so in 1940. The pioneer public housing units built in the 1940s during the Stapleton era—Las Casitas, Lincoln Park, Platte Valley and Arapahoe Courts—overflowed after the war. Mayor Newton tripled the number of low income, subsidized housing units with the Westridge, Newton, Sun Valley, Columbine, Curtis Park, South Lincoln Park, Westwood and Stapleton projects. Since 1955, a half-dozen other low-income complexes have been developed. But the Denver Housing Authority is progressively switching to scattered individual units that are more compatible with the surrounding neighborhoods.

Denver's poor were shortchanged politically by the practice of gerrymandering—creating city council districts according to the number of registered voters only. In many poorer neighborhoods, voter registration was low, particularly in Mexican-American areas with many aliens and non-English-speaking people. Middle- and upper-class white neighborhoods with higher voter turnouts thus maintained disproportionate power in the city council. This policy, as Councilman James Fresquez pointed out, "meant that the people with the greatest problems were not even counted in the drawing of district lines." In 1951, the Council districts were re-drawn to reflect the total population. As a result, previously unrepresented or underrepresented Mexican-Americans gained council seats. In the 1970s, they also began to elect many more representatives to the Colorado General Assembly.

By 1970, Denver's Spanish-surnamed population was 86,345 or 16.8 percent of the total. A decade later, they comprised 22 percent of the population of Denver city and county and looked forward to the 1980s as the "Decade of the Spanish Americans."

Dr. Daniel T. Valdes, professor of sociology and chairman of the behavioral sciences division at Denver's Metropolitan State College, claimed Denver "is in the forefront as far as [upward] Hispano mobility is concerned...far ahead of Los Angeles, San Diego, New York and other cities with large Hispano populations."

Rodolfo "Corky" Gonzales, who founded the militant Crusade for Justice in 1965, disagreed. "We've still got a long way to go," Gonzales said in 1979. "Right now we're getting forced respect, and that creates antagonism. Respect for a human being creates reciprocation. And that's what we're after." Even most militants, however, agree that progress has been made since the 1940s.

In the 1940s, many Denverites were less concerned with minorities than with acquiring automobiles. The result was increasing traffic congestion. The police department tended to cope with traffic jams by putting up a few more streetlights and stop signs and passing out more tickets. According to former city councilman Ernie Marranzino, traffic signals "were just put in when a businessman asked for one to get people to stop near his store."

To unscramble the thickening mass of autos, streetcars and pedestrians, Mayor Newton established a traffic engineering department and hired one of Denver's most controversial bureaucrats to head it—Henry A. Barnes. He was a former truck driver, jig-saw puzzle salesman, policeman and traffic engineer from Flint, Michigan. In six years, he transformed a town geared to streetcars into a smooth-flowing automobile city. When Barnes first proposed one-way streets to the city council, he was shocked to find 250 irate citizens at the Monday-night meeting. Despite protests, Barnes began transforming residential streets as well as major arterials into one-way streets. Not only did Barnes install one-way streets, he converted

them to speedways by installing a traffic computer, a central "brain" that would change each light to green as the traffic got to it.

Synchronized traffic signals on one-way streets aided commuters, but they still found downtown traffic snarled. Denverites increasingly avoided the ordeal of driving and parking downtown by heading out to the new shopping centers that accommodated post-war suburbanization. Newton was unhappy that Denver was losing sales taxes as shoppers headed for suburbia. Barnes, as usual, had an answer. He proposed that downtown be included in the one-way street system.

Businessmen were wary of the change. Reluctantly, they allowed the conversion of two downtown streets on an experimental basis. Traffic flowed so much more smoothly that the business leaders agreed to convert much of the central business district to one-way streets.

Another Barnes innovation still befuddles newcomers. They are astounded to find traffic lights placed in the middle of blocks instead of at the intersections. The purpose of the mid-block traffic light, Barnes wrote in his autobiography, *The Man with the Red and Green Eyes*, "is to discourage straggler cars by forming them into groups which—at the proper speed—will then move through the signal system without stopping. It's also a great help getting cross-street and pedestrian traffic through with a maximum of safety."

While one of these mid-block lights was being placed in east Denver, Barnes received a telephone call from a lady. "Since you have been in Denver, Barnes," the lady said, "you've put two no-parking signs in my side yard, a stop sign and a one-way sign in my front yard, and a fire hydrant next to my driveway which I hit when I back the car out. You've moved my trees twice in the past three years, in order to change the width of the intersection, and now you're installing a red light right next to my bedroom window!"

Barnes, who never seemed to be at a loss for words, shot back, "I think that is pretty good service. Most 'ladies' have to furnish their own red light!"

Hank Barnes (as the folks at City Hall came to call the salty and outspoken engineer) generally sided with motorists. He sacrificed trees and

Rodolfo "Corky" Gonzales, born in Denver in 1928, won 65 of 75 professional fights and became a top contender for the World Featherweight title. Corky, shown with his manager George Zaharias (below), has become a champion of Chicano rights, writing: "I am Joaquin in a country that has wiped out all my history, stifled all my pride. My knees are caked with mud. My hands calloused from the hoe. I have made the Anglo rich. Here I stand Poor in money Arrogant with pride."

CITY RECREATION: Cherry Blossom
Festival time in Sakura Square (above);
playing in Burns Park (left) and cycling
on Boulder Mall (below).

lawns to street widening, quiet neighborhoods to one-way streets and endangered pedestrians by untangling and speeding up auto traffic. Yet Barnes did grant pedestrians one major concession.

"The time has come," Barnes announced after establishing one-way streets in downtown, "to give the pedestrian a 30 to 70 percent chance of getting across the street alive." The traffic engineer presented his scheme to Mayor Newton and the business community. They scratched their heads and said no. Barnes pleaded for a trial and promised to resign if the idea backfired.

So early one morning at Seventeenth and Stout streets, Barnes and his assistants tinkered with the traffic signals. A few early morning winos were amazed to see all the auto traffic lights go red at once and a lot of new pedestrian signals that all read "Walk." With these new installations, pedestrians had total possession of the intersection during their turn to cross.

Businessmen pouring onto Seventeenth Street that morning were curious yet cautious. Some went a block out of their way to avoid the newfangled signal system. Then a secretary strutted diagonally across the vacant intersection, taking a parade of more timid men with her. Slowly, the idea caught on. Some became ecstatic with their new freedom. They crossed and re-crossed, trying all the straight and diagonal possibilities. By the end of the day, secretaries and executives, attorneys and oilmen from all over downtown rushed down to Seventeenth and Stout to enjoy the "Barnes Dance."

After revolutionizing Denver traffic in six years, Barnes moved on to Baltimore and ultimately to New York City. There the traffic tamer met his

CIVIC DEVELOPMENT: Steps in patterns of black and white lead to the Colorado Heritage Center (top) where visitors find multi-media exhibits, dioramas, a research library and the offices of the State Historical Society founded in 1879. The Phipps family (above), with patriarch Senator Lawrence C. Phipps at the head of the table, has influenced many aspects of Denver's development, from Cheesman Park high-rises and Phipps Auditorium at City Park to fox (coyote) hunting and a winning team of Denver Broncos.

Champa Street: Preservation of the past

Historic Champa Street at the edge of the Skyline Urban Renewal Zone provides one of the best preserved insights into old Denver. At the Cherry Creek end of Champa Street is the Auraria Higher Education Center. The campus arose in the 1970s in the oldest part of the city as a novel idea—having the University of Colorado at Denver, Metropolitan State College and the Denver Community College share the largest higher education complex in Colorado.

On the east bank of Cherry Creek, Champa Street borders the monumental Denver Center for the Performing Arts and Mayor Speer's grand old auditorium.

CHAMPA HALLS: Charles Boettcher's white Ideal Building faces the red sandstone Boston Building (above); the Mountain States Telephone Building (below); Denver Gas and Electric Company (center right); and the Oddfellows Hall (lower right).

At Fourteenth Street, the 1929 Telephone Building (Denver's second skyscraper, after the Daniels and Fisher Tower) features foyer murals by Allen True, arched iron entryways, marble wainscoating, coffered ceilings and a glistening terra-cotta skin.

A block away at Fifteenth and Champa, the Denver Gas and Electric Building (now the Insurance Exchange Building) originally housed the predecessor of the Public Service Company. When constructed in 1909, its exterior lighting illuminated the architectural features and curved cornice of the terra-cotta ten-story building.

At 1525-27 Champa, the 1917 Filbeck building houses the award-winning Changing Scene Theatre. Next door are the 1891

Rogers Mortuary Building and Union Lodge No. 1 of the Oddfellows. Since 1887, the Oddfellows Hall has been a favorite meeting and eating place. It once housed the celebrated Dutch Mill restaurant.

The architectural firm of Fisher & Fisher—a prominent Denver firm that designed many early twentieth-century downtown buildings—drew up the plans for the University Building at Sixteenth and Champa. New York architects designed the Symnes Building across the street (now part of the world's largest Woolworth store.)

Denver architect W.J. Edbrooke, brother of the Frank Edbrooke, designed the W.H. Kistler Stationery building at 1636-46 Champa.

The four corners of Seventeenth and Champa streets are occupied by the old Colorado National Bank, the Railway Exchange, the Ideal Building and the Boston Building—four landmarks that have all made the intersection the heart of

the central business district. These four masterpieces were built of Colorado Yule marble, Colorado red sandstone and limestone. They lend variety and humanism to the surrounding glass and concrete towers.

The old Chamber of Commerce Building (renamed the Ross Building) at 1726 Champa is a classic revival jewel decorated with now empty sockets where 7000 light bulbs once helped Denver earn the nickname "City of Lights."

One of the city's few surviving art deco treasures is the Buerger Brothers Building at 1732-40 Champa Street. It was built in 1929 of glazed terra-cotta with floral and geometric tile trim. On Eighteenth

ALONG CHAMPA: The U.S. Post Office (above); the Buerger Brothers Building and the old Chamber of Commerce, now named the Ross Building (left); restored Queen Anne house in the Five Points neighborhood (below); and the French horns of the Denver Symphony in the new Denver Center for the Performing Arts.

Street, the main branch of the United States Post Office sits in neo-classical splendor. The main entrance is guarded by two Rocky Mountain bighorn sheep by Denver sculptress Gladys Caldwell Fisher, wife of architect Alan B. Fisher.

Upper Champa Street, before it ends at Downing Street, contains many Victorian residences. Curtis Park National Historic District be-

gins at 25th Street with over 50 venerable homes on Champa Street alone. City fathers—working with bankers, realtors, business people and Historic Denver—have turned the one-time Curtis Park slum into a showcase of core city restoration.

This revitalization of inner-city homes, coupled with the preservation of commercial buildings on lower Champa, helps make downtown Denver a vibrant residential as well as a commercial neighborhood.

match. In 1968, at the age of 61, Barnes was found dead, sitting behind his desk at the Queen's traffic control center. Heart attack, they said. "His temper had been as quick as a yellow light," mourned the *New York Times*, "his wit as irreverent as a traffic-snarled truck driver's and his pipe as fuming as the back of a bus."

Mayor Newton easily won re-election in 1951 but declined to run again in 1955. After an accomplishment-filled stint as president of the University of Colorado, he, like Barnes, moved to New York City. He headed the Commonwealth Foundation for years before moving to Palo Alto as a senior consultant for the Henry J. Kaiser Family Foundation in the 1970s.

Subsequent mayors continued to alternately promote and struggle with the Denver boom. Mayors Will Faust Nicholson (1955-59), Richard Yates Batterton (1959-63), Thomas Guida Currigan (1963-69) and William Henry McNichols Jr. all alternately promoted and wrestled with the problems of growth. The Denver Chamber of Commerce continued to court new commerce and urged that the United Nations be moved to the Queen City of the Mountains and the Plains. If Denver did not get the United Nations, it did get the UN building's developer—William Zeckendorf.

A high-rise builder from New York, Zeckendorf decided to raise Denver's profile. Until his arrival, the 5,280-foot-high metropolis had thought itself high enough. Mayor Speer's mountain view ordinance limiting edifices to eleven stories had been observed with the exceptions of the 1911 Daniels and Fisher tower and the 1929 Mountain States Telephone Building. Zeckendorf and Denver collaborators used the Courthouse Square Park (former site of the Arapahoe County Courthouse) to erect the downtown Hilton and May D & F Store. Two blocks up Sixteenth Street from these box-like structures, Zeckendorf and others constructed the Mile High Center, which became the headquarters for the United Bank of Denver.

While Zeckendorf, the Murchison brothers from Texas and financiers from Denver and various Canadian and United States cities took turns blocking each others' view from uptown towers, exciting things were happening in old lower downtown. Denverite Dana Crawford spearheaded the resurrection of Larimer Square. Elwood Brooks, a Kansas school teacher turned banker, renovated the old Central Bank building. He and his son Max initiated Brooks Towers, the first of many lower downtown

LARIMER SQUARE: The rejuvenated heart of old Denver accommodates everything from expresso and Italian ices to bicycle races and film festivals to markets and promenades.

161

high-rise residential units to alter the skyline.

After the Denver Urban Renewal Authority erased much of deteriorating lower downtown with the Skyline and Auraria projects, citizens became more appreciative of the surviving architectural heritage.

The successful Larimer Square experiment in rehabilitating historic buildings for retail and office space encouraged other developers. They began to restore and renovate long-abused but still sound structures on Market, Blake, Wazee and Wynkoop streets. Among the buildings reborn to adaptive use were Market Center, Market Street Mall, Blake Street Bath and Racquet Club, the Wazee Exchange, the Wazee Supper Club and the Elephant Corral.

The Equitable Building at Seventeenth and Stout streets—often called the city's grandest office structure—also sustained a facelift. Inside this architectural heirloom, America's first nationally chartered women's bank opened its doors in 1978. Two years later, the bank's assets reached $17 million, second only to the Women's Bank of New York City.

The Denver National (formerly Security National Bank) led the 1980s return to resurrected lower downtown. Denver National Bank's move to a glistening new aluminum tower and plaza at Seventeenth and Lawrence confirmed the metamorphosis of skid row. Two-bit flophouses bowed to $200,000 condominiums. Pawn shops, secondhand stores and shot and beer saloons succumbed to trendy boutiques, cabarets and havens of *haute cuisine*.

By 1980, old downtown had re-emerged as the most exciting part of Denver. It combined old landmarks with new urban renewal developments required to give 40 percent of their surface area to people space. For a centerpiece, the Skyline Urban Renewal Project featured a sunken park that allowed pedestrians to escape street traffic amid splashing fountains that erased the sounds of the city.

Downtown sparkled. And the city's rebirth seemed to be insured by surrounding developments—the Platte River Greenway to the northwest, the Curtis Park and Clement historic districts to the northeast, the restoration and stabilization of the Capitol Hill residential neighborhood and park-like Civic Center to the southeast, the Denver Center for the Performing Arts and the Auraria Higher Education Center historic districts to the southwest.

The Auraria campus opened in the 1970s as a unique experiment. The Auraria branch of the Community College of Denver, Metropolitan State College and the University of Colorado at Denver operate different but mutually supportive programs. They share facilities, including a library, bookstore, student center and recreation center. Despite fears of one state legislator that bringing Colorado's largest student body and squad of professors to Denver might cause riots, Auraria has become one of the most economical, popular and diverse educational opportunities in the Rocky Mountain West. By 1979, enrollment figures for the Community College (3,563), Metropolitan State College (13,351) and the University of Colorado at Denver (8,744) meant that one out of every five college students in Colorado was on the Auraria campus.

The University of Colorado at Boulder, the north campus and Red Rocks campus of Denver Community College, and Arapahoe Community College in Littleton add to the metropolitan area's importance as a regional center for education. Private colleges and universities include the University of Denver, Colorado Women's College, Loretto Heights College, Regis

Despite a spring snow storm, Mayor William H. McNichols Jr. launches St. Patrick's Day parade festivities by changing Larimer Street to Clancy Street. Born into one of Denver's most distinguished political clans, the mayor is the son of a former city auditor and brother of an ex-governor. With hearty support such as McNichol's, Denver has made its St. Patrick's Day parade the second largest in America. After the parade, Irish brethren gather at Sullivan's Bar to chase the cold away.

College, Denver Free University and dozens of technical, vocational and religious training schools. On the primary and secondary education levels, the Denver public schools are complemented by a dozen private schools, numerous parochial schools and the free or nominal cost courses of the Emily Griffith Opportunity School "for anyone who wants to learn."

Many of these schools offer a wide range of programs for all segments of the community—Elderhostel for the elderly, seminars for business and professional people and continuing education courses for everyone. Denverites seeking higher education can study full or part time, day or night, particularly at the Auraria campus which draws many older, working and married students.

Dedication of the multi-million dollar, 169-acre Auraria Higher Education Center in the Colorado centennial-bicentennial year of 1976 climaxed the joint efforts of diverse community groups that had not always worked together so harmoniously. The three institutions and the Colorado Commission on Higher Education worked with the Denver Chamber of Commerce and Downtown Denver, Incorporated. The city also worked with the state, and Denver Urban Renewal Authority worked with Historic Denver to preserve St. Elizabeths, St. Cajetans, Emanuel-Sherith Israel Chapel and another spiritual center—the Tivoli Brewery. Historic Denver renovated a block of old Ninth Street and donated it as a park-like heart of the campus.

Today the green, well-landscaped, low-profile campus is a monument to Denver's faith in the future. It is located on the oldest historic site in the city. For it was in Auraria that William Greeneberry Russell party first found gold in 1858 and planted the settlement that grew into the Rocky Mountain metropolis.

MOVING BOOKS: After the 1955 completion of the new main branch of the Denver Public Library on Broadway, books were moved from the old library by conveyor belt (above). Eleanor Gehres (inset), chief of the Western history department of the public library, presides over one of the finest collections of Western Americana.

163

CITY, COUNTY, STATE CLASSICS: The architecture and sculpture of the Civic Center complex (facing page); and the governor's mansion (left). The Daniels and Fisher Tower, once a dominant landmark, is now surrounded by modern skyscrapers (above).

Old glory, Denver.

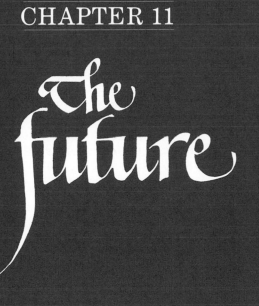

CHAPTER 11

The future

Denver's greatest resource is its
citizenry—a well-educated,
energetic and proud population.

Denver faces the future with more optimism than many cities. In 1980, this seemed evident in an increasingly vibrant downtown where half a dozen skyscrapers and the Sixteenth Street Mall were under construction. Contagious optimism even moved into inner-city neighborhoods such as Curtis Park, City Park, Capitol Hill, Auraria, Baker and north Denver where renovation and historic preservation were countering urban blight.

Yet it is not buildings—but people—that make a city livable and likable. Denver's greatest resource is its citizenry—a well-educated, energetic and loyal population. Most are Denverites by choice rather than by birth. Census figures for the 1970s show Denverites to be the second most highly educated metropolitan population in America, with an average education of 12.6 years.

At a time when many urbanites have been unwilling or unable to invest in their communities, Denverites have approved key municipal bond issues and a sales tax to support the Regional Transportation District. In the 1960s, voters approved the $5.3 million Auraria Urban Renewal effort and the even larger Skyline Urban Renewal project to revitalize the two oldest parts of the Rocky Mountain metropolis.

In 1972, Denver voters defied conventional political wisdom by approving $87.6 million in bond issues for the largest capital

The Grant-Humphreys Mansion (above) is the home of Historic Denver, Inc., the largest private city preservation group in the United States. Construction began in 1978 on the Amoco Tower (below) at Columbia Plaza.

construction program in municipal history. Voters shouldered increased indebtedness to provide their children and other future Denverites with a better and more beautiful city. Despite this huge undertaking, Denver municipal bonds retain good brokerage house ratings as a wise investment in a stable city.

Voters approved the 1972 bond issue by a substantial majority. It included $1.5 million for expanding branch libraries, $10 million for housing development, $9 million for park and recreational facilities, $6 million for the Denver Center for the Performing Arts, $21 million for a new criminal justice center and fire stations, $20 million for sanitary and storm sewers and $10 million for the McNichols Sports Arena.

These projects demonstrate how far the Mile High City has come since the townbuilding days of the pioneer era. Unfortunately, the bond issue did not solve all problems, especially since inflation has reached two-digit figures. For example, the Denver Public Library has sustained drastic cuts in purchases, programs, personnel and operating hours. Yet the addition of new branch libraries in the 1970s and a still excellent, if over-crowded, main branch are a considerable improvement over the early-day saloons and churches which offered the only free reading materials.

The $10 million voted for public housing has been invested in updating old projects, restoring single-family homes and apartment houses for the poor, and building new units scattered about the city.

Housing has become tight during the postwar boom, just as it was during the gold rush beginnings, despite hundreds of new suburban subdivisions, dozens of high-rise apartment houses and the rehabilitation of thousands of nineteenth-century homes.

Even with much newer, multiple-unit housing, Denver remains largely a city of brick homes surrounded by private lawns. There are relatively few row houses, duplexes and common-wall structures. Denverites have always prized elbow room and translated this into free-standing homes surrounded by lawns, flower gardens and vegetable patches.

The bond issue's $9 million for park and recreational facilities and subsequent appropriations demonstrate an on-going interest in beautification and recreational outlets. During the 1970s, over a dozen new parks and recreation centers were built.

Probably the most important park program is the privately assisted greenway project—the conversion of Denver's waterways and gulches into a network of parks connected by paved recreational paths. Cherry Creek and the South Platte River, whose floods are now controlled by Cherry Creek and Chatfield dams, are once again scenic attractions and alternative transportation routes. Bicyclists, runners, walkers, roller-skaters, skate-boarders and tricyclists use the river and creek bank bike paths while new boat landings and passages cut through dams facilitate canoeing, kyaking, row-boating and tubing.

Typical of Denver's commitment to beautification is the landscaping of ever-expanding Stapleton International Airport. It is now fringed by rolling hills of grass, trees, shrubs and floral displays.

After Denver lost almost 60,000 elms to disease, a major tree-planting campaign began in the 1960s. The Denver Board of Realtors, American National Bank, the Denver city forester and the Park People —either gave away trees or subsidized planting. Because of such efforts, Denver remains green—as anyone viewing it from an airplane can attest. Despite Major Stephen H. Long's report in 1820 that the "Great American Desert" was unsuitable for agriculture, the Mile High City has emerged as a verdant metropolitan oasis surrounded by farms and ranches.

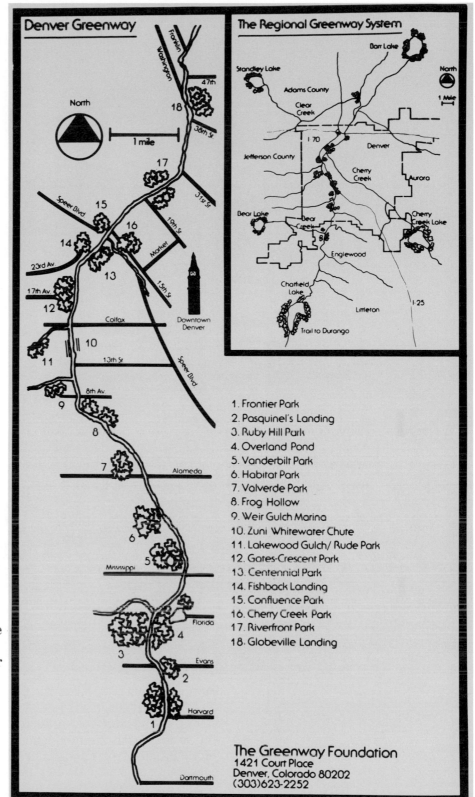

1. Frontier Park
2. Pasquinel's Landing
3. Ruby Hill Park
4. Overland Pond
5. Vanderbilt Park
6. Habitat Park
7. Valverde Park
8. Frog Hollow
9. Weir Gulch Marina
10. Zuni Whitewater Chute
11. Lakewood Gulch/ Rude Park
12. Gates-Crescent Park
13. Centennial Park
14. Fishback Landing
15. Confluence Park
16. Cherry Creek Park
17. Riverfront Park
18. Globeville Landing

The Greenway Foundation
1421 Court Place
Denver, Colorado 80202
(303)623-2252

Of course trees will not grow without water, any more than people can live, industry flourish or agriculture survive. H_2O continues to be a precious liquid, just as in the days of wells and bottled water wagons. The Denver Board of Water Commissioners has struggled with this problem since 1918. That year, the city bought out the Denver Union Water Company (which had absorbed at least 30 other private water companies over the years).

From their new headquarters completed in the late 1970s—a building wrapped around an inside courtyard and waterfall—the water commissioners map strategy for Denver and many of the surrounding

STAR ATTRACTIONS: Film and stage stars appear weekly during summer stock performances at Elitch Gardens, a Mile High City landmark. The summer stock theater (inset) is America's oldest; the accompanying amusement park (above) provides rides, flower gardens and entertainment for all ages.

suburbs. Construction of the Strontia Springs dam and the Foothills Treatment Plant in the 1980s will enable the city to keep growing (although not all Denverites are enthusiastic about more growth.) Denverites now enjoy deliciously cool snow melt from the Rockies, but any discussion of the city's future involves consideration of the surrounding Great American Desert. It may have its own reclamation plans.

During Denver's puppy days, efforts to bring culture and the performing arts to the frontier resulted mostly in burlesque, dubious music and "leg art." A century later, however, the opening of the Denver Center for the Performing Arts brought newspaper critics from the *New York Times*, *Los Angeles Times* and other major national newspapers to their feet for an ovation. They hailed the modern complex of cement and glass as one of the most innovative new American homes for music, drama, dance and cinema.

In 1980, the Denver Center for the Performing Arts was complemented by numerous little theaters including the Changing Scene, Elitch's, Gaslight, Germinal Stage, Heritage Square, Mercury Cafe, Paramount and Rivertree. Theater arts programs also thrived in nearby Arvada, Boulder, Central City, Evergreen, Golden and Littleton. Yet the most spectacular stage in Colorado remains the natural outdoor amphitheater in Red Rocks Park. There Coloradans and visitors hear fresh-air concerts in a pink sandstone setting that millions of years ago was a sandy beach.

The greatest spectacle in pioneer Denver was gun-slinging violence that fostered in the citizenry a vigilant—and sometimes vigilante—concern for law and order. A century after the police department was organized as a paid, professional force under a police chief, Denver's blue coats moved into a new Criminal Justice Center that has drawn praise from architects, city planners and law enforcement officials across the nation. The 1972 bond issue that financed the justice center also provided a half dozen new fire stations. Well-equipped smoke-eaters give Denver one of the lowest fire insurance rates in the country. They have kept Denver free of a major blaze since the great fire of 1863.

Dedication of the $10-million McNichols Arena in the 1970s provided spacious, sleek quarters for Denver's big league basketball and ice hockey teams. Expansion of Mile High Stadium to 75,000 seats accommodated the National Football League's Denver Broncos and the Denver Bears baseball team. It also increased chances that the Bears will be replaced by a major

Colorado State Capitol interior.

171

SPORTS AND ARTS: Mile High Stadium, where the Denver Broncos' quarterback Craig Morton passes against San Diego's Chargers. Since 1965, the Denver Chamber of Commerce has sponsored the Colorado Sports Hall of Fame, annually honoring individuals who have achieved distinction in the field of athletics. Previous inductees include Jack Dempsey, Peggy Fleming, Bill Toomey, Byron R. "Whizzer" White, Babe Didrikson Zaharias and Louis Unser. Denver's cultural scene is set in its new Center for the Performing Arts (facing page).

Harry Tufts (right), founder and director of the Denver Folklore Center, joins fellow musicians on a tune or two.

league team during the 1980s. Particularly after the Super Bowl appearance of the Denver Broncos in 1978, Denver has been noted for spectator as well as participatory sports.

Passage of the bond issues behind these improvements and Denver's high rating among city watchers has been due at least in part to the city's mayor since 1968. William H. McNichols Jr. is the silver-haired, rosy-cheeked, cigar-chomping scion of a famous Irish political clan. His father was city auditor for 24 years, and his brother Steve was governor of Colorado from 1956 to 1962.

After serving as his older brother's executive secretary, McNichols entered Denver politics. First as manager of public works and then as mayor, the younger McNichols has steered Denver through times bad enough to bankrupt some American cities. "The mayor," according to one lobbyist, "is not flamboyant or highly visible, but he is a deft politician in the best sense of the word. He knows how to shake the tree and get the apples to fall."

By providing steady stewardship, Mayor McNichols has fostered a healthy urban climate for many interest groups. He is adept at handling the nuts and bolts—the urban services that keep a city running and liveable. Denver is one of the smoother running American cities when it comes to operations such as trash collecting and dog catching, street cleaning and floral displays. Diligent meter maids quickly ticket illegally parked cars, and violators who fail to pay up find their vehicle immobilized with the dreaded Denver "boot."

Of course Denver still has headaches. Precarious financing troubles the public library, health and hospitals, the natural history museum, zoo, parks and recreation, performing arts center and athletic facilities. In many cases, only the generosity of individuals and foundations keeps these programs alive. The basic problem is that Denverites can no longer afford to maintain these assets by themselves. Yet tourists and other Coloradans—who constitute two-thirds of the patrons of Denver's facilities—do not fully share in their upkeep. Without more help from the rest of the metropolis and the state legislature, Denver's municipal amenities face cutbacks.

The capital city's racial frictions have been eased by the integration of many work and play places, the public schools and many neighborhoods. Blacks continue to be concentrated in northeast Denver and Hispanos in northwest Denver. Only in token numbers have minorities moved into other city neighborhoods and suburban communities.

Air, water, nuclear and noise pollution remain major concerns. The Rocky Flats nuclear weapons plant and the poison gas stored at the Rocky Mountain Arsenal lie uncomfortably close to the city. Whether or not to move Stapleton International Airport continues to be debated although most seem willing to tolerate the noise and safety problems for close-in convenience. The automobile-caused "brown cloud" lingers overhead on breezeless days as lawmakers pass air quality controls and then relax them. Consequently, Denver's air pollution is second only to that of Los Angeles. Denver is the nation's 21st largest metropolitan area. The rapidly expanding city is confronted with a dwindling amount of open space. Without more city, suburban, state and national parks and wilderness areas, Denver may lose a major charm—spaciousness. Yet the other crucial shortage—water—may mandate growth restrictions that will protect the remaining open prairies and unfenced mountains.

Post-war suburban flight, accelerated by those families fleeing integration of Denver's public schools, ate into the city's tax base. It left a concentration of college students and young people, the poor, the ailing and the elderly who needed urban services but in many cases paid little, if any, property taxes. The Mile High City's problems mounted in the mid-1960s when a major company was forced to lay off 40 percent of its work force.

Business leaders formed the Forward Metro Denver coalition, an arm of

Mile High City construction workers, modern mountain men.

the Denver Chamber of Commerce, to combat urban economic problems. Since its formation in 1965, Forward Metro Denver has helped persuade several hundred corporations to move to the capital city.

Johns-Manville and Anaconda were among the New Yorkers to move their world headquarters a mile higher. Former president W. R. Goodwin said Johns-Manville chose Denver over 24 other cities because they wanted "a good quality lifestyle for employees." Johns-Manville built a $70-million plant in the foothills within view of mule deer herds and roosting eagles. Delighted with the move from the Big Apple to the Colorado foothills, Goodwin added that relocation was not only aesthetically worthwhile "but also a definite corporate success."

The Anaconda Corporation, which does a billion dollar a year business in metals such as aluminum, copper and uranium, likewise relished its move to Denver's Seventeenth Street after over 50 years in New York City. Various other major companies have also established national or regional headquarters in Denver.

Denver's emergence as a center for extracting oil, oil shale, natural gas, coal and solar energy during the 1970s attracted hundreds of energy firms, including many small, innovative and rapidly growing companies. To assist commerce, industry and the community at large, the federally supported Denver Research Institute, National Center for Atmospheric Research, National Bureau of Standards and Solar Energy Research Institute are conducting research, publicizing results and helping to solve economic and environmental problems.

New firms and numerous oldtime companies have kept the unemployment rate below the national average. Colorado employers traditionally have paid lower wages because people prefer to live in the state—even if it means lower salaries. But paychecks from the federal government and national and international firms that do not vary from region to region have raised the average income considerably.

In his 1980 survey of major American cities, Pulitzer-Prize winning Paul Gapp of the *Chicago Tribune* wrote that "Denver is booming, energy rich"

POINTS OF INTEREST: *Denver Zoo (top left); Museum of Natural History in City Park (top center); Daniels and Fisher Tower (top right); Botanic Gardens (center left); sculpture on Denver Art Museum grounds (center right); sculpture on Public Library grounds (right), with Denver Art Museum in background; and the Molly Brown House (far right).*

and "blessed with some of the most magnificent mountain scenery on earth...It is one of the most appealing big cities in the United States, deserving of the high ratings it gets in national quality-of-life studies."

Like this Chicago journalist many come to see the Colorado excitement for themselves. And as in the past, many who come as investors and tourists find themselves seduced by the invigorating climate, the open spaces and the spectacular Rocky Mountain backdrop that provides (within an hour of downtown) trout-fishing, back-packing, powder-snow skiing and wilderness solitude.

The energy crisis of the 1970s uncorked a new mineral rush. Thousands of oil wells have been sunk and thousands of tons of coal mined. But the biggest bonanza may lie in the oil shale on Colorado's Western Slope. Multi-national oil companies are testing the Colorado soil, experimenting with new extraction technologies and looking for the necessary water and human resources. If and when the long projected shale oil boom comes, Colorado may have enough of the black gold to end America's reliance on foreign suppliers. That day may come sooner than most realize. In 1980, one oil company executive predicted that the industry would spend $500 billion in the next few decades to develop Rocky Mountain oil shale. While some count the fortunes to be made, others consider the irretrievable damage such a massive project could do to the landscape, air, water and the communities involved.

Perhaps the greatest challenge of the future will be to achieve more effective regional planning, cooperation and sharing of services within the

ON CAMPUS: The Mary Reed Library at the University of Denver (above) and Evans Chapel, originally located downtown and moved, stone by stone, then reassembled on the DU campus.

Artist's rendering (above) and map (below) of the proposed Sixteenth Street Mall.

seven-county Denver metropolitan area. Within Denver, Adams, Arapahoe and Jefferson counties alone, there are 26 municipalities and numerous water, sanitation, school, fire and park and recreation districts.

The Denver Chamber of Commerce, the *Denver Post*, the League of Women Voters and other progressive voices have called for bigger, faster steps toward metropolitan cooperation. Some local officials have not responded with enthusiasm. Nor has the state legislature shown an inclination to promote state-wide or inter-county cooperation in dealing with planning, pollution, water, sanitation and other issues.

Although the solution to regional problems will not be quick or easy, some groundwork has been laid—notably the Regional Transportation District, the Denver Regional Council of Governments and cooperative sewage, drainage and flood control efforts. The need for metropolitan co-operation was recognized in the 1960s when Governor John Love appointed a commission to study regional approaches to metropolitan growth. In the late 1970s, efforts began for a metropolitan council to more efficiently and economically combine a number of regional services.

Some Denverites feel that the postwar boom has been too fast and too reckless. Among the concerned are many newcomers who came to Colorado for an environment and a life style they now find threatened. The 1972 vote on holding the Winter Olympics in the Centennial State was a turning point. Fearing overdevelopment of both mountains and plains and the enormous expense to taxpayers, Denver voters joined other Coloradans in a resounding "no". Richard D. Lamm, a Denver representative in the

Colorado legislature and a leader of the anti-Olympics coalition, was subsequently elected governor. Coloradans re-elected Lamm on a platform of restricted growth and greater environmental sensitivity in 1978.

Each generation builds both well and ill, hoping that its children will preserve and cherish the best of the past. Many of the office buildings, hotels, churches, schools and homes built to stand forever as monuments have been demolished. Proud structures expressing their builders' fondness for and confidence in Denver have been replaced by bigger but not always better buildings designed only to make money. Some come to Denver—as the miners did a century ago—to "git and git out." Others have come to improve the urban environment as well as their own lot.

Rows between developers and preservationists in the 1970s were instructive to both sides. Many came to realize that not every old building should be replaced with a shiny new one and some others came to realize that not every new development is a nightmare. Out of sometimes heated growth-versus-no-growth debates, a new wisdom may be emerging. It is the blending of the best from the past and the present that gives Denver a charm and vibrancy that are the envy of many a Gotham.

Denver arose at the confluence of the South Platte River and Cherry Creek because of the riches of the earth. After exhausting the gold and silver that could be mined profitably, the city continued to rely on other treasures of the earth—agriculture, coal, brick, stone and a handful of precious minerals. Wise leaders realized that the town could not survive if dependent upon the extraction of non-renewable resources alone—dozens of ghost towns made that clear. They made Denver a transportation hub and a diverse industrial and commercial center.

In the 1980s, Denver is once again a booming center for the extraction of the treasures of the earth. And there is even talk of a new gold rush as the price of precious metals skyrockets. Up in the old mountain town saloons, wrinkled miners and young fortune seekers share the old golden visions.

Yet most residents of the Rocky Mountain metropolis now look elsewhere for their gold. Black gold—oil and coal—has sparked the eruption of downtown skyscrapers and suburbs that flow for miles over the prairie and splash into the mountains. White gold—powder-snow slopes of four dozen ski areas—has transformed Colorado into a year-round tourist mecca. Golden sunshine in generous doses (300 days a year) has made Denver one of the population magnets of the sun belt and a national center for development of solar energy.

Over a century after the original gold rush, a second boom has found a maturing metropolis more aware that the riches of the earth are exhaustible. Denverites are learning to use more conservatively the salubrious air, the limited water, the sunshine and majestic mountains and plains that are today's and tomorrow's Rocky Mountain gold.

Mayor William H. McNichols Jr.

Urban walls (right), and true Rocky Mountain gold (facing page).

HIGHER EDUCATION: *The Auraria Higher Education Center (AHEC) is unique in that its 169-acre campus is home to three separate institutions of higher education—Community College of Denver at Auraria, Metropolitan State College and University of Colorado at Denver—all sharing facilities. Important historic structures have been preserved and incorporated into the plans of the campus, located on the site of the old township of Auraria.*

The Ninth Street Historic Park, oldest intact block of residential structures in Denver, now houses administrative and faculty offices.

St. Cajetan's Center, established in 1926, is now the single largest auditorium on campus.

Tivoli Brewery is scheduled to be renovated for commercial uses compatible with the functions of the educational institutions.

180

The first Denver Chamber of Commerce building at the corner of Fourteenth and Lawrence Streets. The building was constructed by Peter Gumry who also supervised the construction of the State Capitol. The Chamber moved into the building in 1885.

Partners in progress

Index to partners in progress

Denver's economic community: A little gold and a lot of partners

From Denver's earliest days, history clearly demonstrates the contributions and vision of business leaders in building a city.

Platted on a jumped gold claim at the edge of the "Great American Desert" and at the foot of the soaring Colorado Rockies, the remote townsite of Denver City was not a likely location for the building of a great city.

Yet a few dreaming, determined town builders saw the potential in the settlement beside the confluence of Cherry Creek and the Platte and made their plans. They backed their dreams with hard work, money, luck and cooperation.

Cooperation has been the key to Denver's success from the beginning when *Rocky Mountain News* editor William Byers joined feuding citizens of the Auraria settlement and Denver City into one unified Denver in 1860.

It was the cooperation and coordinated efforts of business leaders that kept Denver from becoming a ghost town in the 1860s. The railroad, essential to growth and development of the fledgling city, unexpectedly decided to bypass Denver and cross the Rockies in less-rugged southern Wyoming. Businessmen, led by territorial governor John Evans and William Byers, rallied and formed the Denver Board of Trade, the forerunner of the Denver Chamber of Commerce in 1867. Its sole mission was to bring the railroad to Denver. By 1870 the line from Cheyenne was finished, connecting young Denver to the intercontinental route.

In 1884 the Board of Trade became the new Denver Chamber of Commerce. The goal of those business leaders was to "promote general prosperity in all the varied interests of Colorado and Denver," a goal that is still a primary part of the philosophy of the Denver Chamber of Commerce.

Charter members of the Chamber included famed silver king Horace A. W. Tabor and Governor John Evans.

In the 1880s Denver's economy was still founded on mining, but the Chamber had already begun efforts to diversify the growing town's principal employment base. During that decade, the Chamber sponsored an exhibition of manufacturers to stir interest in Denver's products and raised the money to build Fort Logan, which for a time housed six companies of the U.S. Cavalry.

EARLY INVESTOR: J.T. Cornforth (above) was an early Denver businessman and investor in the Chamber of Commerce. His place of business was the Birks and Cornforth Market (right) on Fifteenth between Wazee and Blake Streets. His Chamber membership was documented in an 1884 membership certificate (top).

The silver panic of 1893 painfully taught Denver the necessity of economic diversification as fortunes tumbled with the falling price of silver.

Chamber business leaders not only launched economic programs such as the vigorous promotion of the infant sugar beet industry, livestock sales and tourism, but also were called on to keep the peace during those trying times. Nearly 2,000 unemployed people flooded into Denver seeking relief from the depression caused by the silver collapse, but there were no jobs in Denver, either. The city established a camp at River Front Park for the destitute men, but tensions rose between the city's citizens and the unemployed. Denverites thought the influx was getting out of hand and feared riots. The city wanted to get the destitutes out of town and when some expressed interest in floating down the Platte, the Chamber and the city provided the supplies and lumber for flatboats.

The Chamber also formed a citizens committee to settle a small civil war that was brewing in the city between Populist Governor Davis Waite and a band of Denver police commissioners. When the police and deputies had barricaded themselves inside city hall, the governor called in the infantry and light artillery to force them out. The Chamber's committee finally persuaded the governor to take the case to court instead.

The Chamber's efforts were usually not so dramatic, yet many have been of long lasting benefit. The Chamber started the city's first free public library in its offices in 1884. In 1896 it devised a plan to bring the U.S. Mint to Denver. In 1898 the Chamber proposed and submitted plans for the Museum of Natural History in City Park and raised funds to keep it going during a troubled period at the beginning of the next century.

As Denver grew into a city, it faced urban problems. Air pollution was an early issue. By 1916 the Chamber's Smoke Abatement Committee drafted a smoke ordiance (which the city council adopted) to reduce the black clouds believed caused by "wasted" factory fuel.

Tourism and conventions have long been a mainstay of Denver's economy and the Chamber played a major role in making Denver and Colorado a popular destination. In 1904 the interested members of the Chamber formed the Denver Convention League, the forerunner of today's very successful Denver and Colorado Convention and Visitors Bureau. It directed efforts to build adequate facilities for the increasingly important convention business, including the Denver Auditorium at 14th and Champa Streets. It raised money to build roads to develop tourism for Denver and the state and urged the creation of the State Highway Commission in 1907.

The Chamber also saw the need for improved medical facilities. In 1918 the Chamber raised the funds to purchase 600 acres of land to lease to the U.S. government (at $1 per year) as a federal military recuperation camp. In 1936 the Chamber board transferred the land—site of Fitzsimons Hospital—to the U.S. government.

The Chamber supported efforts to preserve the cliff dwellers ruins in Mesa Verde and the mountain wilderness

Postcards helped make tourism a major Colorado industry.

Astronaut's manned maneuvering unit backpack, being built at the Martin Marietta Denver Aerospace center (below).

around Longs Peak as national parks. A Chamber charter member, John Brisben Walker, envisioned mountain parks for the citizens of Denver, and in 1911 the Chamber began a successful lobbying effort to establish Denver's chain of high country parks.

In 1920 the Chamber began work on a project that continues today—adequate air transportation. Its committee, including Postmaster Benjamin F. Stapleton (soon to be mayor), began researching the creation of a "flying field." By 1924 the Chamber had raised $35,000 of the necessary $40,000 for an army air field for the city (which later became Lowry). Then it turned its efforts to searching for sites for a commercial aviation field and in 1929 helped dedicate Mayor Stapleton's "Folly"—the Denver Municipal Airport.

During the Great Depression, the Chamber launched a campaign to make Denver the "little capital of the U.S." by bringing federal offices into the city. Denver became the headquarters for the Rocky Mountain Region. By 1945 a writer in the *New York Times Magazine* went so far as to propose Denver as the national capital!

After World War II, Denver boomed. Unprecedented numbers of new people and industries moved into the city. The Chamber of Commerce geared up to match the influx, seeking the so-called "clean" industries, such as medical research and aerospace development. There was even a move to bring the United Nations headquarters to Denver.

The Cold War brought the relocation of the Air Force's Command Headquarters from New York to the "safer" Rocky Mountains and the establishment of the Air Force Academy in Colorado Springs.

During Denver's mid-'60s economic slump (caused by major employment cutbacks in the aerospace industries), business leaders responded by creating Forward Metro Denver. Its goal was the creation of 100,000 new jobs for metro Denver by 1970. The goal was met, and the Chamber's Forward Metro Denver Group continues today to work for a strong and well balanced economy.

In the last few years, the Chamber has worked to expand air routes into Denver and to plan for future Stapleton growth. It has encouraged educational development at many levels, including backing the creation of the Auraria Higher Education Center. It has spotlighted improved public transportation through such programs as ride sharing and the study of transportation systems. And it has continued to encourage accountable, efficient government and to support small business.

The Denver Chamber of Commerce is financed by the voluntary membership investments of more than 2,000 business firms throughout the metropolitan area. The membership provides the resources and expertise required for the implementation of Chamber programs.

The histories of some of Denver's more prominent firms are found here. Their financial support has made *Denver: Rocky Mountain Gold* possible.

American Salesmasters, Inc.

Developing today's leaders today

During a single week a bank in London, a real estate company in Sydney, a direct sales organization in Stockholm and an insurance company in Washington, D.C. could all embark on a new training venture — using American Salesmasters films, videotapes and audio cassettes.

On any given day, the Denver international headquarters office may ship a new 16mm film in Spanish to Madrid or a set of audio soundtracks in Japanese to Tokyo.

American Salesmasters is a multinational sales and management training firm unlike any other. Its materials hurdle geographic borders and language barriers. The company "created" its own industry and now stands unparalleled.

The firm was founded in 1964 to provide salespeople the opportunity to share ideas with the world's leading authorities in selling. Its first activities centered around the conducting of seminars, called American Salesmasters Congresses, featuring widely known business, management and motivational personalities. These seminars quickly gained acclaim. As a part of the program, in response to the need for public recognition of outstanding professional salespeople, the "Oscar of Salesmanship" awards were presented. Recipients were nominated and selected by their peers on the basis of outstanding contribution to the profession of selling.

Over the next few years, 100 congresses were conducted in 35 major cities. But before long, demand exceeded supply. To reach greater numbers of people, Salesmasters turned to other media, pioneering the use of audio cassettes as a training device. Cassette portfolios were created on a wide variety of topics — from real estate, automotive and retail sales to management, career development, recruiting and personnel selection.

Concurrently, Salesmasters created its own sales magazine, *Perception*. It became one of the finest sales publications in the United States before being converted to a film production company in preparation for Salesmasters' next expansion step.

In 1969 the company and its training concepts began to receive national attention. In the next two years, Salesmasters was featured in *Business Week* magazine, *Nation's Business* magazine and NBC's "Today" television show.

In the early 1970's American Salesmasters launched the film production effort that has created an entire library of sales, management and motivational films and videotapes. By 1974 the company had so grown that the American Salesmasters Building was constructed and, with its five American flags flown continuously in front of the building, had become a familiar landmark along burgeoning Hampden Avenue.

American Salesmasters recognized that the same needs it had been meeting for U.S. salespeople existed in other parts of the free enterprise world. In 1974 it began to license firms in other countries to market its products. Distribution was begun in Australia, New Zealand, South Africa, Japan, the Philippines and Canada. Later Spain, West Germany, Scandinavia, the United Kingdom and Singapore were added as international outlets, with plans drawn for expansion into other countries.

In recognition of the company's growing position as an exporter, Salesmas-

Collection of Film Leader's Guides from Spain, Japan, United States and Scandinavia.

ters received the 1979 Governor's Award for Excellence in Exporting, the first time that a Colorado service company had received this prestigious award.

American Salesmasters continues to believe in the great potential of the human spirit and the power of the individual to shape the present and future. Finding that potential and turning on that power is the objective of American Salesmasters training. The ultimate goal? — *developing today's leaders today.*

An American Salesmasters film being made.

Atlantic Richfield Company

Denver becomes company's base for mining, mineral activity

Denver is an almost perfect location for an earth-resources company headquarters. The hub of a great many mining and mineral operations, it is strategically located near the Rocky Mountain "Overthrust Belt," a rich potential source of new oil and gas discoveries. It is an attractive place to live — facilitating company recruiting efforts — and boasts excellent transportation facilities.

Thus R. O. Anderson, Atlantic Richfield Company chairman of the board, felt the city was a natural choice for his company's new and expanded base of mining and mineral operations. Headquartered in Denver are Anaconda Copper a division of ARCO subsidiary The Anaconda Company; ARCO Coal Company; and a district office of ARCO Oil and Gas Company.

Atlantic Richfield Company, the twelfth largest corporation in the nation, maintains its corporate headquarters in Los Angeles, California. But a set of fortuitous circumstances in the late 1970s brought a significant part of the company's operations to Denver.

In 1976 Atlantic Richfield Company announced its decision to acquire the New York-based Anaconda Company, a century-old mining and manufacturing corporation. Once a strong money-maker, the company had been dealt a severe blow by the Allende government's expropriation of their Chilean

The Neversweat Mine at Butte, Montana, about 1913. The Butte, Anaconda & Pacific train is in the foreground.

copper holdings. ARCO could provide the new subsidiary with much-needed capital investment, while at the same time itself benefitting from diversification into earth resources other than petroleum and natural gas.

ARCO's management reorganized Anaconda into three separate divisions — the mining company, Anaconda Copper, a manufacturing company, Anaconda Industries and the Anaconda Aluminum Company. These now are three of the ten operating companies created under the Atlantic Richfield corporate umbrella.

When The Anaconda Company announced its intent to move its corporate headquarters from New York City to Denver in April 1977, its new home was already under construction. Sheathed in smoke-colored reflective glass, the 40-story Anaconda Tower now dominates Denver Square, the heart of the down town financial district.

The Anaconda Copper Company is more than its name might imply: it explores for, produces and processes a variety of nonhydrocarbon minerals, including copper, uranium oxide, molybdenum, lead, zinc, silver and gold. Its new Carr Fork underground copper mine near Tooele, Utah is considered among the world's most modern and

Anaconda's Butte, Montana mines circa 1900.

efficient, and promises to produce relatively low-cost, fairly high-grade copper ore at a capacity of 60,000 tons per year.

Anaconda Industries is a diverse organization. Its Brass Division is the nation's leading producer, manufacturing around 100 copper alloys. In the short space of 25 years Anaconda Aluminum has grown into the nation's fourth-largest producer of primary aluminum. Operations are vertically integrated, from mine to finished product.

ARCO Coal Company's main focus is on North American coal and synthetic fuels. Its holdings include two mines in

The Anaconda Tower in Denver Square.

Wyoming's coal-rich Powder River Basin and extensive undeveloped oil shale resources in northwestern Colorado.

ARCO Oil and Gas Company explores for, produces and sells oil, natural gas and natural gas liquids in North America. The company's Denver District, one of nine in the United States, functions almost as an independent oil and gas company, operating in nine states.

Atlantic Richfield Company believes that Denver is rapidly moving toward becoming the nation's energy capital — and ARCO plans on being an integral part of that growth.

Blue Cross and Blue Shield of Colorado

Fifty cent health plan was basis of today's concept

As the nation stood on the brink of the Great Depression in 1929, Justin Ford Kimball, the administrator of Baylor University Hospital in Dallas, Texas, looked at the plight of the local people and realized that they could little afford to pay for medical expenses. His solution was to organize a prepaid system for health care coverage.

For the cost of 50 cents per month subscribers were guaranteed 21 days of hospital stay at the university hospital when they required medical treatment. Kimball first developed the program for Dallas school teachers, but the idea spread quickly to other groups and to other sections of the country. His far-reaching concept laid the groundwork for what would later become the Blue Cross and Blue Shield Associations, the largest providers of health care protection in the world.

In Colorado the Blue Cross Plan began when members of the Denver business community decided there was a need for a voluntary health care prepayment plan. Originally called the Colorado Hospital Service, Blue Cross of Colorado was established in September 1938 with William McNary as its executive director.

The first group to enroll in the plan was the May Company. Coverage at that time was called T-1 and cost only 75 cents per month. By the end of 1938, 94 groups and six hospitals had joined the program. Colorado Hospital Service opened its first offices at the Insurance Exchange Building at 810 Fourteenth Street.

In 1939 Colorado Hospital Service was officially accredited by the American Hospital Association and authorized

Blue Cross and Blue Shield of Colorado quickly became the largest provider of health care coverage in the state. The two separate plans merged in 1978 to form the present corporation.

700 Broadway

The all-glass headquarters of Blue Cross and Blue Shield of Colorado forms an impressive landmark on downtown Denver's south quadrant.

to display the Blue Cross emblem. The plan had enrolled 565 groups with a membership of nearly 25,000 people. Branch offices were established in Pueblo and Grand Junction. Nineteen hospitals were now members.

Recognizing that a prepaid health plan for medical services was also needed, a group of concerned Denver physicians formed the Colorado Medical Service, Inc., the corporate name for the Blue Shield Plan in 1942. Dr. John W. Amesse Sr., a founding member, became the first corporate president.

During the '40s and '50s the two plans enjoyed phenomenal growth. By 1944 Blue Cross of Colorado had enrolled one-fourth of the state's population. New services were offered to subscribers. Community enrollment was made available to people who were not eligible for group enrollment. A Mobile Enrollment Program used vans to travel throughout the state, offering coverage to people in remote rural communities.

By 1955 the Blue Cross and Blue Shield Plans were so widely accepted that the Southern Ute Indian tribe of Ignacio, Colorado enrolled in the plans and became the first Indian tribe in the nation to pay for its own health care protection.

The 1960s brought a closer association of the two Colorado plans with both the state and federal governments. In 1958 the plans were selected by the state to administer the medical program for the aged. When the Federal Employee Program was introduced in 1960 the Colorado Plans ranked third highest in the nation, enrolling 80 percent of the federal employees residing in Colorado.

The Colorado plans were selected to administer both the Medicare and Medicaid programs. Contracts with the state and federal governments today account for approximately 60 percent of the total number of subscribers.

As the plans grew, larger accommodations were needed. The current headquarters at 700 Broadway was opened in 1974. The two plans consolidated in 1978 to form Blue Cross and Blue Shield of Colorado, which is governed by a twenty-member board of directors.

Today, Blue Cross and Blue Shield of Colorado is the largest provider of health care protection in the state. Its operations have expanded to include eight branch offices, which serve 700,000 members. It is part of the National Blue Cross and Blue Shield Associations, the largest health care organization in the world, serving more than 110 million people annually. The slogan "The good health people" demonstrates the organization's commitment to the people of Colorado and to their healthy future.

Boyd Distributing Company, Inc.

The cornerstone of business is service to the customer

In 1944 Cecil Boyd was the aggressive manager of a B. F. Goodrich tire store at 51 South Broadway on Denver's "Miracle Mile." But Boyd wanted more. He dreamed of owning his own business. That lifelong ambition became a reality in the fall of that year when, with financial help from two close friends, Dr. Earl J. Boyd and Carl G. Hoffman, Boyd Distributing Company was founded.

Cecil Boyd opened his business at 20 West Thirteenth Street with just one line, Motorola radios, and just one employee — his secretary. Selling, receiving, shipping, warehousing — they did it all in those early days, and the business began to grow.

Diversification became Boyd's goal. The company expanded into the portable electric appliance business with such lines as Sunbeam, General Electric, Toastmaster, Oster and others, and into the record business with Capitol Records.

In 1951, the company experienced one of the greatest business booms in its history — the introduction of television broadcasting to the Colorado market. Business exploded and Motorola TVs were shipped by the hundreds to waiting dealers. Business was frantic and sets of every description and style were shipped as quickly as they were received. This boom launched the company into a dynamic and stable position in wholesale distribution — a posture it has maintained since.

Expansion continued into the major appliance business in the mid-1950s with the addition of Philco T.V. and Kitchen-Aid appliances.

The company outgrew its original location on West Thirteenth Avenue and in April 1953 moved into a new building at 1661 West Third Avenue. This 30,000 square-foot facility was ideal as growth and diversification continued.

The Boyd Marine Company was created in the mid-'50s and an addition was built to the Third Avenue facility. The boat and accessory business was

The company founder, Cecil Boyd, is shown at left facing the camera in a 1953 gathering which featured Boyd's various product lines.

exciting and the company added such lines as Chris-Craft and Glasspar boats, Voit water skiis and West Bend outboard motors. Business in boats and marine equipment boomed for several years, but in 1958 the division was closed in favor of other opportunities in appliances and television.

Dan Boyd, son of the founder, completed his business degree at the University of Colorado in 1962 and joined the corporation as advertising and sales promotion manager. Five years later the younger Boyd was named vice president and general manager when Dick Brown retired and became secretary-treasurer of the company on a part-time basis.

Boyd Distributing continued to look for ways to diversify. The company moved into the power equipment business in the mid-'60s and bought out a longtime power equipment dealer, Carson Bros. Inc., in 1967. This acquisition ultimately added three divisions to the

company — outdoor consumer power equipment, led by the Jacobsen mower line; commercial mowing and turf maintenance equipment, with the Jacobsen turf equipment line and many others; and a golf car division representing Harley-Davidson golf cars.

It became apparent in the late-'60s that consolidation was needed. Growth in all areas had expanded the company to its limits. The firm moved its facilities from 1661 West Third Avenue to the former King Soopers building at 1400 West Third Avenue and was restructured into five divisions — the electronics division, representing Sony products; the major appliance division, representing KitchenAid and Litton appliances; the outdoor consumer power equipment division, with Jacobsen, Poulan chain saw and WeedEater products; the commercial power equipment division; and the golf car division.

The former King Soopers facility, with more than 150,000 square feet of warehouse, office and shop facilities located near the heart of Denver, proved to be an ideal location for the growing company.

189

Cecil Boyd became chairman of the board and Dan Boyd was named president of the company in 1976. The business has continued to prosper. In 1979, with sales of nearly $17 million, the company employed 80 people, with an annual payroll in excess of $1.5 million.

Boyd is committed to remain diversified and in every way provide the best possible service to the customer, the cornerstone of the business.

Boyd's headquarters building at 1661 West Third Avenue, April 1953.

The Brown Palace Hotel

Tradition strong as its granite walls, contemporary as today's sunrise

When Henry C. Brown, an itinerant carpenter, arrived at the settlement along Cherry Creek in July 1860, he could not have envisioned a city called "Denver" nor a hotel that would still carry his name more than 120 years later.

In three years he had prospered enough to take out a pre-emption claim on 160 acres on the bluffs east of the growing community. Part of this land he donated to the new State of Colorado in 1876 as a site for its State House; the remainder he platted as Brown's Addition to the City of Denver, leaving a triangular plot bounded by Broadway, Tremont and Seventeenth Streets.

On this triangle where his milk cow grazed, Brown planned his most ambitious venture. Denver was now attracting visitors from eastern cities and Europe and Brown felt that his adopted city needed a quality hotel.

The project was begun, but quickly ran out of money, leaving only a gaping excavation. Finally, in 1888 Henry Brown decided to build the hotel himself. Four years later, having cost nearly $2 million to build and furnish, The Brown Palace Hotel stood ten stories tall on the site of Brown's old cow lot.

The Silver Panic of the 1890s brought hard times to Henry Brown and led eventually to the sale of the hotel to W. S. Stratton, a Cripple Creek and Colorado Springs mining millionaire. In 1912 it was sold again to an eastern syndicate and ten years later, Horace W. Bennett and Associates acquired the property. In the late 1930s, a partner in that firm, Charles Boettcher I, founder of a pioneer fortune, and his son Claude K. Boettcher acquired sole ownership of The Brown Palace, which today remains a totally-owned subsidiary of the Boettcher Foundation.

The Brown Palace has always played a prominent role in the history of Denver and Colorado. Buffalo Bill roamed its lobby. Evelyn Walsh McLean kept an apartment there. Queen Marie of Rumania visited in 1926 and required that a special door be cut to permit her to walk from her limousine to the elevators without encountering the public. The Brown has been host to nearly every president since Theodore Roosevelt. During President Eisenhower's administration, the hotel was known as "The Summer White House" because the president and Mrs.

The Brown Palace Hotel from an etching of 1892.

190

Eisenhower made it their headquarters on annual visits to Mrs. Eisenhower's mother.

Prohibition not only closed the bar in which one Harold Frank Henwood shot Louis Von Phul over the affections of a lady named Mrs. Springer, but it also caused Room 929 to be padlocked for the duration when federal agents got word that some Spanish-American War veterans had negotiated with a local bootlegger. Upon repeal, the Ship Tavern opened, decorated with models of clipper ships famous in U.S. history. After World War II, the hotel was the scene of another shooting when a disturbed veteran opened fire, killing two men.

The award-winning Palace Arms restaurant was opened in 1950.

The 22-story Brown Palace Tower, connected to the original building by an air-conditioned, carpeted bridge over Tremont Street, added 300 more guest rooms in 1959. At the same time, air

The onyx lobby of the Brown Palace Hotel.

conditioning was added to the main building, making use of flues that had served the fireplaces which had been part of every room's decor when the hotel first opened.

In the early 1960s the second floor guest rooms in the main building were converted to meeting rooms.

The hotel operates its own bakery, upholstery, carpentry and print shops as well as a beauty salon, barber shop and flower shop.

Employees of The Brown Palace take pride in their long association with the hotel. Three employees, including President and General Manager Karl W. Mehlmann, have 40 years of service and ten others have more than 30 years.

Today, as Denver moves into its role as a leading energy center — much as when gold and silver mining dominated its economy — The Brown Palace remains more than ever the place "Where the World Registers."

Burlington Northern Inc.

On track for the future

Although headquartered in St. Paul, Minnesota, Burlington Northern Inc., a transportation and natural resources company, has roots in Denver that date back to October 1861, approximately six months after the Territory of Colorado was established.

On October 11, 1861, the Apex and Gregory Wagon Road Company obtained a special charter to construct a road from Denver toward Berthoud Pass along the banks of Clear Creek. Due to various financial reasons, the A&GWRC was never able to construct anything, but the firm holds the distinction of being the oldest corporate ancestor of what today is The Colorado and Southern Railway Company.

The history of Colorado and Southern and Burlington Northern is closely identified with the history of Denver and the State of Colorado. First there was Colorado and Southern, which today remains the only Class One railway operating in the state that is a Colorado corporation. Next came the Chicago, Burlington & Quincy Railroad, which, in 1908, purchased the majority of C&S common stock. Today, the words "Burlington Northern" appear on the big green locomotives and rolling stock seen with increasing frequency throughout the Denver area.

Burlington Northern was formed by the merger of Chicago, Burlington & Quincy with the Great Northern, Northern Pacific, and the Spokane, Portland & Seattle railways on March 2, 1970. Burlington Northern's predecessor companies brought a rich heritage to the new enterprise. These pioneer lines, which played a major role in the opening of the West, were traditionally carriers of farm, forest, and mine products — still the backbone of Burlington Northern's commerce. Non-rail natural resource activities assumed increased importance as the years passed.

In fact, Burlington Northern's natural resource assets have widened the scope of interest in the company in today's resource-conscious society. These assets include significant timber, land, and energy holdings. Burlington Northern's prudent management of them enables the company to contribute significantly to many of this generation's basic economic needs. A philosophy of responsible stewardship assures future generations of a continued yield of vital

A Colorado and Southern coal train south of Denver.

Burlington Northern's mini-train entertains thousands each year in the Denver Saint Patrick's Day Parade.

"Piggypacker" at Burlington Northern's Denver Trailer-on-Flat Car Facility.

commodities from its resource base.

Burlington Northern is a diversified transportation company *and* a growing natural resources company, offering a unique combination of assets to a world facing increasing shortages of food, fiber, energy, and minerals.

The first tracks of what is now part of Burlington Northern's Colorado division connected the cities of Denver and Golden. Records show the first train arrived in Denver on September 23, 1870. Promoters of the project were citizens of Golden as well as residents of mining districts in the nearby mountains. By 1882 the line reached Black Hawk.

Meanwhile, the Chicago, Burlington & Quincy Railroad was looking to expand its rail network into Colorado from Nebraska. In the summer of 1881, the road's board of directors authorized construction from McCook to Denver. Thanks to a mild winter, construction advanced to Brush by April 1882, and the line was completed the following month. Approximately 250 miles of track had been laid in 229 working days.

During this period, various transactions, acquisitions and foreclosures created a Colorado and Southern rail network that ran from Wyoming to the Texas border. Chicago, Burlington & Quincy eyed the new C&S with the idea of acquisition in 1899, but fruition of the purchase wasn't realized until nine years later.

Today, Colorado and Southern operations are integrated into Burlington Northern's Colorado division, headquartered in Denver. The city also serves as location for the company's Denver region offices. The region covers a seven-state territory.

Major BN facilities in Denver include two freight car classification yards, a locomotive repair facility and a trailer-on-flat car loading and unloading facility. In addition, BN Transport, Burlington Northern's common carrier trucking operation, has its national headquarters in Denver. BN Transport holds one of the broadest general commodities operating authorities of any rail-owned carrier. Two other subsidiary companies, Burlington Northern Air Freight and Burlington Northern Land Development Corporation, maintain Denver offices and operations.

Capitol Federal Savings and Loan Association

'Think happy' — the culmination of a dream come true

The place — Denver. A thriving town at the foot of the majestic Rocky Mountains.

The time — 1925.

The event — Entrepreneur A. W. Hiner walked out of a meeting being conducted by the incorporators for the new United States Building and Loan Association, not wanting to be a part of the new organization.

As one of the original incorporators, this seemed to be a step backward for the Kansas ex-schoolteacher with a propensity for business and a keen interest in Denver's future. But it took Hiner only long enough to round up some old Kansas friends and his son A. W. Hiner, Jr. before officially chartering the Capitol Building and Loan Association on September 11, 1925.

Timing couldn't have been better. Denver was growing fast. People were arriving in town from everywhere, seeking fortunes. Hiner knew that his company could help these people with their dreams by providing sound, economical home financing and promoting thrift through saving. Capitol was permitted to make only long term home mortgage loans and some home im-

provement loans. But this created a solid base for the development and stability of the community through home ownership. Back then, Capitol retained traveling salesmen to solicit accounts and offer home loans door-to-door.

The fledgling company operated from the second floor of the old Cooper Building at Seventeenth and Curtis, a well regarded location at the time. Shortly thereafter, a choice spot was obtained in Denver's Flatiron Building, 1665 Broadway, across from the well-known Shirley Savoy Hotel. There, with a frontage of approximately 30 feet, Capitol's credibility as a lending and thrift institution was reinforced.

On December 27, 1937, Capitol Building and Loan Association became a mutually owned and federally chartered association. With that distinction also came a name change to Capitol Federal Savings and Loan Association. Soon after, A. W. Hiner, Sr. stepped down from the presidency and his son, friendly and well-known A. W. Hiner, Jr., occupied the position of managing officer and shortly after, president. The same command change was in store some years later for Hiner, Jr.'s son, A. W.

(Bill) Hiner, III. The Hiner family participated in Capitol's management until recent years.

As its 25th anniversary approached, Capitol Federal had established a position of leadership in the community. This was a natural role. Capitol had developed a sound, profitable institution by serving the residents of Denver and environs. Assets reached a whopping 4.5 million dollars. Capitol's leadership also extended to innovative financial advertising and promotion.

Capitol Federal was one of the first associations to sponsor a radio news program and did so for more than ten years. It also sponsored the longest continuous locally-produced program on television. The show, called *Masthead*, lasted more than 20 years and became Denver's top-rated news program. Many residents still remember when the line in front of the Court Place office extended three blocks during the grand opening in 1952, where for the first time in Denver's financial history, a television set was awarded as a grand prize. More recently, the memorable "Think Happy Today" theme, used by Capitol for the past eight years, has become an everyday phrase creating instant recognition of the association.

Management knew that to be successful in the booming Denver economy it was necessary to expand with the growth of the city. In 1960, Capitol laid the foundation for its first branch office at 2625 South Colorado Boulevard. This new office, which was to become Capitol's home office, marked the beginning of continuous, planned expansion into the fast-growing suburban areas.

The 1970s were busy years for Capitol Federal. The association was authorized to create First Capitol Corporation and First Capitol Mortgage Company...both designed to provide new services to customers. This was also a time for mergers. Dome Insurance Company merged with Capitol Insurance Agency forming Capitol Insurance Service, Inc. And, Home Savings of Boulder, established in 1921, became a part of Capitol Federal. Since Capitol's inception in 1925, thousands of families have been helped to own their own homes. Additionally, the association is an active participant in Denver's commercial, construction and rehabili-

Capitol Federal Savings' downtown office at 1665 Broadway in the Flatiron Building, 1927.

Artist's rendering of Capitol Federal's first branch office established in 1960 at 2625 South Colorado Boulevard, later remodeled as home office.

tation loan programs. Millions of dollars have been allocated for the upgrading and preservation of older neighborhoods and urban planning.

The decade of the '80s presents new and important challenges for the savings and loan industry. Capitol Federal is meeting these challenges with innovations including automated teller machines, interest on checking accounts, sixteen branch offices in Denver, Boulder, Colorado Springs and Evergreen and solid assets of more than one-half million dollars.

Capitol Federal Savings' record of the past and vision of the future has been and will continue to be a prime moving force in Denver's growth and success.

Central Bank of Denver

A commitment to innovative, convenient financial services

Central Bank of Denver has been a child of destiny as resilient as the constituency which it serves.

Founded as the North Side Savings Bank, the bank opened on April 12, 1892 with a paid-in-capital of $25,000. Just as it was getting settled, the Panic of 1893 struck Colorado. Twelve Denver banks closed their doors, but little North Side Savings survived.

Central Savings, which it became after an infusion of additional capital and a name change in 1907, showed a steady gain each year for the next several years. However, in 1923 depressed prices of cattle and sheep threw Denver into a deep recession causing a run on several banks, including Central.

Central suffered along with the rest of the nation during the stock market crash of '29, but was still in business when the bank moratorium was declared in 1932. In 1934, however, stockholders were assessed 70 percent of

Chairman of the Board Elwood Brooks and President Max Brooks celebrate the remodeling of Central Bank in 1958.

their holdings and the bank borrowed $200,000 from the Reconstruction Finance Corporation. The downtown trend was halted, but the die was cast. Downtown Denver had fallen victim to creeping paralysis and once-proud Larimer Street was becoming a slum area.

At the end of 1942, a Kansas school teacher-turned-banker paid a visit to Denver with checkbook in hand, huddled briefly with the bank chairman, and a completely new era in Denver banking came into being. Elwood Brooks became president of Central Bank in January 1943 when the bank was 50 years old, had fewer than 50 employees, and total assets of over $8 million.

After changing the bank's name to Central Bank and Trust Company, Brooks immediately instituted an innovative program to assure everyone of complete banking facilities in a relaxed and comfortable environment. During Brook's first year, Central began what was then unheard of in Denver banking — an extensive advertising and public relations program to attract the small depositor and businessman.

At the same time, Brooks began a series of innovations which became known as Central's "firsts" — pay-as-you-go checking accounts; a Veterans' Loan Department in 1944; Installment Loan and Real Estate Departments; the first "drive-in" banking in downtown Denver and a walk-up window for pedestrians.

A milestone was reached in 1955 when the bank's total resources topped the $100 million mark. Central's new image was highly visible. It was Denver's friendliest, most easily accessible and most customer-oriented banking operation. Deeply committed to community affairs, Central became the sponsor of the Denver basketball team in the National Industrial Basketball League — a team that later gave way to the professional Denver Nuggets.

In January 1957, Elwood became chairman of the board and his son Max was elected president. Shortly thereafter, the decision was made to enter a several-million-dollar expansion program. Across the street, Brooks Towers, a 42-story apartment complex was being built and the new Denver branch of the Federal Reserve Bank was on the drawing board.

Abruptly on February 5, 1965, Central Bank faced one of its darkest hours. After putting in a full day at the bank, Elwood Brooks collapsed and died at his apartment. The following month Max Brooks was elected to the dual position of chairman and president. He not only continued but intensified the philosophy and policies of his father Elwood Brooks. By the end of 1965, the bank's resources reached an all-time high.

Central Bank moved into its new Park Central home in 1973.

Central's management team, in 1967, was expanded and Don Hoffman was elected president while Max Brooks remained board chairman. The bank's growth and earnings potential made it a prime target for major corporations seeking diversification. Central considered several offers before allowing the D. H. Baldwin Company of Cincinnati, Ohio to acquire about 99 percent of Central's stock for $18 million, in mid-1968.

In 1973 the bank moved into the block-long Park Central complex which it occupies with Rio Grande Industries. By this time, the parent D. H. Baldwin Company had formed a multibank holding company which put Central in the position of lead bank for a statewide banking complex. President Don Hoffman assumed the additional responsibility of chief executive officer in 1976, and by 1980 Central's total resources were near the three-quarter billion mark.

An innovative and progressive leader among financial institutions in the Rocky Mountain West, Central Bank of Denver enters the '80s with renewed dedication to its motto, "Better Bankers."

The Children's Hospital

83 years of caring "for a child's sake"

It looked like the circus had come to Denver's City Park in the summer of 1897. Several rows of tents had been erected at Eighteenth Avenue and York. But the scene was deceptive. The tents housed an outdoor children's clinic staffed by Dr. Minnie C. T. Love and a corps of nurses. Here, the sick and crippled children in the Denver area, regardless of race or social standing, received medical treatment, nourishing food, sunshine, fresh air and tender loving care. But the clinic was forced to close at the end of its first year when donations and volunteer efforts were directed toward the Spanish American War.

Ten years later, Denver needed a children's hospital more than ever. According to historical accounts of the late 1800s, the sickness and death rates in Denver were inordinately high because of inadequate garbage and sewage disposal. Epidemics also were common among children because of contaminated milk and water.

Dr. Love and a handful of equally dedicated women were determined to make a children's hospital in Denver a reality. Articles of incorporation were written and signed in 1908, and full-scale fund raising began with picnics, bazaars, and requests for personal gifts. The people of Denver opened their hearts and pocketbooks to these resourceful women.

In 1910, a remodeled home at 2221 Downing Street was purchased for the first Children's Hospital. It had 35 beds. A nurse training school was established in an adjacent building, with its first class of three nurses graduating in 1912. During the hospital's first year of operation, the average length of stay per patient was 24-and-a-half days, and the average cost per day was $1.46.

In a short time, the demand for treatment exceeded the hospital's capacity. In 1917, The Children's Hospital moved to a newly constructed facility with 135 beds at its present location, 1056 East Nineteenth Avenue.

Spiraling growth continued. Even in its earliest stages of development, Children's was building its reputation as an outstanding pediatric medical facility. The success of The Children's Hospital in meeting the medical needs of its patients was attributed to the generous support of the men and women in the Denver community, in addition to the skills and faithful services of the health care teams within the institution.

The history of the hospital would be incomplete without recognition of Agnes and Harry H. Tammen. On Christmas Day 1921, the Tammens donated $100,000 for an addition to the hospital. This new wing would provide spacious quarters for treating orthopedic cases and various other diseases on an outpatient basis. At the 1924 opening ceremony, Harry Tammen, co-founder of *The Denver Post*, dedicated the Agnes Reid Tammen Wing "for a child's sake," in hopes that no child would ever be turned away.

Tammen died five months later, and half his estate was endowed to The Children's Hospital. With Mrs. Tammen as executor, this generous endowment served as the nucleus to funding the high level of care for indigent patients. Because of the Tammens, thousands of

A sampling of the proceeds of the 1916 Donation Day included bolts of material, which later were transformed at sewing bees into linens, nightgowns and other useful items.

Helen Adair at the Fourth of July celebration, 1937. Miss Adair was a longtime employee at The Children's Hospital, serving as an anesthesiologist and medical records clerk.

children have had their health restored, modern equipment has been purchased, and additional wings have been constructed.

To meet the need for a modern, centralized nurses home, the Tammen Hall Training School of Nurses was opened in 1932. Four years later an addition to the Agnes Reid Tammen Wing was acclaimed one of the finest therapy units in the United States. An isolation wing that opened in 1942 was designed to accommodate all forms of contagious diseases.

Because of community support, The Children's Hospital has changed dramatically over the years. In October 1979, a 130,000-square-foot patient care addition was opened, bringing the bed capacity to 210.

The Children's Hospital continues its efforts to meet the ever-changing needs of the children it serves from Denver, Colorado, and twelve surrounding states in the Rocky Mountain region. Treatment methods and medical science have advanced, but the task of alleviating human suffering remains constant.

Colorado National Bank

The first hundred years were the hardest

The Colorado National wasn't always "the bank that looks like a bank." In 1862 it rented the right front corner of Cheesman's Drug Store at Fifteenth and Blake streets. This is where Luther Kountze first assembled his gold scales and hung out his banker's shingle.

It took no more than several wheelbarrows in 1863 to move the bank to a more spacious location — a corner in a general store called The Mercantile House of Tootle and Leach. That was the bank's last stint as a tenant. In 1864 Luther and his brother Charles built the Kountze Brothers Bank, a two-story building that stood at Fifteenth and Market streets.

In 1866, a decade before Colorado became a state, the bank received its national charter and was renamed Colorado National Bank. Growing with the city and the times, the bank moved into a four-story cut-stone building at Seventeenth and Larimer in 1882. Denver was on the move, and the Kountze brothers were a part of the action. They played a leading role in bringing the railroad to Denver — a development that put the city on the map.

In 1915, as downtown Denver flourished and stretched to the south-

Colorado National Bank Building under construction, October 17, 1914.

east, CNB again outgrew its quarters and moved with the flow of growth — to the then-fashionable residential area at Seventeenth and Champa. The new bank building featured classic Greek pillars that inspired the slogan "the bank that looks like a bank."

Designed by W. E. and A. A. Fisher, the classic architecture slowly began to take shape during the spring and summer of 1915. Originally intended to be several stories high with plentiful office space, the building was constructed on a foundation that extends some 26 feet below the surface of the street. The structure boasts some twenty fluted columns of Colorado marble and bronze window grilles. The interior was finished in terrazzo marble from Italy. The Bronze vault door presented a major problem — it weighed 73,000 pounds, with support walls required to be 3.5 feet thick. Quite a chore for sheer manpower to install! In the vaults of Colorado National Bank today, the door alone weighs 62,000 pounds — or twenty times the weight of the complete vault and safe of 1874. The main building has undergone a series of alterations through the years, including a refurbished lobby and an addition to the west end of the building that includes a skylight.

In 1925, during the second renovation, artist Allen True was commissioned to paint fourteen murals on the walls of the main lobby. These murals can still be seen today. They represent a series of dream interpretations entitled "Indian Memories."

The bank continued to prosper during World War I and into the twenties. Colorado National survived the Crash of 1929 and the Bank Moratorium Crisis of 1933. Denver continued along its sleepy, unhurried pattern of growth until 1941 — and World War II. Marked changes occurred then because of the nationwide war effort. New military bases opened in Colorado and war plants were established throughout the state to handle the increasing demands for supplies of raw materials and metals. The bank helped to finance many war production loans.

Through the next three decades, CNB stepped into the era of computers and space-age business with the same tenacity that brought Luther Kountze to Denver years before.

Today, Colorado National Bank still stands for community service. And with all the changes 118 years can bring, Colorado National Bank — a part of the past — is a force of the future that "makes big ideas happen."

Conoco Inc.

From petroleum products marketer to international energy company

F.D. Stafford, an employee of Continental Oil Company in the Rocky Mountains, probably would not have guessed in 1888 that in less than 100 years the firm he worked for would become an international energy company generally regarded as the ninth largest in the world.

At that time, Continental — now Conoco Inc. — was a petroleum products marketer, and Stafford's job was to deliver kerosine to 24 grocery stores in nine Colorado towns that made up his territory. For $100 a month, plus expenses, Stafford worked out of Greeley, Colorado, pushing a 300-gallon tank wagon and one team of horses. Stafford kept a diary account of his job. Here's how he described it:

"Load up tank wagon with kerosine and drive to Evans, Colorado, to supply three dealer accounts. Gasoline carried on tank wagon in five-gallon can and many days returned to bulk plant with half can left. Kerosine wholesaled for 25 cents per gallon and retailed for 35 cents. Gasoline price 50 cents per gallon, and average sale consisted of a half gallon. Only diversion on these trips between towns was killing of rattlesnakes. Carried a six-foot length of chain for this purpose."

But Stafford couldn't have known how Denver would grow and mature, and that the company he had worked for would grow up with the city. He couldn't have foreseen that the company would merge with an Oklahoma oil firm and or that a Continental Oil Company building on Seventeenth Street would dominate what would become known as "energy row" in Denver.

Today, Conoco's offices in Denver are the nerve center for western operations as well as the world headquarters for the company's minerals department.

Conoco's heart remains with the Rockies, where as Continental Oil Company it was a petroleum products marketer. Its legacy, however, lies in Ponca City, Oklahoma, where E. W. Marland managed to revolutionize an industry while riding to the hounds or playing polo.

Marland, whom many called eccentric at best and a fool at worst, had the audacity to apply a science known as geology to oil exploration. In the early 1920s, Marland began dealing for land leases with the government of Mexico. His reason? Marland was convinced that the United States would one day run out of oil.

The Oklahoma oilman's vision and technical expertise meshed well when his company and Continental merged. The old "red triangle" that symbolized Marland Oil was used with the new company name — Conoco.

By 1940, Conoco diesel was being pumped into the famed Super Chief train, and the company already had drilled a well to a depth of 15,004 feet, bringing home the fact that America would have to dig deeper to slake an ever-growing thirst for oil. Boats began to look for oil under water, and seismograph technology was being fine-tuned in the swamps of Louisiana.

Conoco's march toward becoming a full-energy company continued in the 1950s, with petrochemical advances, extensions of pipelines and serious entry into offshore exploration. The company held almost 60 million net acres outside the United States by the end of 1956. In that year, Conoco developed its "VIBROSEIS" system that substituted mechanical means of producing low-range sound waves for dynamite detonations. It was a development regarded as a major breakthrough in oil exploration.

Conoco still lives in Denver, but it has come a long way since the days of F.D. Stafford. Oil, gas, minerals, chemicals, coal and the means to process, transport and market them are all a part of the business.

But the company's main product hasn't changed much since former Chairman Howard Blauvelt said in the 1970s:

"The company, in the final analysis, is the aggregate of everything — good or bad — that you and I do. People are our most vital asset."

Charles Lindbergh refuels his "Spirit of Saint Louis" in the Rockies, 1927.

Trinidad, Colorado bulk plant employees in 1909. In the buggy is U.S. Hollister, vice president from 1894 to 1912.

Continental Airlines
The airline that pride built

On July 15, 1934, one of three single-engined, four-passenger Lockheed Vegas owned by the Southwest Division of Varney Speed Lines lifted off the runway at El Paso, Texas, on a 520-mile flight to Albuquerque, New Mexico, and Pueblo, Colorado.

The plane carried 100 letters, but no passengers, and in the next 15 days the little airline flew only nine cash customers. Since there were eight employees on the payroll, it seems fair to say that things were off to a less-than-soaring start. In fact, only 600 passengers were carried during the first year of operation.

Today, those eight employees have become 10,500; the three Lockheed Vegas have become a fleet of 67 jets; the 600 annual passengers have become nine million, and the company's name has been changed to Continental Airlines.

Robert F. Six, who joined the company as operations manager July 5, 1936, and who replaced Avery Black as

Baggage loading the way it used to be! The aircraft is a Lockheed Lodestar, and it first saw service with Continental in 1940. It carried fourteen passengers and had a top speed of 205 mph.

president February 3, 1938, remains as chairman of Continental's board of directors. The company still flies between El Paso and Albuquerque but its routes cover the Mainland U.S. and extend south to Mexico and west to Hawaii and beyond to Fiji, American Samoa, New Zealand and Australia, and to Micronesia, Guam and Japan.

Continental's growth from its small beginning into a regional carrier, then into a major trunkline, was slow but sure.

In 1936, the little airline purchased the Denver-Pueblo route of Wyoming Air Service and moved the company's headquarters from El Paso to Denver. Later the same year, the company's name was changed to Continental Airlines.

Through a series of awards from the Civil Aeronautics Board beginning in 1939 and covering more than a dozen years, Continental's basic Denver-El Paso route was extended throughout the Southwest and Rocky Mountains.

In 1955, absorption of the routes and operations of Pioneer Air Lines added cities in Texas and New Mexico, and Continental began service between

Passenger jetways were still a thing of the future in 1956 as passengers walked out to board a Continental Convair 440. The aircraft carried 44 passengers and had a top speed of 270 mph.

Interior of Continental Convair-Liner (CV-340), April 1952.

Chicago and Los Angeles via Denver and Kansas City, turning the company into a major trunk carrier. With annual sales of just $16 million and assets of only $14 million, Continental ordered $64 million worth of DC-7Bs, jet powered Viscount IIs and pure jet Boeing 707s to operate over the new routes.

Continental continued to grow in the 1960s, adding service throughout the western two thirds of the Mainland U.S., and to Hawaii in 1969 and in 1971, Continental and its affiliate, Air Micronesia, were certified for a route from Hawaii through Micronesia to Guam and Okinawa.

In the last few years, Continental has become an international airline with routes to Japan, Australia, New Zealand, Fiji, American Samoa and Mexico's west coast resort cities of Cabo San Lucas, La Paz, Puerto Vallarta, Manzanillo and Acapulco. During the same period, east coast service was added bringing Washington, D.C. and Newark/New York on-line.

In May of 1975, at Six' recommendation, the airline's board of directors named Alexander Damm president and chief operating officer of Continental. Six was elected chief executive officer and chairman of the board.

In December of 1979, Six announced that on February 1, 1980, after 43 years at the helm of Continental, he was turning the reins over to A. L. Feldman as president and chief executive officer. Prior to that, Feldman had been president and chief executive officer of Frontier Airlines. Six will remain as chairman of the board of directors until July, 1982, when he retires.

The Denver Dry Goods Company

Progressive retailer bases success on service, grows with Denver

The Denver Dry Goods Company, 1907.

Denver has been a progressive, cosmopolitan town ever since its birth. Many diverse cultures were brought together by the lure of silver, the vast agricultural resources and the entrepreneurial opportunities such an influx of people presented.

Among the earliest entrepreneurs was M. J. McNamara, a leading citizen of the infant town. In 1886, just 28 years after General William Larimer built the log and mud cabin that was Denver's first residence, McNamara opened The McNamara Dry Goods Company on the site of the cabin — now the corner of Sixteenth and Larimer streets.

From the first, McNamara proved himself a retailing pioneer in a pioneer town, with a business philosophy that is still active today at The Denver. He believed that the key to a successful store was service. And he served the community by providing it with the wide variety of goods and conveniences it needed — from sturdy roughwear for the miners and ranchers to fine silks, china and crystal for the elegant mansions going up on Capitol Hill; from scales on the counters to accommodate the miners' gold dust to a carriage entrance to protect ladies' skirts from the muddy street.

The McNamara Dry Goods Company prospered along with the town it served. By 1889, Denver's population exceeded 100,000 and McNamara's store was rapidly outgrowing its quarters. A far-sighted real estate man persuaded McNamara to move uptown to the corner of Sixteenth and California streets — at the time, a quiet residential neighborhood — by offering to build for him the finest department store building west of St. Louis. McNamara accepted, and the store that was to become The Denver Dry Goods Company led the move that made Sixteenth and California the center of town.

The demonetization of silver in 1893 hit hard in a state whose principal industry was silver mining. It wiped out great fortunes overnight and might have wiped out McNamara's store along with them. With faith in Denver's future, however, a group of businessmen joined forces and reorganized the store. In 1894 it was renamed The Denver Dry Goods Company.

With the discovery of gold in Colorado, prosperity returned to the Queen City of the Plains and to The Denver Dry Goods Company. By 1900, The Denver was sending its buyers regularly to New York and Europe in search of the world's newest and best for its customers, building a four-story addition to the store, and startling Denver and the world with yet another innovation in service — the first motorized delivery truck, a light steam vehicle from the White Motor Company.

By 1906, The Denver again found it necessary to enlarge the store, extending it along California Street to Fifteenth, making it the largest department store between the Mississippi and the West Coast. Among the modern conveniences of the new building were an escalator and a whole fleet of the new Model T Ford trucks. The event was so ahead of its time that pictures of it were published worldwide.

Surviving the panic of '93 gave The Denver Dry Goods Company sound experience with which to weather the ups and downs of the new boom times, depressions and wars that assaulted the world.

Following World War II, The Denver Dry Goods Company, reflecting the changing needs of Denver, began a long term series of modernizations and improvements — new escalators, new elevators, a handsome new fashion floor, a youth center. There was also a new, modern warehouse that included facilities for the custom manufacture of draperies, slipcovers, upholstery and carpet finishing — still one of the few such workrooms in the country maintained by a department store.

Then, in 1953, The Denver pioneered the branch store movement with its Cherry Creek store, the first and largest complete branch store in the country.

Since then, The Denver has added eleven more stores, continuing to grow with Denver and reaching out to serve its customers in six Denver suburbs, five other Colorado cities and one out-of-state store in Billings, Montana. As each new store is added, McNamara's legacy of warm, personal service grows with The Denver.

Empire Savings

The oxen-drawn Conestoga wagon a symbol of growth within Colorado

The oxen-drawn Conestoga wagon became Empire Savings Association's symbol in 1948.

The nation was still reeling from the "crash of '29," Herbert Hoover was president and every third American home had a new means of communication and entertainment — the radio. The year was 1931 and Empire Savings was founded that spring. It took energy, courage and a pioneering spirit to establish a new financial institution in the midst of the Great Depression — Balmore F. Swan, the founder of Empire, possessed those qualities.

The original Articles of Incorporation for the association were drawn on March 30, 1931 by Swan, J. Herschel White and Edgar McComb. A state charter followed and the doors to the small, storefront building on Welton Street in Denver opened in April. In a matter of five short years, the association had ac-

The expansion of Empire's home office in 1959 – Denver's Centennial year – was disguised by 1859 storefronts.

cumulated assets of nearly $1 million. Property adjacent to the original building was then purchased and the facility doubled in size.

In 1948 an oxen-drawn Conestoga wagon, carrying a pioneer family west across the Great Plains, became the symbol of the association as Empire again moved into new quarters at 1654 California Street. This handsome building — after two expansions — still houses the association's home office today. By 1953 Empire's assets had grown to more than $18 million. Empire established its first branch operation in the new community of Broomfield, Colorado in 1956. The second branch office

in Longmont was opened in 1957, followed by another northern Colorado office in Loveland in 1959. With resources exceeding $58 million, Empire's network was spreading throughout the Denver area to offer greater convenience and service to the association's customers.

The expansion of the home office facilities in 1959 coincided with the Denver Centennial. The old Carson Building and Empire's existing headquarters were combined to form a modern office complex with a western motif including a flagstone floor and fireplace, walnut paneling and two bronze doors with bas-relief scenes of the Old West. Since the remodeling occurred during the Centennial celebration, the construction was disguised with a facade of 1859 storefronts. Customers entered Empire through the Overland Stage Office and found employees dressed in Old West costumes. The two-week grand opening attracted thousands of visitors from Colorado and neighboring states and whetted Empire's appetite for further growth.

The pioneering spirit was to gather momentum in the '60s. In 1960 branches were opened in Greeley, Lakewood and the University Hills area of Denver, followed by Bear Valley in 1962. By 1963, its 32nd birthday, Empire was the largest state-chartered savings and loan association in Colorado with resources in excess of $100 million. The decade of the '70s proved to be a continuing success story for Empire. Within a ten-year span the association opened 26 offices. In the year 1979 alone the association claimed the most extraordinary growth of the decade with an increase of eight full-service offices. By the end of 1980, 37 Empire offices were operating throughout Colorado.

Empire Savings was acquired in 1968 by D. H. Baldwin Company. Ten years later, Baldwin merged with The United Corporation, a closed-end investment company, and commenced operations under the name Baldwin-United Corporation. Much of the corporation's $3 billion in assets are now employed in Colorado, servicing the rapidly expanding Rocky Mountain region. In addition to savings and loan, principal areas of Baldwin-United's operations include insurance, banking and musical instruments, the latter being the original business of the D. H. Baldwin Company. A fifth area of operation — other financial services and investment — includes installment financing, leasing, mortgage banking and income from foreign investments. The management of Baldwin-United, working closely with Empire's management team, is committed to support the superior quality of growth and home ownership in Colorado.

Today, with assets of over a billion dollars, the spokes of the Conestoga wagon symbolize the association's expansion throughout the state. Empire Savings is growing with Colorado to help its citizens plan and build for the future.

The Fairmount Cemetery Association

Third generation descendants continue founders' tradition of beauty and service

Decoration Day, May 30, 1893, dawned cool and clear, with just enough breeze to rid the city of its usual haze of smoke. Five and a half miles east of Denver, in Baron von Richthofen's grandiloquent suburb of Montclair, a crowd of people gathered at the intersection of Center Avenue and East End Boulevard, eager to board a train that would take them to the Queen City's most celebrated patch of green — Fairmount Cemetery.

The day was special enough — Denver was justifiably proud of its sons who had served in the Grand Army of the Republic — but making the day even more exciting was the long-awaited inaugural of the "Cemetery Express," a steam railway company owned and operated by The Fairmount Cemetery Association.

Ever since the founding of the Association three years before, the board of directors had made repeated attempts to persuade various cable and electric rail companies to build a spur line out to Fairmount, thereby linking the cemetery to the rapidly expanding city-wide transit system. Denver's booster press, always ready to promote civic improvements, regularly heralded the building of the "New Fairmount Line," speculating that not only would it provide lot owners and visitors with a necessary mode of transportation but also would open vast tracts of land to real estate development.

Local newspapers had good reason to expect the directors to be successful in their negotiations with the rail companies. All were well-known to the people of Denver — many were pioneers of the early gold rush days — and were intimately involved in all aspects of the city's growth. And yet, in their talks with railway officials, they came away with nothing but empty promises.

Finally, after resorting to horse-drawn "hacks" to carry the more than 2500 people who weekly visited the

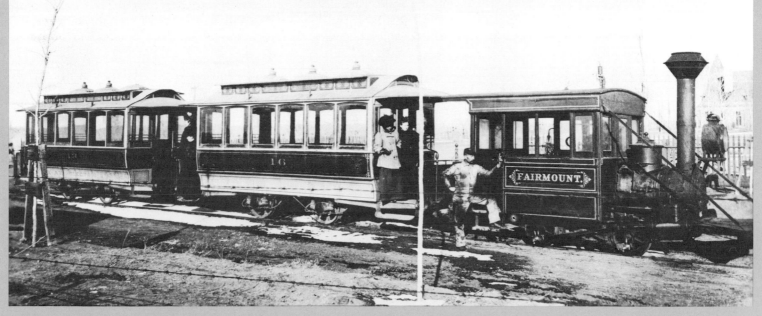

The Fairmount Railway, 1893.

201

cemetery, the directors, in the spring of 1893, announced that the Association was going into the railroad business. The line would be ready by Decoration Day.

And so it was.

Now, as the train moved slowly up the steep grade passing the Agnes Phipps Sanitorium, passengers sat comfortably in their seats, enjoying the magnificent panoramic view of the Front Range of the Rockies — Pike's Peak clearly visible to the south, and to the north, the snow-capped splendor of Long's Peak.

When they arrived at Fairmount, further expressions of wonder could be heard from the passengers as they climbed down from the cars. For here, on the fringe of the fabled Great American Desert, were hills of green, brightly-hued flower gardens of every size and description, and, perhaps most surprising of all, a forest of trees — thousands of trees, including seven variety of oak, maple, elm, honeylocust, sycamore and many other species once thought unfit for Denver's arid climate.

To make the desert bloom, the direc-

tors had engaged the services of Reinhard Schuetze, a landscape architect from Eberswald, Germany. In the spring of 1891, Schuetze planted nearly 5,000 trees and over 2,000 shrubs and vines. His success was such that when his work at Fairmount was completed, he went on to pioneer the greening of Denver, designing City Park, Cheesman Park (the site of the city's original cemeteries), Washington Park and the state capitol grounds.

Enhancing this pastoral scene were two sandstone structures designed by Denver architect, H.T.E. Wendell. On their way to the grounds, the visitors walked under the archway of the Gate Lodge and in the distance they could see the picturesque Ivy Chapel with its flying buttresses and gable roof surmounted by a tower 90 feet in height.

More than a thousand people visited Fairmount on that Decoration Day, strolling the tree-lined circular drives and private walking lanes, to pay tribute to their honored dead.

Today, nearly 90 years since that first train ride, Schuetze's embryonic forest has grown into Colorado's most exten-

The Fairmount Gate Lodge, now an official Denver landmark, with the Agnes Phipps Sanitorium in background.

sive tree arboretum, and the Gate Lodge and Ivy Chapel have been designated as official landmarks by the Denver Landmark Preservation Commission. And, in harmony with this tradition of beauty, new developments have been added, including the Mausoleum, Memorial Terrace and Wind Chimes Tower — all making Fairmount a fitting burial ground for the more than 140,000 people who, in their own way, helped shape the history of Colorado and its Queen City of the Plains.

The First National Bank of Denver

First a mint and first a bank

The only known financial institution in the history of the United States to conduct commercial banking and minting activities simultaneously was located at Sixteenth and Market Streets in Denver.

On July 20, 1860, in a settlement called Denver City, an enterprising trio from Leavenworth, Kansas opened the only financial institution in the history of the United States to conduct simultaneous commercial banking and minting activities.

Founded by brothers Austin and Milton Clark and Emanuel Gruber, the bank was first called Clark, Gruber & Company. Then, after selling the minting operation to the U.S. Mint, the trio moved to quarters on Fifteenth Street between Market and Blake. In 1865, their company became the newly-chartered First National Bank of Denver — now the Rocky Mountain region's largest financial institution.

The bank and its leaders have been an integral part of the growth of Denver and Rocky Mountain West — spurred by the contributions of such notables as David H. Moffat Jr., Walter S. Cheesman, George W. Kassler, Jerome B. Chaffee and A. V. Hunter, early-day bank executives.

One major contribution came in 1868 when Denver lost half its population because of a decision not to serve the

First permanent location of The First National Bank of Denver was The National Block, Fifteenth and Blake Streets.

had clerks display bags of gold, silver and currency in the windows to discourage a run. That, combined with the last major gold discovery in Colorado, helped the state survive the depression better than most.

The bank continued to grow. By October 1897, it recorded $10,962,000 in deposits, making it the 27th largest in the country and the second largest in the western two-thirds of the nation. The bank relocated in 1896 to the Equitable Building on the southeast corner of Seventeenth and Stout streets, and again in 1911 to the southwest corner of the same intersection in the state's then tallest skyscraper — the eleven-story First National Bank Building.

In 1912 the second merger occurred, with Capitol National. And in 1958 First National Bank merged with the International Trust Company to form the largest commercial bank and trust operation in the Rocky Mountain region. That year, the bank occupied four floors in the newly-completed First National Bank Building, Seventeenth and Welton streets.

Ten years later The First National Bancorporation, Inc., a registered bank holding company, was formed and, in 1973, First of Denver became the first billion-dollar Colorado bank with total assets of $1,031,277,834, as of December 31, 1973.

Then in 1974 the bank moved a substantial portion of its operations into the lower sixteen floors of the First of Denver Plaza Building at Seventeenth and California streets, linked to the former structure by seven floors of a connecting addition.

And how times have changed. The previous site of the International Trust Company building adjacent to both skyscrapers has become a half-acre brick-paved plaza, one of daytime downtown Denver's "people places," with a variety of activities held throughout the year.

The bank's founding fathers would be pleased to see the people-oriented tradition they established continue so successfully.

community with a transcontinental railroad. The group spearheaded efforts to establish the Denver Pacific Railroad, linking Denver to Cheyenne — then a railhead of the Union Pacific — and saved Denver from probable demise.

In 1876 Colorado gained statehood and The First National Bank of Denver moved into prestigious quarters on the northwest corner of Sixteenth and Larimer streets. Shortly thereafter, H.A.W. Tabor emerged as the region's silver king in the Colorado mining town of Leadville and became the largest single shareholder in the bank, as well as a director. His contributions to the state's economy bolstered growth and provided a highly colorful chapter in the region's history.

During the Tabor era (1882), Merchants National Bank became part of The First National Bank of Denver —

the first of three mergers in the institution's history — and three years later the bank moved again to larger offices across the street.

As the First National moved upward and forward, there were those who tried to stifle progress — such as the man who confronted President David Moffat in his office on March 30, 1889. He pointed a .44 revolver, displayed a bottle he claimed contained nitro-glycerine, escaped with $20,000 in bills and $1,000 in gold — and was never caught.

Independent sources subsequently confirmed that the robbery was masterminded by Tom McCarty, whose accomplice was allegedly Robert Leroy Parker, later known as Butch Cassidy.

Another setback was the silver crash of 1893, which caused a several-years-long nationwide depression and the closure of several Denver banks. It is said that Moffat liquidated $2 million of his personal government securities, placed the cash in The First National Bank and

Frankel Manufacturing Company

Innovators in the fast-paced office products industry

At the turn of the century, a young student at Denver's East High School, Henry Frankel, had but one goal in mind — to become an attorney. He never imagined that he would instead

become a pioneer in the office products industry.

In the summer of 1906, Henry Frankel Sr. and his wife opened a retail stationery store on Larimer Street in

Denver and young Henry performed delivery chores after school. Business was good in bustling young Denver — sales totalled $6,000 that year.

But three years later the Frankels'

bright future was dimmed by the death of the elder Henry. Determined to carry on, his widow continued to operate the business while raising her family. Her son, Henry, assisted every moment that he wasn't in school earning a law degree.

Upon graduation, Frankel decided to devote his full attention to the family business. In 1914, he broke away from the role of retailer and began his own manufacturing operation — the first of its kind in the region. The company's first products were fine typewriter ribbons made from imported cotton. The product line was soon expanded to include one of the world's first silk ribbons.

The success of this manufacturing venture quickly led to the creation of new products. In 1923, Frankel began the manufacture of mimeograph stencils, which were in great demand, as the prosperity of the '20s led to explosive growth in America's administrative activity. This product presented Frankel with a challenge. The patents for the conventional nitro-cellulose stencil coating processes were held by a Chicago firm, thus a new technique was necessary.

Working in a laboratory in his basement, Frankel developed a protein stencil base. "I didn't learn too much about chemistry in school" he later said, "so when the time came, I just had to sit down and start reading books." Such was the start of his firm's self-styled pioneering leadership in office products.

Keeping up with the dizzying pace of

Nineteen-year old Henry Frankel, left, and associates in Frankel Stationery office, 1910.

change in this field proved to be no problem for the company with its "KLEAN WRITE" product line. In 1930, Frankel introduced the film-top stencil which produced an unparalleled quality of printing. This development was largely responsible for the company's prosperity during the Great Depression. During that bleak period, the firm grew so large that several branches in other states were opened to streamline distribution.

The tables were turned on Frankel and his company during the Second World War. Legal entanglements with imitators of Frankel stencil innovations, along with the channeling of most commercial activity in the direction of the war effort, siphoned the firm's resources and cut into its sales.

Undaunted, Frankel and his son-in-law, Eugene J. Weisberg, who had recently joined the company as general manager, turned their attention to new ventures after the war. The Frankel Company introduced the first usable nylon ribbons in 1945 and the perforated film stencil in 1950. The high quality and innovative nature of the company's products fueled a strong, sustained period of growth to the late 1960s.

But, by the beginning of the 1970s, photo-copying technology had largely eclipsed the mimeograph stencil market, and typewriter and computer makers were designing machines using polyethylene-based carbon ribbons instead of inked fabric ribbons. Rather than devote all its resources to its formerly dominant products, the company again diversified. In 1971, after two years of intense research, Frankel introduced not only its own line of ribbons but an entirely new technology for mak-

Executive Vice President Eugene Weisberg, left, and Henry Frankel, second from right with Colorado Governor Lamm and Denver Mayor McNichols at 1979 ground breaking ceremony.

ing them. A complete line of ribbons to supply the burgeoning computer and word processing industry soon followed.

Throughout its history the Frankel Company has depended heavily on its human resources — 80 percent of its manufacturing machinery has been designed and built by its employees. The firm has been known for its progressive employee programs and has been a leader in employment of minorities in Denver. In addition, the company has been active in such community activities as the United Way, and Henry Frankel was a founder of General Rose Hospital.

At the dawn of the 1980s the Frankel Company is still family-owned, with three generations participating in its management. The firm, which now employs 400, is completing a new facility in North Denver and has begun a new plastics manufacturing division.

"In business, you can't stand still," Henry Frankel once said. "If you stand still, the world moves on past you."

Frederic Printing

More than 100 years
of quality and innovation in printing

In the days when Denver was a boom town overflowing with wealthy miners and railroad men, money changed hands rapidly. It was a time when fly-by-night operations must have had a heyday making a quick buck. But respectable merchants in those days were more far-sighted. They realized that quality and honest service could assure them and their families a fine livelihood for generations.

One such man was John Frederic. In 1878, he responded to the increasing communications needs of burgeoning Denver by opening a print shop near Tenth and Curtis, downtown. He painstakingly handset his own type in the manner of old world craftsmen and fed the sheets into his small letterpress.

These presses were remarkable for their simplicity and durability. In fact, they survived their westward passage in spite of extremely rough travel. Many fell into rivers and rolled over cliffs, only to be retrieved by printers with the pioneering spirit to assure the communications needs of the West would be well met.

The year 1878 in Denver was a good one for John Frederic to start his business. It was a big political year, and the Republicans won with the Honorable Frederick W. Pitkin becoming governor. There was renewed activity in business and building operations, and merchants were making money. Real estate became active and strong, and railways were taxed to their utmost capacity. So John Frederic was undoubtedly a busy man printing business letterheads, cards and advertising broadsides for a receptive public. He was committed to excellence in his craft, and his ideals have seen his business endure here in Denver for more than 100 years.

By 1923, there were 150 printing and publishing businesses in Denver, employing over 1300 people. Clearly, the craft was thriving, and it was not long before a more refined printing process was sought. The improvements came with offset printing — which offered better quality than the letterpress method. Cold type or photographic typesetting was a boom, too, and increased the speed at which printers could work.

Bob Frederic took up the printing trade in his family's business when he

Curtis Street, downtown Denver in the late 1800s – the approximate location of where Frederic Printing first began business.

was 21 years old. He learned the traditional aspects of the craft, but he had an eye out for the advances in technology that would make printing the sophisticated art it is today.

In 1965, Frederic Printing converted to color offset lithography and even invented its own registration system for four-color printing. It was the first in the region to bring in a 40-inch four-color press. Frederic Printing also pioneered, on a regional basis, 300 line duotones and 200 line separations to provide even truer depths of continuous tone. As part of its ongoing goal to assure customers the finest product, Frederic Printing has also added a full bindery and diecutting capability to the operation.

In 1978, Frederic Printing celebrated its "Heritage 100." The sophistication of the printing art after 100 years would boggle the mind of founder John Frederic. But the company still adheres to his credo of "high-quality printing and on-time delivery." It has served well for more than a century.

In fact, it was Frederic's commitment to consistent quality, service and innovation that won the firm Colorado's only membership in the Creative Printers of America in 1969. Constant contact with other members of this select organization has meant continual access to the latest printing technologies all over the country. To customers that has meant tangible results in the way of benefits.

Frederic Printing now resides at 4290 Holly Street in Denver. The 41,000-square-foot plant was designed to create an environment conducive to smoother work flow and increased efficiency. It is a result of the knowledge that truly advanced technology is not just modern equipment, but a continuing process involving both minds and machines — minds always seeking to develop new techniques to provide the best in service, quality and innovation.

Frederic takes pride in its community heritage. In the best tradition of its predecessors, it honors the philosophy handed down from more than 100 years of experience — that of creativity, innovation, quality and dependability in its work. As John Frederic knew, it is a philosophy for all time.

Frontier Airlines

Air-linking Denver with 92 cities in 26 states, Canada and Mexico

As World War II wound down, new "feeder" air services for the communities of Main Street America were okayed by the Civil Aeronautics Board. One of the fledgling airlines selected to complement the established trunk carriers was Denver-based Monarch Air Lines. Founded by Raymond M. Wilson, a Colorado aviation pioneer, Monarch inauspiciously inaugurated its first certificated route on November 27, 1946, with one daily round trip between Denver and Durango, Colorado.

Three years of criss-crossing the Continental Divide with its small fleet of 21-passenger DC-3 aircraft proved discouragingly unrewarding. In an attempt to strengthen its wobbly financial position, Monarch's management merged with two other struggling "feeder" carriers: Challenger Airlines, also based in Denver, and Arizona Airways, headquartered in Phoenix. This effort at corporate survival brought into being, on June 1, 1950, a new company — Frontier Airlines. The newly-merged airline now spread its costs and its wings across seven states to 50 communities of the Rocky Mountain West and Southwest.

Red ink continued to flow with dismaying regularity on the pages of Frontier's corporate books into the late 1950s. Then a four-state route award in the Midwest and acquisition of Convair 340 aircraft capable of carrying 44 passengers began attracting additional users.

Between 1962 and 1967, change in the ownership, management and corporate philosophy catapulted Frontier into an era of expansion and profitability. Low cost fares induced thousands of travelers to start using the airline's services. Then the carrier's Convair fleet was upgraded with turbine engines. Designated the Convair 580, the aircraft cruised at 350 miles per hour, had cabin pressurization, inflight meals and additional seating. These traffic stimulators were introduced by Lewis W. Dymond, president of Frontier at that time. Ownership of the airline again changed in 1965 when RKO General, Inc., a subsidiary of General Tire and Rubber Company, acquired controlling interest.

During the mid-1960s Frontier ambitiously sought long-haul routes. Ser-

Flagship of Frontier Airlines' fleet is the 106-passenger Boeing 737, a twin-engine jet capable of cruising at 520 miles per hour. Frontier has the second largest Boeing 737 fleet in the world with 43 of these planes in service by the end of 1980.

Exchanging their service uniforms of World War II for the caps and wings of Monarch Air Lines, this gung-ho group of pilots line up with the airline's founder and first president, Raymond M. Wilson (rear row - center), in front of two of the carrier's DC-3 aircraft. These planes were converted from World War II C-47 troop carrier aircraft.

vice was inaugurated from Denver to St. Louis and Kansas City in June of 1967, using Boeing 727 jet aircraft.

In the fall of 1967, the CAB approved Frontier's plan to merge Central Airlines of Fort Worth into its system. This extended Frontier's routes into Texas, Oklahoma, Arkansas, Kansas and Missouri.

After this heady five years of route expansion, merger and jet fleet acquisition, Frontier began to experience extensive financial reverses, and the drain on the company's resources continued into the early 1970s. Contributing to this unprofitable situation were: a general down-turn in the national economy, high start-up costs of new route development and jet fleet expansion, a costly write-down in book value of aircraft acquired in the Central merger, plus a significant

reduction annually in the federal subsidy needed to service smaller communities.

By the spring of 1971 RKO General decided that a more innovative management was necessary to again make Frontier profitable. Fresh from a successful management performance with Aerojet General Corporation came A. L. "Al" Feldman to become Frontier's president. Along with him came Glen L. Ryland, who became vice president of finance. Feldman and Ryland immediately introduced Frontier to the concept of "management by commitment." Individuals and departments were to be judged and rewarded by performance results alone.

Total team effort evolved with fresh approaches to dependable, on-time flights using "real world" scheduling for maintenance, ground services and flight operations. The jet fleet was standardized with Boeing 737-200 aircraft, which featured first class meals, ample leg room and a standard fare.

Innovative marketing programs aimed at discretionary travel, increased flights in selective markets, and incentive fares strongly improved Frontier's appeal to potential passengers while increasing market share on competitive routes.

These management-by-commitment efforts paid off on the bottom line. During the first full year under the Feldman/Ryland leadership, Frontier turned a healthy profit. Aggregate net earnings from 1972 through 1979 totaled $92.7 million. During this six-year period, major new destinations were added to Frontier's expanding system and the airline extended its reach to 26 states, Canada and Mexico.

From its inauspicious beginnings in 1946, Frontier enters the '80s as an airline industry leader in profitability, safety and passenger service.

In January 1980 Glen Ryland succeeded Al Feldman as president and chief executive officer. In the decade ahead, Ryland forecasts further expansion of the airline's routes, jet fleet and contributions to the growth of Denver as the energy and marketing center of the West. But he won't lose sight of Frontier's underlying philosophy — run on time, be honest with people and provide quality service.

The Gates Rubber Company

From leather tires to number one in belts and hose

In 1905 Charles C. Gates Sr., a graduate of the Michigan College of Mining and Technology, ventured west to pursue a career in mining. Once in Denver, however, Gates opted for a career connected with the fast-growing automobile industry. In October 1911 he purchased, for $3,500, the Colorado Tire and Leather Company at 1025 Broadway in Denver.

The firm manufactured the Durable Tread, a steel-studded band of leather which could be fastened over worn auto tires to extend their wear.

Charles' younger brother, John G. Gates, came to work for the company soon after its purchase and invested $3,000 to help keep the faltering business going. In February 1912 he became a partner, and the business moved to 1320-40 Acoma.

The brothers then made horse halters from the leather scrap. Buffalo Bill tested them in his wild west show and reported that they never broke. Using the name Never Break and the cowboy's endorsement, within three years the company became the largest producer of halters in the U.S.

By 1914 the Durable Tread gave way to the International Half-Sole and the company moved to its present location at 999 South Broadway. The International Half-Sole was a tread cover but made from rubber and fabric to be cemented over worn treads to extend their wear.

In the summer of 1917, John Gates bought a new Cole coupe. He discovered V-shaped pulleys powered by rope turning the radiator fan. It was then that the world's first rubber and fabric V-belt was created. John's invention soon became a standard in the industry.

The company's name was changed to The International Rubber Company in 1917, then to The Gates Rubber Company the following year.

In 1919 Gates introduced its first balloon tire, the Super Tread. Specialized rubber products followed in 1921. Those were items shaped by a mold during curing. In 1927 Gates began making hose — first steam hose for locomotives and then garden hose, followed by automobile radiator hose.

During the Great Depression, because of its product mix and as a supplier to many original equipment and replacement markets, the company was able to maintain a status quo. The first industrial products were Vulco

This Cole coupe led John Gates in 1917 to the invention of the rubber and fabric V-belt which launched The Gates Rubber Company on the road as the world's number one producer of belts and hose (right).

The Colorado Tire and Leather Company's first product in 1911 was the Durable Tread which sold for $9.60 to $38.50 depending on the tire size. Horse Halters were sold later for $1.25 (below).

Ropes — heavy duty V-belts. Introduced in 1931, they replaced chain and gear drives.

During World War II, Gates made more than 1,000 products specifically for the war effort. Products for all three services ranged from gas masks to tires and molded parts for ships, tanks and airplanes.

Beginning in 1954, additional plants were built in the United States and foreign countries. The company began diversifying in 1962.

Subsidiaries included the A Bar A, State Line, and Big Creek ranches (cattle raising and a guest ranch); Financial Programs (mutual funds management);

Gates Learjet (executive jet aircraft), Gates Land Company (residential land development); Gates Energy Products (rechargeable lead-acid batteries).

After the death of Charles Sr. in 1961, his son Charles C. Gates became company president. John died in 1969 and Gates sold the tire business in 1973.

Presently the company is the world's largest producer of belts and hose, with thirteen plants in ten states and nine more located in five foreign countries. The son of the founder remains president and chairman of the board of this family-owned company. Corporate sales are expected to exceed $1 billion by the end of 1980.

Johns-Manville Corporation

From a basement beginning to a worldwide business

Johns-Manville is a $2.3 billion multi-national company headquartered in the foothills of the Rocky Mountains southwest of Denver. The firm employs some 33,000 people at more than 100 mines, plants, and sales and administrative offices around the world.

For more than 120 years, Johns-Manville has provided products that meet society's needs. These include insulation products that conserve energy, control sound, and provide fire and heat protection; roofing products for agricultural, industrial and municipal needs. The company also mines and processes minerals such as diatomite, used in such specialties as filters for beer and wine. In addition, J-M recently has added paper, packaging systems and lumber to its extensive product mix.

The first half of what was later to become Johns-Manville was founded in 1858 by Henry Ward Johns, a 21-year-old entrepreneur who launched a roofing, coatings, woods, metals and fabrics business in a New York basement.

The other half of J-M was founded in 1886 in Milwaukee, Wisconsin, by Charles B. Manville and his sons. The Manville Covering Company produced pipe coverings and insulation for heating and cooling systems. Manville soon became the major distributor for Johns products, and in 1901, the two merged into the H.W. Johns-Manville Company. On January 1, 1927, J-M became a public corporation under its present name.

Since that time, J-M has experienced steady growth, even during the Great Depression. The company developed new products and gained greater market penetration for its major products through the 1950s.

In 1958, J-M added a new dimension to the company's existing insulation and roofing business with the acquisition of the L.O.F. Glass Fibers Company in Toledo, Ohio. The acquisition set the stage for J-M's major growth over the next 20 years. Fiber glass insulation and fiber glass roofing quickly became an integral part of the company's total operation.

The acquisition in 1979 of Olinkraft — now Manville Forest Products — a wood and paper products company, was a major step in implementing J-M's philosophy of operating in basic product areas that are woven into the fiber of everyday life.

Johns-Manville moved its corporate headquarters from New York to Denver in 1971, relocating more than 1,000 families to the area in one operation. On July 4, 1976, J-M moved into its present award-winning headquarters on the 10,000-acre Ken-Caryl Ranch.

Today, Johns-Manville is a highly diversified multi-national corporation with more than 1,200 products in seven major business areas: fiber glass products, pipe products and systems, roofing products, non-fiber glass insulations, asbestos fiber, industrial and specialty products and services, and forest products.

J-M's present corporate headquarters in foothills near Denver (inset).

"87 Marden Lane" – New York headquarters in 19th Century (below).

But J-M still looks to the future. Like many corporations, it finds itself at a crossroads as the '80s begin. The company expects vast market potential for a wide range of products, but it faces a multitude of challenging problems that will require dedication, determination and action if it is to achieve its goals for the coming years.

Johns-Manville's top management is confident the corporation will succeed because of the inherent strengths of its people and its businesses.

The Jolly Rancher Candy Company

Where good taste is a timeless tradition and total commitment

The old barn which was the beginning of the candy manufacturing plant 1942.

In 1942 airline pilot Bill Harmsen, his wife Dorothy and year-old son Bill Jr., left their urban lifestyle in Minneapolis and moved into a 75-year-old farm house on ten acres west of Denver.

Farming was a new experience for the Harmsens, who assumed management of the farm and its perennial fruit and flower crops after the birth of their son Robert two years later. For Mrs. Harmsen — who guided the farm's ventures while her husband continued his flying — managerial responsibilities had to be interwoven with those of running a household and raising sons Bill, Robert and later, Michael. A near disastrous fire in the basement of the house nearly ended the venture entirely — but the Harmsens pressed on.

Bill Harmsen soon gave up flying to take advantage with Mrs. Harmsen of the reportedly lucrative soft ice cream business.

The Harmsens opened the first Jolly Rancher Ice Cream Store in 1949 in nearby Golden, Colorado. The name "Rancher" seemed suitable for a western motif and "Jolly" had a hospitable, inviting connotation — thus the name "Jolly Rancher" was copyrighted.

From left, top, the Harmsen boys – Bill Jr., Mike, Bob, and father, Bill Sr. – and candy makers. From left, bottom, Dorothy Harmsen and candy dippers and packers.

Rumors of great wealth in the business were unfounded. After the first summer the Harmsens discovered they had more liabilities than assets, and the $4,000 borrowed against the farm had been invested in inefficient ice cream manufacturing equipment. Survival during the next winter months was accomplished by adding a high quality line of bulk and boxed chocolates. The store prospered and several franchised candy and ice cream shops were opened in Colorado, Wyoming, and Nebraska.

Two years later, the Golden store was sold. But the Harmsens were still responsible for supplying the franchise stores with a quality line of chocolates. The candy had been provided by a manufacturer in Denver, who could no longer meet the demand. Also, requests for the five-cent hot cinnamon taffy stick, now known as "Fire Stix" (the recipe had been developed by the Harmsens while in Golden), became so numerous that Dorothy and Bill realized they had a "red hot" opportunity, and

decided to do something about it.

In three months the Harmsens had completely renovated the old barn on the farm site, hired a candy maker and dipper and hung up a sign giving the ten acres a new name — "Sugar Bar Ranch."

Eventually, the flowers and fruit made way for a parking area and new kitchens were added to the barn. The bunkhouse became the office and a later addition connected it to the plant. The remodeled house remained the Harmsens' home until 1968. All of the additions to the barn were built and decorated to maintain the atmosphere of the old west, painted barn red with white trim.

"That's how it all began" back in 1949 by two Colorado "late" pioneers, who could be called 20th century '49ers.

The year 1966 brought the merger of Jolly Rancher with Beatrice Foods Company of Chicago, which resulted in a new impetus for further expansion. Rising costs made complete automation in the manufacturing and office systems necessary and the manufacture of the famous chocolate candy line was terminated, rather than sacrifice the fine quality. Jolly Rancher now is known worldwide for its "Famous For Flavor" line of hard candies.

In 1977 Bill Harmsen retired as president of the company. Dorothy Harmsen still is active as the editor of the company's trade publication, *Sugar and Spice.*

The Jolly Rancher offices, expanded into the ranch house, are a virtual repository of western art as paintings cover the walls from ceiling to floor.

The second Harmsen son, Bob, who grew up in the family business, became general manager in 1977. Today, he is the genial president, surrounded by quality

Bill and Dorothy Harmsen pondering the possibilities of changing the pneumatic kneaders to an automated method –1960.

candy and western art. The candy plant is efficient and immaculate, bustling with activity 24 hours a day. Harmsen reminisces about his parents' early days in the candy business — "Mom and Dad would wait for the mail man each day to bring in the orders that kept the factory working for that particular day. Dad would deliver the local candy orders in town, while Mom oversaw the candy maker and chocolate dippers, and kept the books. A day in town meant that Dad returned with 100 pounds of sugar, always on credit, in the old station wagon."

Jolly Rancher candy is shipped into all

50 states, Puerto Rico, Canada, Mexico and other foreign countries. The company operates a fleet of 25 transport trucks, carrying over one million pounds of candy per month. The atmosphere of the west, is promoted through reproductions of original western paintings on the truck trailers to all areas of the United States.

It is, indeed, a success story of two people who reached their goal and are continuing to reap their rewards through their son's able management of Jolly Rancher, a company built with quality, honesty and 400 faithful employees.

KBTV, CHANNEL 9
A station of the Gannett Broadcasting Group

Commitment to community service secret of station's success

"All is fine at Channel 9" according to headlines in the July 11, 1953 issue of *"TV and Radio Weekly"* which featured a special edition saluting KBTV on the opening of its new studios at 1089 Bannock Street.

Celebrity guests at opening day festivities for the station included local civic leaders, members of the press, stockholders and comedian George Jessel.

However, the real story of KBTV starts back in 1951 when owners of radio station KVOD and a group of Denver businessmen formed the Colorado Television Corporation and laid plans to build a transmitter on Lookout Mountain and apply for a license for Channel 9. In a joint statement in their request for a license, they stated, "We intend to put the accent on public service and will always make our facilities available to every worthwhile cause as well as offer a facility for the airing of political and important controversial matters of the day." On July 11 the FCC granted Colorado Television Corporation a license for Channel 9 and Denver viewers got their first taste of TV with the October 12, 1952 broadcast of "The Jack Benny Show."

While the station still stands at Eleventh and Bannock Streets, its studio has been significantly expanded and modernized since its early days housed in this former Packard dealership building.

Much of the expansion and modernization of the station must be

The chance meeting of KBTV's John Mullins (left) and Bill Zeckendorf on a train ride in 1956 resulted in a profitable partnership for Channel 9.

laid to the talents and creative marketing strategies of Oklahoma businessman, John C. Mullins, who moved to Denver and purchased Channel 9, an ABC affiliate, from the Colorado Television Corporation in 1955.

Through an acquaintance with Oral Roberts, and a chance meeting with real estate tycoon, William Zeckendorf — aboard a train bound for Cheyenne Frontier Days — Mullins was able to obtain financing to improve and strengthen the station in the 1950s.

Over the next decade, Mullins turned his energies to acquiring additional

broadcasting facilities in Little Rock, Arkansas. He also put Denver's first "all news" radio station, KBTR, on the air, purchased the Barbre Production Company, and added outdoor electric and sign companies to his corporation. Mullins died in 1969, and in 1972, KBTV was sold to Combined Communications Corporation of Phoenix, Arizona. At that time, Alvin G. Flanagan was named president of CCC's broadcast division. Flanagan held the position continuously — with only a title change to that of president of the Gannett Broadcasting Group following the merger of Combined Communications with Gannett Co., Inc., in 1979.

During the seven year period of ownership by Combined Communications, Channel 9 made significant impact upon and inroads into the Denver market by being first on the scene both with technical advances and with innovative programming of public affairs and news. KBTV offered the first hour-long news broadcast; put Sky 9, the first Denver news telecopter in the air; installed the first ColorRadar weather-scanning equipment, including the only wholly-owned weather satellite feed; and opened the first full-time television news bureaus in northern and western Colorado.

Mindful of the original incorporators' commitment to community service and public access, Channel 9 annually produces documentaries ranging from hour-long specials on Colorado's energy problems, to public opinion polls and the consumer protection news feature, 9 Wants to Know.

In addition, the station sponsors two statewide events of special interest to Coloradans: "9 Who Care," which honors nine outstanding volunteers selected from hundreds of nominees at an annual televised awards banquet, and the "9 Health Fair." This year nearly 10,000 medical and non-medical volunteers provided free health screenings to 55,000 people at 176 sites in communities across the state.

Now, 29 years after the "All is Fine at Channel 9" headlines and innumerable advances in the industry, television viewers in the Rocky Mountain region testify to KBTV's modern-day motto — "It's all right here on Channel 9."

The former home of KBTV-Channel 9.

KOA Radio

A leading source of news, sports and information since 1924

At 8 p.m. on December 15, 1924, KOA Radio went on the air in Denver, Colorado. The opening broadcast featured music by the Public Service Company of Colorado "Saxaphone Band," numerous speeches and musical solos. The inaugural program proved a little too much for the transmitting tubes and an interval of two minutes followed while the

Krameria Street studios and transmitter.

station went off the air temporarily, "to let them cool off."

Founder of the station was the General Electric Company which termed its Rocky Mountain Broadcasting Company a public service. The avowed purpose of the new radio station was "to serve with special intimacy the states that lie in the great plain — from the Dakotas and Minnesota to Texas — to the Mississippi and beyond, to spread knowledge that will be of use to them in their vast business — to further their people's cultural ambitions — to give wider play to their imaginations and make melody in their ears — to bid them lift up their eyes unto these western hills whence comes new strength."

The early day statement went on to say, "Also, to those of The Great Divide, who in little scattered communities are adding to the nation's wealth, the voice of KOA will bring news of the nation's doings, the strains of its music and the measure of its dance, the message of its teachers, the thrill of its drama and an opportunity to unite in the worship of the Church.

"Thus KOA will add to the intellectual, artistic, and spiritual value of the gift that it offers on behalf of the Rocky Mountain States; thus it will strengthen the links of the chain with which Radio Broadcasting binds together the distant places of the earth."

After 56 years of public service in broadcasting, the high purposes stated are still the basic aims of the station.

The first license issued to KOA by the Department of Commerce, the forerunner of the FCC, was for a frequency of 930 kilocycles, 322.4 meters, with an antenna input power "not exceeding 1,000 watts." Since that original grant, KOA has experienced several changes in power and frequency. Its present 50,000 watt transmitter was authorized in 1934.

On February 22, 1927, KOA broadcast a special program, through the facilities of the National Broadcasting Company, honoring Washington's birthday. It was the first network program for the station. On February 3, 1928, KOA officially became an NBC affiliate, an association that lasted until KOA affiliated with the Columbia Broadcasting System in March 1976. In addition to CBS news and sports programming, KOA is the leading source of local news, sports and information for listeners in the vast expanse of territory served. KOA's play-by-play sports broadcasting includes Denver Broncos, Nuggets basketball and Bears baseball.

Known as "The Voice of the Rocky Mountain West," KOA's listeners have responded from every state in the union and from many foreign DX (long distance) fans.

On October 1, 1929, the National Broadcasting Company took over the operation of KOA by lease from General Electric. Until this time, KOA had been housed in a special building at East Fourteenth and Krameria streets. This structure (see photo) was the first in Denver to be specially designed and built for radio broadcasting — one of the first in the nation to be so constructed — containing offices, studios, and the

KOA's first mobile unit in the early 1930s.

transmitter... all under one roof.

On April 7, 1930, the license was assigned to NBC, but GE ownership of the plant continued until NBC bought the transmitter from General Electric in 1941. On December 15, 1934, a decade after the founding of KOA, the studios and offices in the NBC building at Sixteenth & California streets were officially opened. The new KOA home boasted of studios that "floated" within the walls and became known as "Denver's Radio City," patterned after the parent company's Rockefeller Center studios in New York.

A brochure of the period states that "KOA... insures every listener of the

best entertainment the nation affords — three networks — the Red, the Blue, and the Orange." This was before NBC was required to dispose of the Blue Network (now ABC) and the Orange which was a regional group of stations.

Then on March 29, 1941, KOA was reassigned from 830 kilocycles to its present 850 khz. wavelength.

A few months later the United States entered World War II, and KOA plunged into the war effort with special servicemen-interview shows, Red Cross fund-raising drives, war bond drives and virtually every method of keeping listeners fully informed of progress in the war.

KOA's first "sister station," KOA-FM was established on Channel 239 on a frequency of 95.7 megacycles March 12, 1948. A few years later the station was moved to 103.5 where it is today. Known as Q-103, the FM station has become a major contemporary station in Denver.

In June of 1952 the Metropolitan Television Co. purchased KOA from NBC. The board of directors is now composed of several Denver and California businessmen, including Bob Hope, long an entertainer over the NBC network.

Just as it promised, KOA continues to "bind together the distant places" through its radio voice.

KOA-TV

A solemn obligation to serve

During 1952 and through much of 1953, the television license for KOA was debated in comparative hearings between Metropolitan Television Company in conjunction with Hope Productions, Inc. and the Myer family of Denver, owners of KMYR Radio. The Myer family contested Metropolitan's purchase of KOA from NBC, claiming that 50 percent of the station would be owned by Hope Productions, rather than by local people. There was some criticism of the fact that Bob Hope, one of the owners of Hope Productions, was in the entertainment business, but contrary to many comparative hearings before the FCC today, there was no attempt at defaming the character of any of the parties involved. Late in 1953, Metropolitan Television Company, headed by William W. Grant, won FCC approval. Grant — a business leader and humanitarian of long standing in the Denver Community — and his associates determined to keep their affiliation with NBC.

Christmas Eve 1953 was to mark the premier broadcast on Channel 4, but on the sixth of December, fierce winter winds of 80 miles an hour toppled the nearly-completed broadcast tower on Lookout Mountain.

KOA-TV met the challenge by constructing a temporary tower. Programming that night provided Christmas specials and included an episode of "Dragnet" featuring a Christmas theme.

When Channel 4 lit up along with the Christmas lights of 1953, the new KOA-TV station had two established traditions, determination to serve its viewers and dedication to progress.

KOA's Executive Vice President Don Searle commented on the role of tradition in broadcasting, "...we feel that it is clear that the great traditions of KOA Radio are being carried foward in the dramatic new medium of television...We at KOA-TV take very solemnly our obligation to give you the best in entertainment, education and in-

A 1969 KOA-TV newsroom scene with anchorman Clyde Davis.

formation, because we know our success can be measured only in terms of your approval...."

The KOA-TV viewing audience didn't wait long to express its approval of the first color TV program broadcast in Denver. NBC Network color coverage of the Tournament of Roses Parade on New Year's Day 1954 was beamed to the KOA transmitter, which then broadcast color signals for the first time. The Denver Post newspaper called the event "...an historic first" and reported that "Anyone in Denver with a new color receiver...could see the natural colors in the parade and the actual hues of sport shirts and neckties on the sidelines."

In 1955 the current antenna was erected on Lookout Mountain 1,440 feet above average terrain, six miles west of the studio. KOA-TV operated (and continues to do so) with video power of 10,000 watts and audio power of 50,000 watts.

"Thanks for the memories" took on a new meaning in Denver when Bob Hope attended the dedication of KOA's new studios in 1959 — the first constructed in Denver for the exclusive purpose of television and radio broadcasting. The festivities also marked the addition of a television mobile unit to KOA-TV facilities, providing more flexibility in remote (on location) telecasts.

In recalling the early years of television in Denver, Mr. Grant, president of Metropolitan TV stated, "Those were the days when all TV stations were scrambling to establish an effective news format. We also worked on some public affairs programming, but there were taboos against discussing such things as birth control, abortion, and incest. In the late '50s and early '60s we began to see some changes in what types of discussions were acceptable to the public."

In November 1964, ownership percentages were reorganized in KOA's licensee, Metropolitan Television. William Grant continued as president, and Hope productions sold its interest.

Later in an FCC action on June 5, 1968, KOA's licensee, Metropolitan Television Company, was transferred from a group headed by William Grant to General Electric Broadcasting Company for $8.5 million. G.E. took control on July 31. KOA Radio and Television's licensee then became General Electric Broadcasting Company of Colorado, Inc.

The emphasis on news in the early days at KOA became stronger and more competitive in the '70s. According to the KOA-TV News Director in 1972, Jim Reiman, "GE says we have no political ax to grind. We're to present the news 'objectively'...." Early in 1976 the news on Channel 4 was renamed Newswatch 4. Vice President and General Manager Mick Schafbuch discussed the new format and logo in relation to KOA-TV's continuing quest for excellence in broadcast journalism — "We don't intend to put on phony smiles. We're going with...the best reportorial staff in the city...Content has to be the earmark. Newswatch is another way to improve on it."

KOA-TV made a name for itself in news reporting in the Denver community and became known on a national level for its excellence in public affairs. For two consecutive years, 1977 and 1978, KOA Television received national recognition through winning the prestigious Abe Lincoln Awards. KOA-TV was recognized for its innovative policies and interests concerning community affairs, and KOA-TV was the first station in Denver to make its documentaries and public affairs programming available to the public free of charge through Denver libraries.

KOA's current Vice President and General Manager Brian Cobb says, "Our interest in the community, in good journalism, and in a fair and equitable representation of community needs and concerns is a continuing one. It is an interest that increases with time and that stimulates the awareness of our inherent responsibilities to the public we serve."

King Soopers, Inc.

"Our people have made the difference" for more than 25 years

In 1944 an experienced grocer and entrepreneur named Lloyd J. King sold his interest in five Save-A-Nickel grocery stores in the Denver area to join the Navy. Upon returning in 1946, he purchased property with the intent of starting a new Supermarket Chain in Denver. Building materials were scarce, however, and King was unable to obtain a building permit. In 1947 he converted a small meat market in Arvada into the first King Soopers.

From the beginning, Lloyd's philosophy was "sell the best products, at the lowest price, and develop a positive relationship with the customer that surpasses every competitor." With these ideas in mind, Lloyd pioneered the concept of the self-service meat department in his first store, and Lloyd's people sold the idea to the public. Other chains soon followed King Soopers' lead

King Soopers operates 53 Full Service Supermarkets along the front range of the Rockies.

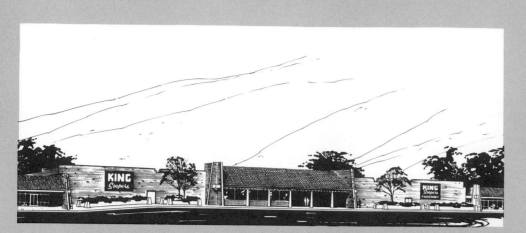

The first King Soopers' store, June 1947, at 38th and Irving in Arvada, Colorado. The self service meat department was pioneered here.

in self-service meat. This was to be the first of many consumer innovations that would, in later years, establish King Soopers as the supermarketing leader in the Denver area and as a recognized innovator in the industry.

After purchasing this third store, in 1949, disaster threatened to end Lloyd King's young company. A fire gutted his second store. A successful fire sale turned a nightmare into an opportunity to stay in business.

The year 1951 marked an important event for King Soopers when it became the first to offer trading stamps. Sales increased dramatically.

In 1957, with ten stores and an oppor-

tunity for future growth, King Soopers merged with the Dillon Companies of Hutchinson, Kansas, under King's direction as president. The support facilities for developing a large network of stores along the front range of the Colorado Rockies appeared quickly. A new grocery-frozen food-dairy warehouse was added in 1957. In 1959, the first central bakery opened. By 1963, a new produce and frozen food warehouse were added, along with a central deli kitchen.

Then in 1968, King Soopers implemented a new marketing strategy — discount pricing. Prices and gross profit margins were drastically cut. Trading stamps were eliminated, while the quality in products and service remained. The move took the market by surprise and before competition reacted, King

Soopers had established a new image as the low price leader.

Discount pricing proved to be the vehicle for accelerated growth in the '70s, with the addition of 23 more stores, a new grocery warehouse, bakery and meat processing plant complex. Additional support facilities included a new frozen food warehouse, a general merchandise warehouse, a photo finishing plant and a complete dairy operation. At the same time, many more consumer-oriented firsts evolved in the King Sooper's tradition — unit pricing, open code dating, in-store pharmacies, prescription drug price posting, generic products and optical departments.

The leadership of the company changed hands when Ray Rose became president of King Soopers, 1972-1979, and Jim Baldwin became president in 1979. Commitment to the customer, to the community, to the employee, to quality products and low prices remained intact. Discount theatre and ski tickets appeared, along with coupon exchange centers, aluminim can recycling and electronic scanning to carry on the consumer-oriented aluminum tradition.

With 53 stores and 11,000 employees in 1980, King Soopers ranked as the second largest employer in the state. For more than a quarter century, the reason for King Soopers' success is best described by the company motto, "Our People Make the Difference."

Howard Lorton Galleries

Family-owned furniture store became focal point of design excellence

Every New Year's Eve for 33 years, Howard Lorton, a man with innovative merchandising ideas, boarded a train at Denver's Union Station bound for the furniture markets in Grand Rapids and Chicago. It was part of his philosophy of doing business to keep in touch with the best sources in the home furnishings field and to provide a very personal kind of service to his customers. His was the first furniture store in the area to have an interior designer on the staff. Lorton and Robert Kuykendall, an accomplished designer, were the only members of the firm when it was founded in 1927. Today, with William Lorton Cook, grandson of the founder as president, there are 43 employees including eighteen designers.

Howard Lorton came to Colorado in 1908 from Roodhouse, Illinois. When he

Howard Lorton Galleries, Speer Boulevard and Acema, 1927.

Entry of show house with interior design by Howard Lorton Galleries. Benefit for The Wallace Village for Children.

was 12 years old, he worked at the St. Louis World's Fair, passing out Heinz pickle watch fobs. It was there that he heard of Colorado for the first time when a boxcar of Colorado cantaloupes backed up to the fairgrounds. Young Lorton came west four years later.

Initially, he was in the camera business in Denver. Later he began a career in furniture merchandising at the Denver Dry Goods Co., where he was buyer for five years.

When he began planning for a furniture store of his own, Lorton first considered a location on Wazee in the heart of downtown Denver. Then, to the surprise of some businessmen of the twen-

ties who considered it "out in the country," he chose the site at Speer Boulevard and Acoma. The land-filled property (a former city dump) looked anything but promising as a business location. But from the first, Denverites found the quiet, leisurely atmosphere appealing. Lorton's was one of the first businesses to move out of the downtown area.

Two years after the store opened came the stock market crash. The business survived day-to-day with a few loyal customers. Bill Lorton, son of the founder, joined the business in 1930. He worked closely with his father in all phases of the business until he died in 1960 at the age of 49.

Obtaining merchandise was difficult during the war years. It was not until after the end of World War II that the turnaround came and the business began to prosper. Expansions in 1947 and 1962 more than tripled the store's floor space.

William Lorton Cook, grandson of Howard Lorton, joined the firm in 1960. He had been studying architecture and had not intended entering the family business. He came to Denver to help out when his uncle, Bill Lorton, died. When his grandfather died less than a year later, Cook took over as president with his mother, Lois Lorton, as vice president. The arrangement continues today.

Under Cook's leadership, growth has been steady and substantial. A new Lorton store was opened in Colorado Springs in 1979 following the acquisition of a well-known design studio. A third of a block of near downtown Denver property at Broadway to Lincoln on Twelfth Avenue was purchased in 1978 with

room for expansion. The summer furniture annex, warehouses and workrooms are located there.

The firm is a strong supporter of the arts and contributes its services to charitable events such as the annual Denver Symphony Guild Show House Benefit, National Jewish Hospital LPGA Pro-Am and the Classic Chorale. Howard Lorton Galleries in 1977 was presented the Denver Advertising Federation's Fame and Fortune award "in recognition of its record of achievement in successfully building one of Colorado's outstanding organizations through sound advertising, selling and merchandising; further, in bringing credit to Denver and the Rocky Mountain region through excellence of its service."

Cook is active in civic affairs. He has served as president of Denver's Advertising Review Council and the Rocky Mountain Better Business Bureau. He also has been involved in statewide marketing affairs as chairman of the Colorado Retail Council.

Today, Howard Lorton Galleries continues as a family business with a close working relationship with the country's most prestigious furniture manufacturers, including Baker Furniture Company since the early '30s and Henredon Furniture, Inc. since 1947. The firm's philosophy remains the same as that stated in the opening announcement in 1927: "Here will be displayed the results of our thorough search of the markets both East and West for objects of interest for the home" and "Personal service is the foundation upon which we hope to build a long-lasting and happy relationship..."

Martin Marietta Denver Aerospace

Titan missile manufacturer evolved into one of nation's leading space centers

Denver Aerospace is the space center for the Martin Marietta Corporation. Established in 1955 (by what was then the Martin Company) to build the Titan I ICBM for the U.S. Air Force, the firm has since evolved into one of the nation's principal industrial contractors for launch systems, spacecraft and instruments, and command and information systems.

Even before the Titan I program was completed, the Air Force awarded Denver Aerospace a contract in 1960 to design and build a second-generation ICBM. Designated Titan II, the still-

operational weapon is the largest and most powerful ICBM in the U.S. arsenal.

The power and reliability of the Titan II made it the logical choice as the launch vehicle for the Gemini manned space program. On March 23, 1965, astronauts Virgil Grissom and John Young — aboard the spacecraft Molly Brown — were lofted into orbit by a Titan II launch vehicle, the first of ten manned space missions launched by the Titans.

The successes of the Gemini program and the development of the Titan III launch vehicles encouraged Martin

Marietta to broaden its activities into space exploration. There have been about 120 Titan IIIs launched since 1964, including the twin Viking spacecraft to Mars, the two Voyager exploratory spacecraft to Jupiter and Saturn, and the two Helios satellites put in orbit around the sun.

Beginning in 1966, Denver Aerospace helped design Skylab, the nation's first space station, launched in 1973. Its mission was to study the earth's resources, geophysics, the upper atmosphere, the stars, the sun, the physical effects of long-duration space flight on the crew, manufacturing in space, and equipment to help man work in space.

Martin Marietta also built and outfitted the multiple docking adapter, the control and display equipment for the earth resources experiments, and the Apollo telescope mount for Skylab.

On July 20 and again on September 3, 1976, the United States landed the Viking spacecraft on Mars, a major milestone in man's exploration of the solar system. These small machines, guided by human genius and the physical laws of the universe, made the eleven-month, 440-million-mile voyage to land on a planet less than half the size of earth.

Martin Marietta was the principal industrial contractor to NASA for the Viking landers, scientific experiments, mission integration, and the Titan III/Centaur launch vehicles.

Martin Marietta is also building an improved version of the Titan III for the Air Force, called the 34D. This launch vehicle will serve the Air Force during the transition to the Space Shuttle and will provide an emergency backup to launch top priority defense payloads.

The assembly, test, and system support contractor for the Air Force's fourth-generation ICBM — Missile X — is Martin Marietta. The mobile system is intended to be hidden in a widely dispersed complex of shelters to create targeting difficulties for would-be attackers.

As prime contractor to NASA for the mammoth external fuel tank for Space Shuttle, Martin Marietta is also building a manned maneuvering unit that will give Space Shuttle astronauts a propulsion system for free flight in space during extra-vehicular activity.

Denver Aerospace's command and information systems product area is the

Martin Marietta's space center southwest of Denver.

outgrowth of nearly two decades of experience in hardware, computer software and electronics development. These techniques are applied to intelligence processing systems, electromagnetic environment simulators, automatic test equipment, military communication systems, and the checkout, control, and monitor subsystems for the Space Shuttle.

The company has also built a wide variety of scientific instruments such as the SCATHA satellite, the space sextant, a faint-object spectrograph for the large space telescope, a cloud analyzer for a Jupiter probe, and a solar wind analyzer.

In 1980, Denver Aerospace had nearly 12,000 employees on its payroll, with approximately 7,500 in the Denver

area. More than 2,400 of the others were in New Orleans at NASA's Michoud facility building the Space Shuttle external fuel tank; about 1,200 were assigned to Vandenberg Air Force Base, working on Titan, MX, and Space Shuttle; and approximately 500 were assigned to the Kennedy Space Center for the Space Shuttle and Titan programs.

The economic impact of Denver Aerospace in Colorado for 1956 through 1979 included salaries of nearly $2 billion, $85 million in taxes, and $355 million in expenditures. Gifts and grants to area charitable, arts, and educational institutions amounted to nearly $1 million as well.

With its more than 400 active contracts, Denver Aerospace finds itself, at the beginning of the decade of the '80s, more flexible, resilient, and prosperous than at any other time in its 25-year history.

May D&F

Merchandising empire built on vision of a dreamer

The May Company was founded in the Colorado Rockies more than a century ago by David May. Born in Germany in 1848, May was destined to become a merchandising giant. The fundamentals were taught by his father, the proprietor of a modest store. At the age of fifteen, on his parents' insistence, David May set out for America — that fabulous land where everyone was free to express himself and free to advance just as far as his own ability and hard work could carry him.

Not totally alone in America, May

settled in Cincinnati to work for his uncle in a clothing factory. His continued interest and enthusiasm in the merchandising field led him to a store in Hartford City, Indiana, where in a year he increased sales from $20,000 to $100,000. In return the store owner gave him one quarter interest. And thus began David May's dream of becoming a merchant prince.

After nine dedicated years, his health was weakened when he saved his merchandise from a fire. His only hope in avoiding tuberculosis was to move to

the dry climate of Colorado. Little did he know this move would become an important stepping stone in his life.

While on a fishing trip high in the Rockies, May heard about the discovery of silver ore in nearby Leadville, a small mining camp. After several weeks of mining, he concluded that his 'mine of fortune' was nothing more than a hole in the ground. He then decided to pursue his lifelong dream.

In 1877 he opened his first store in a canvas shack to sell copper-riveted overalls and red woolen longies to miners. Leadville became the largest silver camp in the world and David May opened "branches" in Pueblo, Cripple Creek and other Colorado mining communities.

On a visit to Denver in 1888, when the mining boom was winding down, May bought a clothing store. That same afternoon there was a brass band in front of the new May store and a crowd inside, buying heavily at bargain prices.

As the Denver May store expanded, David May and three brothers-in-law partners (Louis, Moses and Joseph Shoenberg) subsequently moved to two other cities with the acquisition of relatively small stores which were to grow into major department store operations — Famous-Barr Co. in Saint Louis and The May Co. in Cleveland.

The partnership continued until The May Department Stores Company was incorporated in 1910. May common stock was listed on the New York Stock Exchange early in 1911, and the company has paid continuous quarterly cash dividends ever since — longer than any other department store company listed on the New York Exchange.

May Company of Colorado opened its first branch store at University Hills in 1955. One year later a central distribution facility was built to handle receiving, shipping, distribution and delivery.

A significant year was 1957 — the Colorado May Company acquired Daniels and Fisher, a home-owned company which catered to the elite of Denver and Colorado Springs. This prompted the name change to May D&F. Now a historic landmark, the D&F tower still stands and is undergoing renovation. In 1958 May D&F moved to its new downtown location at Sixteenth Street and Tremont Place, where it has become an integral part of a retail, hotel and parking complex.

The 1960s were growth-oriented for May D&F with the addition of four branch stores — Westland, Bear Valley, North Valley and Colorado Springs. The '70s saw the completion of three more locations — Fort Collins, Southglenn and Aurora Mall, to bring the total to nine.

Over the years, May D&F has stood in support of the Denver community and its arts and humanities. May D&F's Downtown Plaza has been host to an endless variety of events. May D&F has also offered support to the Denver Center for the Performing Arts, the Denver Art Museum, the Heart Fund, United Way, Children's Hospital, the Children's Diabetes Foundation and many other worthy causes.

Today, May D&F and its 2,100 employees serve the merchandise needs of

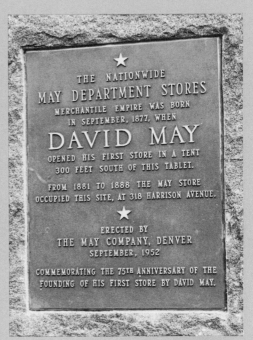

Marker in Leadville, Colorado commemorates the site of David May's first store.

more than one million people. They follow a retailing philosophy which founder David May summarized in these words. "We gave value and kept faith, so purchasers became customers and customers became friends. And there you have the secret of any success in a nutshell."

May believed in advertising. Here, every window of the store bears the legend "$11 Suit Sale."

The A. E. Meek Trunk and Bag Co.

A family tradition for more than 100 years

The Civil War had just come to a close, gold and silver had been discovered in the Rocky Mountains, Leadville was just being incorporated, The Central City Opera House was opening and the first telephones were about to be installed in Denver. In this invigorating spirit of progress, A. E. Meek opened a small trunk and valise factory at Fifteenth and Water Streets, under what is now the Sixteenth Street viaduct. In the late 1860s, three brothers of the Meek family (eight brothers and two sisters) came to Denver from Canning, Nova Scotia, drawn by what they had heard about the area's climate, mountains and attractiveness. Originally school teachers, they liked what they saw and remained to become businessmen in the city of Denver.

Arthur Edmund Meek — a great uncle of the present owner Rupert M. "Mick" Meek — saw that the miners and other settlers in the area mostly carried their possessions in gunny sacks and the carpet bag of Civil War fame. His chance of success, Meek felt, lay in providing these pioneers with sturdy luggage. From this modest beginning, the A. E. Meek Trunk and Bag Co. grew to supply the region with leather valises and trunks of all descriptions.

In 1891, A. E. Meek was joined by his brother L. B. Five years later, in 1896, they expanded to the heart of the retail district, relocating the store at the corner of Sixteenth and Lawrence Streets. After the death of A. E. Meek in 1898, the company incorporated and continued to grow. In 1905, with the addition of the youngest brother, Rupert C. Meek, a new factory was built at 24th and Curtis Streets. In the years following, the company gained national recognition for the quality and durability of its handmade trunks and valises. By 1924 it employed more than 50 people.

In 1921 Rupert C. became president and in 1932 the retail facility was moved to 1035 Sixteenth Street. It remained there until it was destroyed in the Jacobson Building fire in the summer of 1946. The same year, after returning from Air Force duties of World War II, Rupert C. Meek Jr. assumed controlling interest of the business. He sold the factory on Curtis and reopened at 1544 Broadway primarily as a retail store, keeping the best craftsmen to do custom manufacturing and repair work. The golden era of the large specialty trunk was rapidly being replaced by the manufacture of light-weight hand luggage, more suitable for the developing air travel industry.

R. M. Meek, representing the family's third generation in the business, joined the firm in 1969. Shortly afterward, a second location was opened at Cinderella City in Englewood. With the advent of Regional Transportation District

The firm's retail facility and general offices at 1616 Stout Street, 1976.

(RTD) and the Sixteenth Street Mall concept, the main store was moved to its present location at 1616 Stout in the fall of 1976. Since then additional branches have been opened — in Colorado Springs in 1977 and Ft. Collins in 1979.

From these modest beginnings, The Meek Luggage Co. prospered, supplying the Rocky Mountain region with simple carrying cases as well as other custom merchandise. Some of Meek's more interesting custom orders ranged from a matched set of carpet-covered, dome-topped trunks for H. A. W. Tabor's first wife, to a trunk designed to carry 98 pairs of shoes, each in a separate compartment, and a unique club bag made from an entire alligator. The bag won a blue ribbon in the 1893 Chicago World's Fair.

Luggage, however, is not the only business in which the Meeks have participated over the years. Often the luggage store was just a place from which the other brothers ran their businesses. One brother, Fred D. Meek, had a grocery store just off Sixteenth Street at the turn of the century. Leonard B. Meek was extensively involved in real estate in the Denver area, including the development of Barr Lake for northeastern irrigation.

Today, the A. E. Meek Trunk and Bag Co. — never more than one-half block from Sixteenth Street in over a century of business — offers the finest in luggage, leather goods, business cases and gifts. It operates a complete repair facility to service merchandise, and Meek craftsmen custom manufacture specialty items.

The A. E. Meek Trunk & Bag Company remains one of Colorado's pioneer businesses. The Meek family — originally attracted to Colorado for much the same reasons that continue to draw people today — continues its significant contributions to Colorado's business and philanthropic community.

The A. E. Meek Trunk and Bag Factory in 1909.

Steel and the queen city of the plains grow up

The Midwest Steel & Iron Works Company started as a small ornamental shop in 1894. It has since developed into a large and efficient organization for the fabrication and erection of structural steel.

The original location of the company was the old Cyclorama building on Champa Street. The firm soon moved to 1521-1523 Stout Street because of increasing demands for space. Continuing expansion necessitated a move in 1906 to Nineteenth and Blake Streets.

In 1910 Albert G. Fish moved to Colorado and bought a majority of stock in the Jackson-Richter Iron Works Company. On January 17, 1911, Fish was placed on the board of directors and elected president and general manager. Martha Richter served as vice president and Ira C. Bower as secretary.

The company continued to expand its capabilities and personnel and become instrumental in the growth and development of Denver. Fish was active in the Chamber of Commerce, The Manufacturers Association, and other civic groups. In July of 1916, the company's board of directors voted to donate money to the Militia Fund of the Denver Civic and Commercial Association for the various departments of enlisted men of the Colorado National Guard.

When World War I began, Ira Bower left the firm to serve with the U.S. Army Corps of Engineers as an officer. Shortly after his return in 1919, the board of directors discussed changing the name of the company due to the anti-German feelings in the country. So on October 1, 1919, "The Midwest Steel & Iron Works Company" became the firm's legal name in the state of Colorado.

Additional land was acquired in 1922 from the Brown Iron Works Company. The 25 Larimer Street address is the present site of the company offices and

The company's suspension bridge over the Royal Gorge, near Canon City, Colorado, is one of the most unique constructions in the Mountain States area.

Plant No. 1 — visible from the Colfax-Larimer viaduct just to the west of Interstate 25.

A fabricating shop in Pueblo, Colorado — near the Colorado Fuel and Iron Works Company's Mill — was completed in April 1928. It is the present site of Plant No. 2.

During the first year of the Depression, business continued without much difficulty. In 1933, however, the officers of the company reduced their salaries. The federal government — thru the National Recovery Act — progressed on the Fabricators Code, raising wages for shop employees in 1933 and 1934. By June of 1934, business had improved and the company was once again ready for expansion.

When the United States became involved in World War II many men left

the company to serve in the armed forces. John Lumpp, who later became treasurer, served with General George Patton's Second Armored Division in North Africa, took part in the invasion of Normandy and the Battle of the Bulge.

In July 1942 the company entered into a contract with the U.S. Navy to manufacture parts for escort vessels located at Mare Island, California. Other contracted defense projects were Fort Francis E. Warren in Wyoming, Fort Logan, Lowry Field, and Buckley Field in Denver and Camp Carson in Colorado Springs.

In January of 1944 The Midwest Steel & Iron Works Company was awarded the Army Navy "E" for excellence. Its production of hulls for "landing craft, tanks" had carried U.S. troops and equipment ashore in landings in the South Pacific and on the shores of the Mediterranean. In appreciation for the efforts of the company, Mr. Fish received the "E" for excellence from Commander William E. Howard in a ceremony attended by former Governor Carr and Mayor Stapleton.

In June of 1947, Albert G. Fish passed away. Burton W. Melcher was elected president, Frederick G. Fish vice president, William E. Geer secretary, and William E. Bower treasurer.

By the end of 1953 an additional plant was operational — at 48th and Fox Streets — for the heavy fabrication of large steel bridges along the interstate highway system. That facility is today's Plant No. 3.

Upon the resignation of President Burton Melcher in January 1957, Frederick G. Fish became president, William E. Geer vice president, John Lumpp treasurer, and William E. Bower secretary.

Nine years later, in June 1965, the Platte River flooded, leaving Denver in

Midwest Steel & Iron Works Co. operating force in 1940.

total chaos. Eight to ten feet of water flooded the company's office and Plant No. 1. To compensate, a temporary office was set up at the Albany Hotel. After the water had receded, two feet of mud and debris covered the entire lower level of the office and plant. It took three months to repair the damages of about $250,000.

As the old made way for the new in the 1970s Midwesteel's® fabricated steel could be seen in Denver's rapidly changing skyline.

This was also a period of growth within the company. New advances in the construction industry brought challenges in fabrication and finishing techniques. The addition of experts in structural steel fabrication to Midwesteel's employ resulted in a present staff of five registered engineers and seventeen structural steel detailers. The company erects most of its fabricated buildings.

Today the Midwest Steel and Iron Works Company looks forward to the 1980s — the decade of its 90th anniversary and the celebration of 90 years of contributing to the growth of the Queen City of the Plains.

Mile High United Way, Inc.

Pioneering innovation strikes rich vein of community spirit

What we know today as the United Way began in Denver, in 1887. The concept has spread to 23 hundred communities in the United States and Canada, plus a dozen countries overseas.

The idea began with four Denver clergymen when Denver began its growth along the banks of Cherry Creek and the South Platte River. Reverend Myron W. Reed, Monsignor William J. O'Ryan, Dean H. Martyn Hart and Rabbi William S. Friedman recognized their city's welfare problems and the need for cooperative action and decided to work together on a plan for organizing the community's resources.

The result of their efforts was the establishment, in 1887, of the Charity Organization of Denver. In its infancy, it had 23 participating agencies and raised $21,700 its first year.

The Charity Organization grew slowly for six years, then suffered some setbacks in the Panic of 1893. It continued, however, until 1914, when the community looked toward even more inclusiveness and the Denver Federation for Charity and Philanthropy replaced the Charity Organization.

Seven years later, in 1921, the Denver Chamber of Commerce recommended formation of a Community Chest. Under the new umbrella organization were the members of the Federation and numerous other charitable agencies.

The Community Chest moved forward through the '20s and '30s and then

In the depths of the Depression, United Way made a positive approach in its 1934 Campaign Appeal by this poster painted by Walter Beach Humphrey.

became known as the War Chest with the outbreak of World War II. Following the war, the name Community Chest was re-adopted and the counties of Adams, Arapahoe, and Jefferson joined Denver in a four-county unified effort.

In 1952 a study of charitable giving by the Chamber of Commerce resulted in the formation of the Mile High United Funds. This involved one fund drive for the Red Cross, several health agencies, and those agencies already under the Community Chest umbrella. To avoid confusion and supplemental fund drives by the three partners, the trio came together as the Mile High United Fund, incorporated in 1957.

The Boulder United Fund joined in 1961, and the Longmont United Fund brought the northern half of Boulder County under the umbrella of the Mile High United Fund in 1966. All five metropolitan counties were now part of the fund.

The name United Way, accompanied by a new hand and rainbow symbol, was adopted in 1969. The name of Colorado's largest voluntary organization was officially changed to Mile High United Way, Inc. in 1973.

The tremendous growth in population and area served prompted the Mile High United Way to relocate its headquarters. In 1976 the headquarters moved to donated office space in the Inverness Business Park. Upon leaving the downtown area, an outreach office in downtown Denver was created to provide information and volunteer services.

Since 1887, the contributions raised in the Mile High community have risen dramatically. A record $12,402,215 was raised through the 1979 annual fund drive. These funds went to help 76 human care agencies throughout the five-county metropolitan area.

In the Denver of the 1880s there was a spirit of neighbor helping neighbor. That spirit fostered the Charity Organization of Denver and is the very foundation of today's Mile High United Way. The spirit of voluntarism is not only the foundation of the United Way, but the state and nation as well.

Mountain Bell

'Galvanic muttering machine' came early to bustling, growing town

The telephone was less than three years old on February 24, 1879, when service for 161 subscribers began in Denver.

The Denver Telephone Dispatch Company was founded by Frederick O. Vaille, who had procured a license to lease telephones patented by Alexander Graham Bell. The Denver exchange was the first between the Mississippi Valley and the Pacific Ocean.

The fledgling service was greeted with some skepticism by local reporters, one of whom termed the device a "galvanic muttering machine." Another newspaper article was headlined, "The Line Open." It read: "The telephone was in working order yesterday, and the line was well patronized. After the novelty of the thing has worn off, the operators will be able to get some rest."

The company's first headquarters location was in the 1500 block of Larimer Street. Subscribers were on ten-party lines and paid $5 a month for business service and $4 a month for residences.

In 1881 Vaille's business was incorporated as the Colorado Telephone Company. It bought several smaller telephone companies and in 1890 moved its headquarters to 1441 Lawrence Street. A new building at 1421 Champa Street was completed in 1903 and remained as headquarters until 1929, when the present headquarters building was finished at 931 Fourteenth Street.

The late nineteenth and early twentieth centuries were times of growth and expansion for the company and the region. By 1888 the number of customers in Denver had increased to a point where telephone poles were almost 100 feet tall and carried as many as 400 wires.

The year 1911 was a critical one for the company. In July, Colorado Telephone

A turn-of-the-century pole-setting crew in front of the old corporate headquarters at 1421 Champa Street.

merged with the Tri-State Telephone and Telegraph Co. to form Mountain States Telephone and Telegraph. Later that year, Mountain States bought Rocky Mountain Bell, which operated in Idaho, Montana, Utah and Wyoming. Finally, acquisition of the Overland and Arizona Telephone companies expanded Mountain States' service area to nearly what it is today.

Also in 1911, the first line between Denver and New York City was completed. Three years later, the first transcontinental line was finished, with the final splice being made in Wendover, Utah, in Mountain States territory.

Dial service was introduced in 1929, when the company had 180,000 phones in Denver. The Great Depression caused a net loss of 70,000 telephones between 1931 and 1933.

Mountain Bell's corporate headquarters building shortly before it was completed in 1929.

World War II brought new demands for service, but also forced the company to grant military leaves to 1,100 employees.

As the war ended, demands for service reached unprecedented levels. At one point, the company was holding 13,000 requests for service that couldn't be filled even though construction crews were fighting to keep up with the demand.

Growth has continued. Today, Mountain Bell — the fastest growing operating company in the Bell System — serves one-quarter of the land area of the continental United States in seven states and a portion of Texas. It employs about 46,000 people and serves more than 7.5 million phones. The big challenge for the future — changing from a monopoly purveyor of a utility service to a competitive firm offering a wider range of products and services.

C. A. Norgen Co.

Dedicated to setting the pace for industry

The early history of the C. A. Norgren Co. is the story of a promising young engineer and his struggle to develop a small business venture into a progressive and vital industry.

Carl A. Norgren was born in Riverside, South Dakota on November 21,

First C. A. Norgren Co. plant, located at 222 Santa Fe Drive.

1890. He attended and received engineering degrees in electrical and mechanical engineering from the University of South Dakota.

After several successful jobs in South Dakota, Nebraska, Utah and Washington, Norgren moved to the town of Rifle, Colorado for health reasons. After six years of ranching in the high

country, his health improved and in 1925 he and his wife, Juliet, moved to Denver.

Norgren developed a small hose coupling and set up an assembly operation in the kitchen of his basement home. He and his wife, made couplings in the morning and went out to sell them in the afternoons. When sales of couplings grew, they moved the business to a building at 1159 California Street.

But progress was not made without struggle. On numerous occasions the Norgrens had to sell household furnishings and personal belongings to get the capital needed to keep the business running.

As early as 1916, Carl Norgren had an idea on how to lubricate air operated equipment. However, it was not until 1927, while visiting a General Motors plant in Detroit, that his now famous "Norgren Oil Fog Lubricator" became a reality. The theory of automatically applying lubrication directly into the air stream worked, and by 1930 fog lubricators were being built in small numbers.

With the industrial acceptance of the "oilfog" principle, the Norgren Company seemed to have developed a base for success. Just as things looked brightest, shades of the Depression plunged the firm into a difficult struggle for survival.

Twice the company had to use all its

resources to expand. Consequently, it had no financial backlog to carry it through hard times and it was finally sold to a Chicago holding company. After many months of depression, the holding company discontinued business and closed the doors on the fledgling Norgren Co.

In 1932, still believing in their dreams, the Norgrens reorganized the firm. They petitioned the courts to reacquire the company and during the next four years managed to pay off their local creditors and place the company on a sound operating basis again.

In 1936, the first plant specifically designed for Norgren Manufacturing was built in Denver. In the next twelve years seven additions were made to the plant, more than tripling its size.

World War II brought a burst of interest in and a new demand for Norgren products. In 1951 the company again had to move to new quarters, a gleaming new factory and office building in Englewood. Again in 1957, with the development of increased business and expanding markets, the company faced the need for more space, so a 30-acre site in Littleton was acquired and a zinc die casting and manufacturing facility built there.

While still maintaining the Englewood plant, another facility was constructed at the Littleton site and in 1964 the two plants were consolidated into the present location. Like all the other

First Norgren Co. assembly plant located in the basement of residence at 1935 Kearney Street.

Present C. A. Norgren Co. plant at 5400 S. Delaware Street, Littleton, Colorado.

plant sites, this one has seen addition after addition. By June of 1980 the factory had increased to 196,000 square feet of floor space.

Carl A. Norgren died in 1968 after a lengthy illness, but the company he founded continued to grow and prosper under the leadership of his son, C. Neil Norgren, who became president in 1962.

In the tradition developed by his father, C. Neil Norgren continued to seek out new and innovative ideas to make the company an ongoing success. He expanded and broadened the employee benefit program and maintained that the greatest asset of the company was its people. In 1970 he established a four-day work week for all employees.

Under the leadership of Norgren management, the company continued to make major contributions to industry and growth by expanding its worldwide activity. Manufacturing/joint venture licensees or distributors have been established in most major countries of the world.

In 1973 the company was acquired by IMI Ltd., a large British metal manufacturing company. The acquisition by IMI did not affect the status of Norgren employees, management operating practices or policies, but added financial strength to its operation.

Today, Norgren — devoted exclusively to the production of compressed air accessories — has one of the largest plants and the largest industrial operation of its kind in the world.

From its inception the C. A. Norgren Co. has developed an outstanding reputation for sound financial operation and product integrity and it is proud of its contribution to the growth and development of the metropolitan Denver area.

Olinger's

First and foremost a commitment to service

Olinger's Englewood.

In 1890 John and Emma Olinger came to Denver from Santa Fe, New Mexico, and started what is today the Olinger Mortuaries. From their home and business location — in a store building at 2409 Fifteenth Street — the couple's mortuary practices varied greatly from the more sophisticated procedures of the current day. No embalming was done. Instead, ice was used to preserve the remains until the funeral — which usually lasted a full day. The hearse was horse drawn and the funeral director dressed formally, wearing a top hat and white gloves.

John and Emma had one child, George, a remarkable son whose vision and energy made an impact on Denver that has rarely been equaled. Founder of the Highlanders — a group of young boys in Denver who played instruments and marched in precision formations

Olinger's at 29th and Wadsworth.

during World War II — young Olinger made a lasting contribution to his parents' business.

After his father's death in 1902, the young man and his mother devoted much to the business and, in 1908, built a mortuary up the hill at Sixteenth and Boulder Streets. In the following two decades they developed the organization into the foremost mortuary in the Rocky Mountain area.

Olinger was responsible for several advancements in his field over the years, including the founding in 1917 of the National Selected Morticians, an organization which now has members in foreign countries and of which he was president from 1917 through 1919.

Joseph E. Bona, who came to the organization in 1910, later bought eight-tenths of the business. He was joined in the venture by Frank W. Farmer and Martyn H. Temple, who each bought one-tenth. George Olinger in 1920 began development of Bonnie Brae, Welshire, Indian Hills and Crown Hill, to name a few. Olinger sold his interest in 1925 to the organization responsible for these developments and returned to the mortuary, under contract to Bona.

The Olinger Mortuary continued as a family enterprise when Olinger's daughter Gwendolyn came into its employ in 1929. A recent graduate from the University of Denver, she worked side by side with Francis Van Derbur, whom she married on June 13, 1930 and who is currently president of the organization.

Unable to make the required payments to Joseph Bona in 1930, Olinger and Bona reversed their contract but agreed that Olinger would remain president. Bona persuaded Van Derbur to stay and work for him and in 1944 turned the business over to Van Derbur.

Mildred L. Robins, hired by Bona as organist in 1931, is today executive vice president; Ray Harris, Gwendolyn Van Derbur, and Gene Steinke are vice presidents.

The Yeager Mortuary at Speer and Sherman was acquired by Olinger's in 1930. In 1951 Olinger's built at East Colfax and Magnolia and in 1952 took over the Englewood Mortuary at 2775 South Broadway. The firm's fifth mortuary was then built at 29th and Wadsworth in 1970.

Although Crown Hill Cemetery is owned by a Texas corporation, Van Derbur owns the Tower of Memories Mausoleum in its center.

Other interests of the organization include the Olinger Life Insurance Company, founded in 1957, which specializes in funeral benefit policies.

The organization's determination to provide quality service through the years has contributed to its recognition today as a foremost mortuary in the Denver area.

Porter Memorial Hospital

Healthful lifestyle still key goal of unique medical center

The hospital was envisioned by pioneer Denver businessman Henry M. Porter.

A 45-cent refund more than half a century ago led to the founding of a major Denver medical institution.

Porter Memorial Hospital, today a multimillion dollar health care center, was a gift to the community from pioneer Colorado businessman and philanthropist Henry M. Porter. He was impressed with the treatment he received at a California hospital — Paradise Valley Sanitarium, near San Diego — when he fell ill on a West Coast vacation in 1928.

After his discharge from the hospital, operated by the Seventh-day Adventist Church, he was surprised to receive a letter from the institution's credit manager. Enclosed was a check for 45 cents, with an apology for the inadvertent overcharge discovered after Porter settled his account.

Forty-five cents was hardly a significant sum even in 1928. Porter's interest and respect, already aroused by the caring concern he had noted among those who helped restore his health, grew to embrace a bold plan characteristic of "Denver's grand old man," as he was known.

"Can you give me," he wrote to Harley Rice, the credit manager, "the address of the general manager of your various corporations? I would like to correspond with him in regard to establishing a like institution in Denver."

Subsequent correspondence with church officials culminated in a gift of $315,000 and 40 acres of land on which to build a 100-bed hospital. The institution, known then as Porter Sanitarium and Hospital, opened in February 1930. Its original, three-story brick building still stands, though largely obscured by more modern additions.

Although it provided full general hospital services from the outset, the new institution on Denver's southern outskirts reflected a progressive health philosophy common to numerous "sanitariums" operated by the Seventh-day Adventists. Patients frequently entered the sanitarium to stay for several weeks, believing that tensions would be released and their health enhanced by the restful surroundings, vegetarian diet, vigorous physical therapy regimen, and personal counseling afforded by the sanitarium experience.

Over the years, changing economic and social conditions shifted the emphasis at Porter to acute hospital care, and in 1969 the name Porter Memorial Hospital was legally adopted to reflect its modified character. A new name, however, detracted nothing from the institutional commitment to preventive medicine and education in healthful lifestyles.

This unique mission of helping Denver citizens stay well found new fulfillment in a wide range of community health education programs that have since been emulated by hospitals everywhere. Nearly 20,000 participants have benefited from the Five-Day Plan to Stop Smoking, begun at Porter in 1965 as the country's first hospital-based smoking cessation clinic. Weight control, stress management, nutrition, alcohol awareness, physical fitness, and other practical health subjects are regularly taught by the hospital's staff of professional health educators.

Porter continues to advocate a natural diet, high in nutritional variety and low in fats and animal products. Its popular cafeteria, open to visitors as well as the 1,200 hospital employees, features a completely meatless menu. In recent years, however, patients have been given the choice of attractively prepared meat entrees or vegetarian meals.

A new era began with the decade of the 1970s in Porter Memorial Hospital's service to the community and national leadership in health care. An agreement

Its tranquil setting belies the round-the-clock activity of this major medical center.

with nearby Swedish Medical Center provided for the merger of their separate medical staffs into one combined organization, and for the development of shared services and joint planning on a scale unprecedented by any similarly "competitive" institutions anywhere.

By setting aside institutional egos in favor of the highest interests of community health, Porter and Swedish created a service system that was hailed as a model for cost-effective health planning in every urban area. Their consolidated specialty services, by concentrating skilled personnel and eliminating needless duplication, provide documented savings of millions of dollars yearly and helped establish both cooperating hospitals as referral centers for patients from much of the West and Midwest.

The vision of Henry M. Porter and the support of thousands of friends in the ensuing years make it possible today for Porter Memorial Hospital to carry on its historic mission, *To Make Man Whole.*

Presbyterian/Saint Luke's Medical Center

A century of service in the Rocky Mountain empire

The history of Presbyterian/Saint Luke's Medical Center is contained in the development of two separate medical facilities that finally merged in 1979.

Saint Luke's Hospital had its beginnings when John Franklin Spalding, the newly elected Episcopal bishop of Colorado, came to Denver from Erie, Pennsylvania with his wife and five children in February 1874. Early in his tenure, Bishop Spalding realized the "great need for a church hospital." Through his efforts, Saint Luke's Hospital was incorporated on February 12, 1881 under the sponsorship of the Episcopal Diocese of Colorado.

In June 1881, the Grand View Hotel on Federal Boulevard in North Denver was purchased for $7,000 and renovation began on what would be the 60-bed hospital.

It soon was obvious that the hospital needed a site close to the center of the city, and land was purchased at the current location of Nineteenth and Pearl Streets. In spite of a city ordinance prohibiting the construction of a hospital within city limits, supporters of the hospital persevered and a new facility was dedicated on October 18, 1891, at a cost of $74,000.

In 1903, the Greek cross was adopted as the symbol of Saint Luke's Nursing School. But the American Red Cross protested the use of the symbol in 1919. The board of managers, however, argued successfully that Congress had not given the Red Cross exclusive right to use the Greek cross until 1905. Accordingly, the red cross continues to be the graduate symbol of Saint Luke's School of Nursing.

During the difficult post-World War I era, Dr. Isaac B. Perkins, a member of the Saint Luke's Hospital medical staff, became strongly committed to the idea that the city needed more hospital beds. Dr. Perkins, a devout Presbyterian and one of Denver's busiest surgeons, approached the leaders of his church who eventually rallied to the cause of building an additional hospital. The cornerstone of Presbyterian Hospital was laid on June 26, 1921.

The site of the new hospital was just eleven blocks east of Saint Luke's on "Grasshopper Hill," a place that traditionally had been the scene of family outings and where fishermen searched for grasshopper bait. It was March 26, 1926 before the hospital opened, providing 148 adult beds and 22 nursery beds.

A further commitment to nursing education was pledged, and a school began training nurses in 1925 before the new hospital was even ready.

After the Depression and World War II years, the hospital experienced several expansions. The School of Nursing's Dawson Hall opened in 1951; a bequest from Senator Samuel D. Nicholson helped finance a new wing in 1952. An especially memorable year was 1959, marking the completion of the East Wing, the Ira J. Taylor Isotope Laboratory, Park Manor retirement residence, and the North Wing. The hospital's West Wing was completed in 1967.

In the 1970s Presbyterian expanded its commitment eastward with the opening of the 134-bed Presbyterian Aurora Hospital on January 8, 1975.

After several months of intensive preparations, Saint Luke's Hospital and Presbyterian Medical Center merged in July 1979 to become Presbyterian/Saint Luke's Medical Center. The reasons for the merger were manifold, but particular benefits were seen in the areas of cost effective operations, the combination of clinical services, and the increased magnitude of the role which the Medical Center could play in the health planning and regulatory areas.

The Medical Center is now providing in excess of 3,000 jobs and is one of the

The Pathology Laboratory in Presbyterian Hospital during the institution's early years. An early hospital brochure boasted "The equipment is the most modern of scientific apparatus."

A St. Luke's Hospital ambulance in 1897. The next advance was a two-horse ambulance.

top 30 corporations in the state. With well over 1,000 beds, the Medical Center's overriding mission continues to be providing for the health care needs of both business and the community. These responsibilities are typified by such programs as the Senior Citizen's Health Center, the Alcoholism Recovery Unit, the Environmental Care Unit and a network of outpatient clinics in the metropolitan area, as well as in the mountain areas west of Denver.

Public Service Company of Colorado
First Denver utility before Colorado statehood

The first man-made illumination at the confluence of the South Platte River and Cherry Creek, site of the present Denver, was probably an Indian campfire. By the time the great Pikes Peak gold rush got under way in 1859, Denver City was already in existence, overlaying the Saint Charles townsite claimed earlier on the north bank of Cherry Creek. Across Cherry Creek to the south was Auraria. Candles provided the light in those early communities.

A decade later, on November 13, 1869, seven years before statehood, Denver's first utility company was incorporated for the purpose of lighting city streets. Eight prominent businessmen signed the papers of incorporation for the Denver Gas Company in the original offices of the *Rocky Mountain News*, at what now is about 1555 Larimer Street.

On September 20, 1870, crews began laying gas lines, and construction began on huge coal-retort ovens at Eighteenth and Wewatta for manufacturing gas. Gas for the street lights began to flow in a two-mile line later that year. A year later, in 1871, there were eight and a half miles of gas line in use. Denver and its needs were expanding rapidly.

The first electric utility in Denver came into being February 21, 1881. The aim of Colorado Electric Company was to wrest the street-lighting business from the gas company. And it did, but not until 1885.

The first electric-generating plant in Denver was built at 21st and Wewatta streets. That plant's 250-horsepower Wright steam engine can still be seen today on the grounds of Public Service Company of Colorado's Valmont Electric Generation Station near Boulder. "Old Sally" stands as a monument to Colorado's electrical pioneers.

The Daniels and Fisher Department Store, only the tower of which remains at Sixteenth and Lawrence streets, was the first structure to be commercially arc-lighted in 1881. By 1885, Colorado's capital boasted eight iron towers, ranging from 150 to 250 feet in height, used for street lighting. Each of the "lighthouses of the plains" had eight 3,000-candlepower arc lamps. They continued in use only until 1891.

In the meantime, the gas company turned its attention to household lighting and cooking.

Gas and electric companies proliferated during the 1800s. By the end of the decade, all the electric companies had merged into the Denver Consolidated Electric Company. In 1891, the gas companies did the same, producing Denver Consolidated Gas Company. All gas and electric service was brought under one roof with the incorporation of the Denver Gas and Electric Company in 1899, thus eliminating wasteful duplication of facilities and manpower. This produced lower costs of operation and more favorable rates to consumers.

The state was in a depression in the 1890s, but economic vigor revived after the turn of the century. Denver's population increased 90,000 in the new decade, reaching a total of more than 213,000.

Principal source of power in Denver at the time was the Lacombe Station, now the Zuni Station, at Thirteenth and Zuni streets. Some 52 "benches" of coal-retorting ovens produced more than 3.6 million cubic feet of gas per day by 1910. The night sky glowed with the flames belched from the giant retorts.

By 1911, all gas and electric service was being provided by Denver Gas and Electric Light. Its headquarters were in the Gas and Electric Building at the corner of Fifteenth and Champa Streets, now called the Insurance Exchange but still sporting 13,000 exterior lights — infrequently lit.

Gas and Electric Building (now Insurance Exchange) at Fifteenth and Champa.

Across the state, similar consolidations took place. Economy of operation improved with central generation and integrated power-transmission systems. By 1924, the bulk of the state's utilities had been gathered under one management, Public Service Company of Colorado. Its headquarters were also in the Gas and Electric Building.

Today, Public Service Company of Colorado serves more than two thirds of the gas and electric needs of Colorado. The histories of the state and company are closely entwined. Each has profoundly influenced the other.

Headquarters for the state's largest utility company are now at 550 Fifteenth Street, just about one mile from the place where the waters of Cherry Creek and the South Platte still meet and mingle.

Employees of Denver Gas and Electric Company around turn of the century.

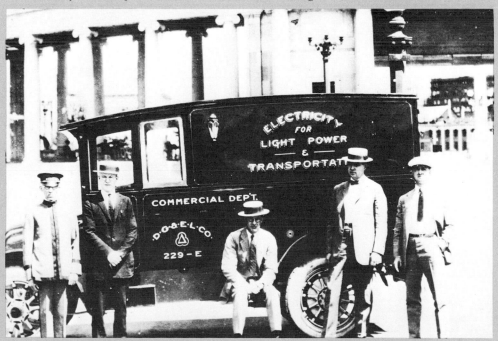

Robinson Dairy

Five generations later, family dream continues

The history of America is the history of countless other places. It is a history of distant cities, towns and isolated countrysides...and the aspirations that were born there; a history of hope, crossing oceans and continents, to find the land where opportunity was equal to the spirits that challenged it.

And so, of course, the history of America is, most accurately, a history of great dreams...and very small beginnings.

You can ask any member of the Robinson family about that. They all know the modest origins; they are all, five generations later, continuing to enrich the great dream.

In 1885, Lewis Robinson brought his family from the recesses of eastern Europe to a location nearly as remote. They arrived in the foothills of the Rockies, and put down their roots in an area now known as Lakewood, Colorado.

Lewis Robinson, with his two sons Morris and Hyman, then proceeded to do what Lewis Robinson did best...with an eye to doing it as well as he could, and better than most.

The family began to farm. And to milk cows. The farming they did for others — creating from their heritage a new enterprise in the new world.

Robinson Dairy Farm prospered, and shortly after the turn of the century, the plant outgrew the boundaries of the Lakewood acreage.

Under a new name, Climax Dairy, the Robinsons built a new downtown Denver headquarters and processing plant.

Robinson Dairy general office, 2401 West Sixth Avenue.

In this location, the business grew until, in 1929, it attracted the attention of, and was purchased by, a larger national company.

Proceeds from the sale, however, went right back to work. Hyman's son, Sam, started a new dairy, naming it Gold Seal Dairy. Sam nurtured Gold Seal to success using what had become the family trademarks — quality and service, morning, noon and night.

Sam sold Gold Seal five years after starting it, but remained in an executive capacity until 1947. In that year, two generations of Robinsons joined forces to launch the family's fourth Denver dairy business, and mark the fourth generation of Robinsons to take part in Lewis Robinson's dream.

Sam's sons, Richard and Edward, went to work with their father under the banner of Robinson Dairy. Today Robinson Dairy is one of the largest independent dairies in the Rocky Mountain area, with customers from Cheyenne, Wyoming, south to Pueblo and throughout the mountains. And Richard, as president, and Edward as executive vice president, have brought a fifth generation of Robinsons into the business. Richard's son John works at the dairy part time while attending college; Edward's daughter Emily does the same, while attending high school.

The main facility of Robinson Dairy is located on the banks of the South Platte River, just west of downtown Denver. In addition, there are Robinson sales branches in Colorado Springs and Silverthorne. From the Silverthorne branch, Robinson serves the needs of

From left, Sam Robinson, Richard Robinson and Edward Robinson.

Colorado's continually expanding ski and resort areas.

Robinson's product line maintains the highest quality in dairy products, including milk, cream, yogurt, ice cream and more. Robinson's recently completed ice cream facility is one of the most modern and best equipped anywhere.

The dairy markets its consumer products through supermarkets and convenience stores. But Robinson also does a major institutional business, serving restaurants, hotels, hospitals, airlines and vending companies. The institutional division has gone an extra length in continuing the family tradition of non-stop service. It does business 24 hours a day, seven days a week, 365 days a year.

While the Robinson family business has made a substantial mark in Colorado, the Robinson family itself has contributed equally significantly. Sam and Edward Robinson serve on the board of the National Jewish Hospital and Research Center and The National Asthma Center. Richard serves on the board of the AMC Cancer Research Center and Hospital, having previously been its president for three years. The Robinson family members have been frequent recipients of civic and professional awards.

Richard and Edward are graduates of Colorado State University with degrees in Dairy Science. Their father Sam attended the University of Colorado.

As the 100th anniversary of the Denver family Robinson's dairy business nears, the dream that began with Lewis Robinson has found its way into the fifth generation of Robinsons who are carrying it forward in ways even the original family dreamer would never have dreamed of.

Rocky Mountain Empire Sports, Inc.

Professional sports in a big league city

Early in 1947 Will and Eddie Nicholson — unrelated but both prominent Denverites and long-time friends — formed Rocky Mountain Empire Sports, Inc., secured a franchise in the newly revived Western League, and presented professional baseball in antiquated Merchants Park.

After one dismal season, the entire operation was sold to the Howsam family of Denver. Bears Stadium, with an initial capacity of 13,000, opened in August of 1948. Almost overnight, the Denver Bears became a major attraction for area sports fans and established minor league attendance records that still stand unchallenged.

As interest in minor league ball dwindled over the years, the Howsams took the bold step of diversifying, with the acquisition of one of the eight franchises in the new American Football League. The Denver Broncos were born. The first year, 1960, was even less successful at the box office than on the field, and the Howsams were forced to sell to a syndicate headed by Gerald H. Phipps and Calvin W. Kunz. Included in this purchasing group was Gerald's brother Allan.

While the new ownership saved both baseball and football for the community, four years of substantial losses led to total disenchantment of all but the Phipps brothers. The final resolution of the resulting internal problem was acquisition of virtually 100 percent of corporate ownership by the Phipps in February 1965.

Tremendous fan support followed quickly, but was not matched by success on the field. While the 1966 merger agreement between the long-established National Football League and the fledgling American Football League increased fan enthusiasm, defeat in March 1967 of a metropolitan district bond issue to replace Bears Stadium (expanded by 1960 to a seating capacity of 35,000) with a 50,000 seat facility left the future of both Denver Bears and Denver Broncos in doubt.

Enter a consortium of citizens' groups, organized into one high-powered committee that within months raised some $1,600,000 in corporate and individual contributions. The funds were turned over to the City and County of Denver, which purchased Bears Stadium from Rocky Mountain, and then floated a $3,000,000 revenue bond issue to expand renamed Denver

Mile High Stadium to a capacity of 50,000. A $25 million bond issue approved in 1974 brought capacity to 75,000 in 1977, with every seat for every regular season game sold for ten straight years.

Slowly but steadily, the football franchise matured. Finally, in 1973, the Broncos produced a winning season, losing a division championship and play-off spot to Oakland in the season's final game. Meanwhile, though still suffering from the minor league label, the Bears continued to provide top level baseball with consistently contending teams, including league champions in 1971, 1976, and 1977.

Qualifying for the NFL play-offs in each of the past three years, places today's Broncos among the most feared and respected organizations in the National Football League. The high point in corporate history was reached in 1977 with an American Conference championship and a valiant though losing effort against Dallas in Super Bowl XII. At this writing, the Bears have achieved the best won-lost record in all of organized baseball, with attendance at the highest level in more than twenty years.

Bears Stadium shortly after it opened in 1948 with seating capacity of 13,000 (right).

Denver Mile High Stadium in 1978 (below).

With a physical facility in all respects meeting major league baseball standards, it is only a matter of time before Denver takes its rightful place in the "bigs," at which point Rocky Mountain Empire Sports will discontinue its baseball operations. In the meantime, the organization is dedicated to providing the very best in triple A entertainment to Denver area fans.

As far as football is concerned, a quality organization, unrivalled fan support, and the beginnings of a winning tradition assure the permanence of the Denver Broncos as an important element in the well-rounded community that is Metropolitan Denver.

The popular Robert "Red" Miller has entered his fourth year as Broncos head coach with the enviable regular season record of 32 wins against 12 losses. He is supported by an able board of directors and officers of the corporation.

Rose Medical Center

A growing tribute to the community

In the mid-1940s, population growth in Denver propelled a group of concerned physicians and community leaders to fulfill the need for a new hospital on the east side.

One community leader, Maurice B. Shwayder, was given the responsibility for the fund-raising drive to finance the construction of the institution. He generated financial support through charity events highlighted by appearances of such celebrities as Jack Benny, Eddie Cantor, Al Jolson and Danny Kaye.

In 1945, General Maurice Rose of Denver — commander of the Third Armored Division and the first to cross the German border and capture a German town during World War II — was killed by a Nazi bullet. It was decided that the new hospital should bear his name. On August 14th, 1946 ground was broken for the main building of General Rose Memorial Hospital.

August of 1948 brought General Dwight D. Eisenhower to Denver to lay the cornerstone for the 250-bed, nonprofit hospital. On March 1st, 1949, General Rose Memorial Hospital opened its doors.

Today, those familiar with the hospital on East Ninth Avenue know it as Rose Medical Center. This name change symbolizes the growth of the center from a community hospital to a major health care institution.

Rose expanded its licensed capacity to 400 beds in 1964, building a new north wing to house the addition.

In 1966, Dr. Abe Ravin, a distinguished cardiologist of international reputation, established Colorado's first coronary care unit at Rose. Rose was also the site for the first coronary arteriography performed in the region. In 1980, the hospital's Division of Cardiovascular Medicine was named in memory of Dr. Ravin.

Rose was first again in 1975, building the Joe and Betty Alpert Arthritis Treatment Center, the only such center devoted exclusively to patient care in the field of arthritis and related rheumatic diseases in the Rocky Mountain region. It has recently been designated by the federal government as a regional center for arthritis treatment.

New labor and delivery suites were constructed in 1976. In addition, a ten-unit intensive care nursery was opened to offer life support and emergency care to newborns and "preemies" in critical condition. Working with the University of Colorado Health Sciences Center, Rose established a nurse-midwifery program. And 1980 saw the start of a prenatal diagnosis program including new, complete genetic counseling services, amniocentesis and chromosome analysis.

The Department of Pathology serves every patient who enters the hospital. It doubled in size in 1978 to occupy most of the lower level of the newly-built west wing. The new wing also provided space for expanded Emergency and Outpatient departments. In 1980, the west wing was named The Alice Levy Pavilion.

Rose Medical Center, a neighbor of the University of Colorado Health Sciences Center, is located on the northeast edge of the university's campus. But the relationship goes beyond mere geography. Rose is the primary private hospital affiliated with the university for post-graduate training. Hundreds of university medical students have received part of their post-graduate residency training in various medical specialties at Rose.

From its very beginning, Rose Medical Center has been committed to serving the needs of a growing community.

Rose Medical Center, 1980.

It is one of the few hospitals experiencing a steady increase in births, recently nearing 3,000 a year.

Dedicated to comprehensive patient care, clinical research and education, the medical staff at Rose fully utilizes its skills and devotes time and effort to such community programs as the

General Dwight D. Eisenhower lays the cornerstone for General Rose Memorial Hospital, 1948.

Mountain Plains Outreach Program, public and professional education seminars and charity care to indigent patients.

On August 31, 1948, General Dwight D. Eisenhower said of the hospital — "I have the very great honor and privilege of dedicating this hospital to the spirit among all the people of this great community — the spirit that has erected this building in the recognition that the community must perform its own tasks if we are to endure."

With the support of the community, Rose Medical Center is now a major health care organization. General Eisenhower's statement echoes today and Rose continues to meet the challenges of fulfilling the expanding health care needs of Denver and the Rocky Mountain region.

Frederick Ross Company

A proud history of leadership in commercial real estate service

When Frederick R. Ross started his real estate and investment firm in 1888, Denver was still a very young city with vivid memories of gold and silver strikes in the mountains to the west. Electric cable cars had just been introduced in Denver... Baby Doe and Horace Tabor were the talk of the town... and the city's new facade of wealth included the elegant Windsor Hotel on Larimer Street and the magnificent Tabor Grand Opera House on Sixteenth Street.

It was in this bustling, often rough-and-tumble atmosphere that Ross opened his first, three-man real estate office in downtown Denver. Now, as the Frederick Ross Company approaches its 100th anniversary, more than 100 employees are engaged in all aspects of commercial real estate service, working from corporate headquarters in the brand-new, 29-story Energy Center on Denver's Seventeenth Street.

Like many others before and since, Frederick Ross came to Denver for his health. He was 23 years old when he moved to Colorado from Waterford, Vermont and entered the real estate business as a member of the firm of Hill, Sage & Ross. In just two years, he formed the Ross Investment Company — which later became the Frederick Ross Company.

Ross entered the property management field in 1909 and quickly established a successful reputation for refurbishing run-down buildings and turning them into attractive, economically-sound units. A short time later, he acquired a partner — a young, one-time rent collector named Cyrus Hackstaff — and the two proceeded to blaze new trails through the fledgling Denver real estate market.

In Hackstaff's words, the pair "did very well" in the Roaring '20s. Although they stayed with real estate, not stocks, the boom-like aspects of the times prompted the partners to put their

The Guaranty Bank Building at Seventeenth and Stout Streets was one of several downtown Denver office buildings managed by the Frederick Ross Company since the 1920s.

money into safe investments. Their conservative nature paid off when the Great Depression of the 1930s hit Denver and the rest of the nation. Says Hackstaff, "We were sitting comfortably, not indebted to anybody."

The team of Ross and Hackstaff survived the Depression and went on to change the real estate map of Denver. They marketed home sites near the Denver Country Club, sold building lots in the vicinity of Colorado Women's College, and helped develop a residential area known as Hilltop in east Denver.

Not only were they successful in business, Ross and Hackstaff set an example as civic-minded citizens. Both men served on the Denver Water Board, were active in the Chamber of Commerce and spearheaded development of the city's public library system. In his will, Ross directed the bulk of his estate to finance construction of four branch

Many of the major office tower buildings in the Denver metropolitan area — pictured here on Seventeenth Street — are leased and/or managed by the Frederick Ross Company.

libraries in Denver. Hackstaff was an early supporter of Children's Hospital and one of the founders of Downtown Denver, Inc.

Over the decades since Frederick Ross' death in 1938, the company has continued to expand and flourish. In addition to management and acquisition of commercial properties, the Ross Company led the luxury apartment building boom in east and southeast Denver; was awarded the city's first urban renewal contract to develop the Avondale Shopping Center in 1962; and prepared for the postwar surge in new office building construction which changed the face of downtown Denver during the '60s and '70s.

Cy Hackstaff retired as honorary chairman of the board, passing direction of the company to his sons, Robert and Allan. In its near-century of service to the Denver metropolitan area, the Ross

Company established a leadership position in office and retail leasing, investment and industrial real estate sales and property management.

As the Denver commercial real estate market fairly "explodes" in the early 1980s, the Frederick Ross Company finds itself at the center of activity, managing and leasing many of the city's largest and most prestigious office towers — Lincoln Center, the First of Denver Plaza, Energy Center, Pavilion I & II, the soon to be completed ARCO Tower — plus scores of smaller office, industrial and retail buildings.

Other divisions of the company are involved in major investment property sales to local institutional and foreign investors, many of whom have a stake in the energy boom which is reshaping Denver's role as the economic capital of the Rocky Mountain West.

All of these accomplishments — guided by a young, dynamic management — are the result of a business philosophy established long ago by Frederick R. Ross. It is amplified by current president, Robert P. Hackstaff, who sums up the challenge to his profession this way: "The stakes are very high in commercial real estate. Nothing less than total performance with absolute integrity will do."

Saint Joseph Hospital

The hospital that grew with Denver

In 1873, when Denver was little more than a dot on a territorial map, Mother Xavier Ross of the Sisters of Charity of Leavenworth, Kansas, sent four sisters to the frontier establishment for hospital work with this challenge: "Look forward for what good is yet to be." With these words, Saint Joseph Hospital, Colorado's first private hospital, was born.

The sisters opened their hospital in a cottage at Fourteenth and Arapahoe streets but soon moved to a brick building at 26th and Holladay, later renamed Market Street. Since this was a short distance from Denver's active red light district, someone mentioned that it was a questionable neighborhood for a hospital. "We'll take the question out of the neighborhood," replied one of the sisters.

The hospital's first patient, Denis O'Morrow, was admitted September 22, 1873, and died one month later of typhoid at the age of 26. Thirty patients were admitted that first year. Of these, eleven were victims of typhoid fever, a killer for many years. Insanity, acute alcoholism, rheumatism, pneumonia, gun shot wounds and "hurt in the head" were also frequent diagnoses.

During these early years the hospital was known as Saint Vincent's. This was changed to Saint Joseph in 1876 when the sisters began construction at Eighteenth and Humboldt Streets on land donated to them by territorial Governor William Gilpin. This site is directly adjacent to the hospital's present location at 1835 Franklin Street.

The first building on Humboldt was a three-story structure accommodating 80 patients. The sisters not only nursed the sick but did the laundry, cooking, scrubbing and fund collecting. Nursing consisted of such common procedures as purging, sweating and bloodletting. Leeches or poultices of soap, sugar and flaxseed were applied to draw out infec-

This 1963 picture shows Saint Joseph's original towers in the shadow of the impressive new twin structures. The old towers were razed to make way for future additions.

tion. Surgery was performed in the kitchen, and sterile technique was unknown.

As Denver grew, so did Saint Joseph Hospital. Construction of the administration building with its famous twin towers — for many years a Denver landmark — began in 1899. The people of Denver raised $10,000 for this building with a "gigantic city-wide bazaar," and a "monster euchre (whist) party," planned by none other than Mrs. J. J. (the Unsinkable Molly) Brown.

Extensive equipment was installed during these years, including a brass sterilizing machine, reputed to be the first of its size west of the Mississippi. X-ray equipment was also added — a remarkable accomplishment since the procedure had just been discovered in 1895.

Throughout the following decades, Saint Joseph Hospital's primary mission continued to be excellence in patient care. Continued construction and addition of equipment to meet patient needs reflected this vital mission. Ground was broken in 1961 for the hospital's current twin tower structures, which were dedicated May 31, 1964. Construction was accomplished in two phases — first, the present towers were built, then the old twin towers were demolished. More recent additions of the old building were remodeled and utilized as part of the new structure.

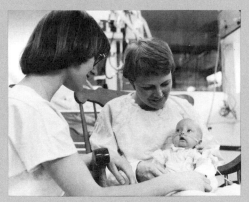

Saint Joseph nurses help parents learn special ways to care for babies in the Intensive Care Nursery.

Saint Joseph began its second century of health care with ground breaking ceremonies September 22, 1972, for new surgery and outpatient department facilities. The hospital's latest major addition, completed in 1977, is the Radiology/Cardiovascular annex, housing the newest and most modern facilities in the mountain states region.

Today, Saint Joseph Hospital is a 551-bed private, non-profit, regional medical center, providing acute care to more than 23,000 patients annually from Denver, Colorado, and neighboring states. Nearly 900 physicians comprise the hospital's medical staff and 73 resident physicians assist in patient care 24 hours a day through residency programs. The hospital is one of the top fifteen employers in Denver and has a strong economic impact in the community.

More than 200 head and body scans are performed each month by Saint Joseph's radiology department. Over 300 open heart surgeries are performed yearly, and the cardiovascular laboratory runs diagnostic tests on more than 1,000 people each year. The hospital also has one of the largest newborn nursery populations of all Colorado hospitals and is designated a regional high-risk maternity care center.

Saint Joseph's dedication to excellence in health care extends beyond patient care in the hospital. The hospital — vitally involved with community health care — provides medical services through its Family Practice Center, free health screenings at health fairs and various other community outreach programs.

Saint Joseph's story doesn't end here. The words of Sister Xavier Ross are still a vital part of the hospital's philosophy. Saint Joseph Hospital will continue to "look forward to the good yet to be" and grow to meet the challenges of decades to come.

Samsonite Corporation

"Golden Rule is guiding principle for company's success"

Jesse Shwayder considered himself just an ordinary man. He based his unusual success on his belief in self-reliance, a dedication to hard work and his belief in the Biblical Golden Rule, "Do unto others as you would have them do unto you." With this strong philosophy, but against considerable odds, Jesse Shwayder founded the Shwayder Trunk Mfg. Co. in 1910. The name was changed to Shwayder Bros. Inc. in 1931 and to Samsonite Corporation in 1965. Its modest beginnings in Denver gave no indication that the seed had been sown that would eventually yield one of the world's major luggage manufacturers, and a leading maker of furniture. Today Samsonite manufactures in ten countries and exports to more than 100 others.

During the early years the Shwayders literally had to learn the manufacturing business from the ground up. But Jesse and his four brothers — Solomon, Mark, Maurice and Benjamin — persevered in producing a distinctive and quality luggage product assuring the consumer the very best value for the money.

Following World War I, major strides were taken toward industry leadership with national distribution and the introduction of color coordinated luggage and increased attention to styling. "Samson," the company's first trade name,

Famous trademark of the five Shwayder brothers demonstrating the strength and durability of their luggage products.

signified quality and durability for which Samsonite products became known. These attributes were dramatically illustrated in an early advertisement showing the five Shwayder brothers standing together on a platform supported by just one Samsonite case. Captioned with the slogan, "Strong enough to stand on," it became the company's first trademark.

In 1924 production was organized on an assembly line basis with the installation of one of the first materials handling conveyors. To meet increasing consumer demand and offset rapidly rising freight rates, the Shwayders opened a second factory near Detroit, Michigan in 1927.

During the Depression, the Shwayders began diversifying as a result of sagging luggage sales. Their most practical and profitable endeavor was the introduction of folding card tables in 1931. Folding tables became the foundation of Samsonite's multimillion dollar Furniture Division — which today produces patio furniture, bar/counter stools, wall systems, office and reception room furniture and a variety of folding and stacking chairs and tables.

During World War II, both the Denver and Detroit plants converted production to wartime materials. Through research, Samsonite found ways to hasten production and improve quality at considerable cost savings. For this the company received the coveted "Army-Navy E" award. Improved quality control and precision manufacturing techniques were to benefit the company's consumer products as well.

Research and innovation have often played important roles in maintaining Samsonite's consistent leadership position. As a result the company has seen

Jesse Shwayder created the Golden Rule Marble as a symbol of the company's guiding principle (inset).

In 1917, the growing Shwayder Trunk Mfg. Co. moved to this three story building at Sixteenth Street and Platte in Denver (below).

many "firsts" — first to use vinyls, to promote fashion colors in luggage, to use hidden locks. The '50s brought two more important firsts: the use of magnesium and sophisticated plastics to produce lighter weight, more durable products. One of these, Samsonite's Silhouette, was introduced in 1958, and is now considered the hallmark of the luggage industry.

In 1961, Jesse Shwayder passed the mantle of leadership to his son, King D. Shwayder. Under King Shwayder's guidance the company continued to flourish. Firmly established as the industry leader in molded luggage and attache cases, Samsonite moved into the casual luggage market. Its international efforts expanded rapidly with the addition of most of its current subsidiaries, and licensees.

In August 1973, after being family-owned and operated for more than 63 years, Samsonite Corporation joined Beatrice Foods Co., as a wholly-owned subsidiary. Today, guided by Jesse's nephew, Irving J. "Bud" Shwayder, president, Samsonite Corporation continues to enjoy and expand its world leadership position in its industry. The Golden Rule still serves as the company's guiding principle.

Seal Furniture & Systems Inc.

Commitment to quality, service, value distinguishes regional leader's dynamic growth

In 1950, Mildred and Galen Seal moved from Topeka, Kansas into a 20,000 cubic-foot office supply store in Denver. Thirty years later the company is approaching a one million cubic-foot complex composed of a furnishings showroom, sales office, design office, audio visual center, drapery division and vertical storage warehouse.

The commitment to service, the positive disposition toward growth and the ability to anticipate change form the basis of success at Seal Furniture & Systems. "It was service that made us different. Everybody had the same access to the same products. We stressed next-day delivery and follow-up," says founder, Galen Seal, who also planted the seeds of growth. "We carefully studied Los Angeles and Denver before moving. We chose Denver for its growth potential."

One hundred years ago only one-tenth of all employees worked in offices. Today

over half do. Information handling, word processing, data processing, software and office landscaping are terms that didn't even exist in 1950. Seal Furniture & Systems Inc. is in the business of creating environments that help people work efficiently and comfortably. These effective working environments provide an optimum setting for the creation, transmission, storage and retrieval of information. Office systems are planned to maximize performance and reduce long-range problems and costs.

Seal Furniture & Systems works with designers, architects and management. Through its design subsidiary, Design Innovations Inc. — established in 1970 — a complete program has been developed to study the needs of each individual office to determine what systems work best. Believing that a good interior is first a functional interior, the staff of Design Innovations applies systems

Efficient, modular work stations increase performance, please employees and reduce costs.

solution expertise to work flow, communication patterns, acoustic space planning, interior architecture and aesthetics.

Seal Furniture & Systems, now under Jon J. Seal, president and sole owner, has expanded into Colorado Springs, Grand Junction, San Diego, Orange County and Los Angeles. With total sales projected at $100 million dollars in the 1980s, Seal Furniture & Systems has become the regional leader in providing businesses with enduring, task-oriented office environments.

As a supplier for one client, Seal Furniture & Systems will order and deliver 3,000 chairs, 600 tables and hundreds of miscellaneous items from more than 30 different suppliers on time and on budget.

Jon J. Seal's view of what distinguishes his company's performance is that "although computerization now helps us to get the tasks done, it is the quality and professionalism in our people that makes the difference. We are expected to advise a client on particular problems and offer viable solutions based on our resources. That means learning both business and customer needs. We are concerned about new management techniques, energy saving ideas and space allocation — not just selling a chair based on looks and price. We create values rather than promote products at a price."

Seal Furniture & Systems represents more than 300 manufacturers of office furnishings and equipment, with each supplier carefully selected for quality and value. Seal Furniture & Systems is the largest dealer in the world for Herman Miller, Inc., the pioneer in office systems furnishings.

Guided by a corporate philosophy which stresses quality, service and value, Seal Furniture & Systems was the first recipient of the American Society of Interior Designers award. The award was presented in recognition of the firm's "high professional standards

Managerial functions are facilitated in an office systems approach.

and outstanding services in the contract design field."

The growth and development of Seal Furniture & Systems parallels the expanding role of Denver and the western states. Seal Furniture & Systems' leadership in introducing new working concepts has taken it from an office supply store to a major regional company, whose growth now is branching internationally with contracts in the Middle East.

The future direction of Seal Furniture & Systems is summed up by Jon J. Seal: "In this kind of economic environment, I think the best products are the ones that prove their worth. Products should be able to prove their value in space savings, improvements in productivity of people and flexibility of settings. Management will continue to buy the best possible facilities that they can afford. That's the way we are structuring our company."

Sears

Has served the Rocky Mountain West for more than half a century

Sears, Roebuck and Co., the largest distributor of retail merchandise in the world today, had a very humble beginning in North Redwood, Minnesota, where Richard W. Sears worked in 1886 as a railroad station agent and consignment watch salesman. He opened the R. W. Sears Watch Company in Minneapolis later the same year.

The next year he moved his business to Chicago and hired Alvah C. Roebuck, an Indiana watchmaker. In 1893 the corporate name of their firm became Sears, Roebuck and Co. Sears has maintained

its corporate headquarters in Chicago ever since and, in 1973, completed construction of the 110-story, 1,454 foot high Sears Tower which, at the time, was the tallest building in the world.

During the intervening years, Sears experienced phenomenal growth under the leadership of two particularly noteworthy men. In 1895 Julius Rosenwald opened the Chicago mail order plant, thereby introducing the Sears Catalog to rural America. He formulated the unique and bold policy of "Satisfaction Guaranteed or Your

The first Sears Store in Colorado opened in 1929 at Seventeenth and Broadway in downtown Denver.

Money Back" in 1905, and later created the famous Savings and Profit Sharing Plan for Sears employees in 1916. He also developed a merchandise distribution system that has revolutionized not only retailing but the world economy in the twentieth century.

In 1924 General Robert E. Wood joined the company and opened the company's first retail store at the time when Americans began their long love affair with the automobile. He accelerated the company's entry into retail merchandising and, during a twelve-month period in 1928-29, the company opened retail stores at the rate of one every other business day. In 1931 General Wood created the Allstate Insurance Company as a wholly owned subsidiary of Sears. In 1942 he introduced Sears into Latin America and opened stores in Cuba, Mexico, 10 other Latin American countries, Canada and Spain.

As a part of this revolutionary growth in retailing, Sears built its first store in the Rocky Mountain West in 1929 when it opened a retail store at Seventeenth and Broadway in Denver, on the site where Augusta L. Tabor's home had been razed the previous year. Located literally at the crossroads of the city, during the next 25 years Sears became a focal point of sound merchandising and outstanding values in the Mile High City.

After World War II, Denver mushroomed in size and by 1954 had a population of 700,000 residents. At that time, First Avenue was a dirt road lined with shacks, wild grass and weeds that led to the City and County of Denver Landfill — the city dump. It was here, at the intersection of First Avenue and University Boulevard, that Sears opened the $3.5 million Cherry Creek Store on Thursday, August 19, 1954. The three-floor structure had more than 200,000 square feet of gross area, a 24-car automotive center and provided almost 1,100 customer parking spaces. Thousands of customers visited the new

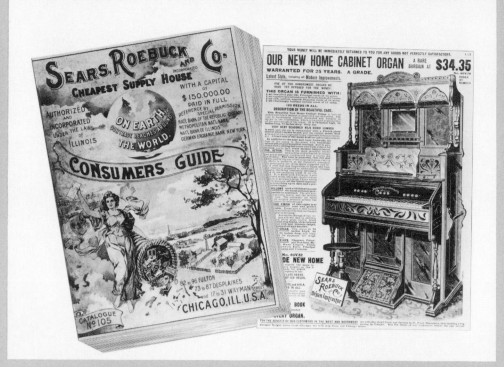

This 1897 Sears catalog confirms that the "Wish Book" provided the "one-stop shopping" of yesteryear as it does today.

store that opening day and demonstrated their desire to "Shop at Sears and Save." Sears and Denver have continued to grow and, 25 years later, that landfill with the Sears Store and the entire Cherry Creek Shopping Center find themselves located at Denver's busiest intersection, with 100,000 cars passing daily.

Today the Cherry Creek Store continues to serve Sears' customers in Denver and also houses the administrative offices for the company's entire operations in Colorado and Wyoming. In addition to five full-line retail stores, two catalog-appliance stores, and credit, service, and distribution centers located in the Denver metro area, Sears has full-line retail stores in Colorado Springs, Pueblo, Fort Collins, and

Grand Junction, and in Casper, Wyoming. Moreover, several additional stores are scheduled to open in the fast-growing Rocky Mountain area during the next five years, making Sears' Colorado-Wyoming group the most rapidly expanding segment of all the corporation's domestic markets.

By the end of 1979, the tiny enterprise that Richard Sears founded 94 years ago had served three generations of Americans, attained almost $18 billion in annual sales, operated more than 800 retail stores, 14 catalog merchandise distribution centers, and employed over 350,000 people annually. It had literally earned the slogan of "Merchant to the Millions."

During the past half century Sears and Denver have complemented each other and shared in the growth and development of the Rocky Mountain West.

Today, Sears is still the store "Where America Shops for Values." It's a story that could happen only in America.

Stearns-Roger

Diversification, performance and integrity created the nation's oldest engineer-constructor

Colorado was still celebrating the news of statehood when Tom Stearns made his first tour of this lively mining-and-cattle region. The young engineer noted an urgent need for reliable processing equipment with the technology

to produce and install it. By 1885 he was ready to launch a company that has continued his business philosophy and emphasized his integrity through a century of ever broader industry activity while concentrating on design and construc-

tion for all industries having processing needs.

In 1885, under the name Stearns-Roger Company, offices were established near the heart of Denver in the 1800 block of Larimer Street. An iron

Stearns-Roger Center Corporate Headquarters Tower at 4500 Cherry Creek Drive.

works was operating in Leadville, a better location for serving the mining camps. While John Roger ran the manufacturing plant, Tom Stearns carried on engineering and construction activities, provided sales representation of equipment distributorships, contacted prospective customers, and made the drawings necessary for designing and installing structures and systems required by ore processing and smelting clients.

In the 1890s the country had begun to accept alternating electric power as the coming energy source and Stearns-Roger was commissioned to build one of the earliest municipal power plants in Colorado, in Canon City. A commercial sugar beet industry also was developing and Stearns-Roger designed and built one of the first sugar factories in the West at Garden City, Kansas. To meet an ever-expanding need for iron and steel fabrications, the company moved the shop equipment from Leadville to a new facility in a creek bottom on the outskirts of Pueblo in 1891, the offices moving to the Engineers Building in the 1700 block of California Street in Denver at the same time.

Disaster struck Pueblo in 1921 in the form of the roaring Fountain Creek flood. The Stearns-Roger plant was destroyed like many other businesses. Some of the equipment was salvaged and hauled to Englewood for rebuilding and installation in a cooperative facility that became known as General Iron Works.

As the West grew into the oil and chemical age, Stearns-Roger added these industries to the staff expertise in power and mineral and food processing. Most of the firm's business continued to be in engineering and construction, and for such projects equipment procurement was an important service, as it continues to be today.

For a number of years Stearns-Roger has ranked among the five or ten largest firms in the design-construction field according to annual listings by a major industry magazine*. In addition to metallic ore beneficiation, food process-

ing, power generation, oil and gas processing and petrochemicals, the company engineers and builds plant facilities for such disparate fields as aerospace, water treatment, coal conversion, solar power, nuclear fuel handling, unit train loading/unloading, paper, water- and air-pollution control and consumer products manufacturing.

The company is unique in several respects. T. B. Stearns, president until his death in 1946, had arranged for his company to become totally employee-owned and operated, as it still is. Stearns was succeeded by Charles O. Voigt, first as president and later as board chairman. Donald E. Provost held these titles until 1980. Currently Wm. L. Storer is president while Provost continues as chairman of the board and chief executive officer. Under their guidance, Stearns-Roger has broken all sales records.

The Denver headquarters presently employs over 2,000 persons, more than 1,500 of whom are performing some phase of engineering work. Over 400 others are in full time field supervisory jobs, 500 more work at General Iron Works, 100 at the Englewood pipe fabricating plant and 250 at the offices and pipe fabricating plant of the Canadian subsidiary in Calgary. The Canadian company was organized in 1955 specifically to serve the growing process and piping needs of this good neighbor. All other operations of Stearns-Roger originate at the Denver headquarters, 4500 Cherry Creek Drive. The twelve-story corporate headquarters building was developed by the staff of Stearns-Roger architects, Ltd., an important part of the total company capabilities.

Although most of the company's projects are outside of Colorado, it is the state's largest engineering-constructor. Stearns-Roger has had a long and continuing impact on the development of Denver and Colorado.

Engineering News-Record.

Engineers Building at 1720 California Street was Stearns-Roger headquarters from 1891 until 1954.

Sundstrand Corporation

A story of growth and balanced diversification

The growth of Sundstrand Corporation — a multi-million dollar, international organization with two major plants in the Denver area — has paralleled the growth of the industries it serves. The company's expansion from machine tools into hydraulics, aerospace, fluid handling, power transmission, and other areas resulted from constant searching for new and better ways to serve these industries.

Sundstrand's birth in 1905 coincided with the genesis of air conditioning, automobile production and American rocketry. And, more important, the launching of the air travel age was important to its later growth.

It was against this background that inventor and machinist Levin Faust and two young toolmakers, Elmer Lutzhoff and Swan Anderson, started the Rockford Tool Company, to manufacture a small chuck for a furniture carving cutter. Four years later two brothers, Oscar and David Sundstrand, and their brother-in-law, Edwin Cedarleaf, bought a small machine shop in the same building. They eventually called it the Rockford Milling Machine Company, and later created a subsidiary, the Sundstrand Adding Machine Company. By 1926 these all merged under the name of the Sundstrand Machine Tool Company. Building on each technological development and through acquisitions, the company diversified from

Sundstrand Fluid Handling plant, 14845 West 64th Avenue, Arvada.

machine tools into machine hydraulics and fuel oil pumps.

And, just as the fuel oil pump — the first truly automatic home heating system — developed as an offspring of machine hydraulics, so did Sundstrand's eventual entry into the aviation field. Sundstrand's program of diversification had prepared it to meet the needs created by World War II, and its engineering capabilities led to the formation of an Aviation Division in 1945.

Sundstrand then developed a constant speed drive (CSD) which made possible a complete alternating current electrical system. The lighter weight system for aircraft also provided greater range and increased carrying capacity — and made aviation history.

Sundstrand constructed its present plant in 1955 at 2480 West 70th Avenue for the manufacture of CSDs and components for defense. The Denver site was chosen from among 27 potential sites.

It was named, in 1957 one of the ten best U.S. industrial plants built during 1955-56 by *Factory Management and Maintenance Magazine*, a McGraw-Hill Publication.

By 1963, Sundstrand Corporation — so named in 1959 — was making a big contribution toward positioning Denver as a focal point for the U.S. space program. Sundstrand launched a major expansion program to accommodate its increasing employee population — nearing 1,400 — and to manufacture and test a variety of new space-age products. To-

Exemplifying Sundstrand's technological and manufacturing expertise is this Electrical Power Generation System, selected for the Boeing 767/757 aircraft.

day, the plant area is more than double the original 168,000 square feet.

In later years Sundstrand Corporation centralized its research and test facilities at home base — Rockford — leaving the Denver facility to concentrate on the exacting manufacturing requirements of the aerospace industry.

The Sundyne® pump — a by-product of some of Sundstrand's space research — also contributed to Sundstrand's growth.

Developed originally for water injection on jet engines, the pump was adapted for the pumping of any liquid. It was tested in the petrochemical field, where it proved successful. By 1970, Fluid Handling was created as a separate division of Sundstrand, although it shared the aviation manufacturing facilities. In 1978, Fluid Handling moved into its new quarters in Arvada, establishing the Denver area as the home of multiple Sundstrand facilities.

Today, Sundstrand serves virtually every commercial and military airplane program in the free world with a variety of high technology components and subsystems. Sundstrand has multiple products on all the jumbo jets, the new Boeing 767/757, and the Airbus Industrie A310 — and on all the current military programs such as the F-16, F-18, F-14 and F-15. It also supplies several critical systems for the Space Shuttle.

Its 1,800 employees in the Denver area are dedicated to the quality product design, production techniques and special marketing skills needed to maintain Sundstrand's leading position as a high technology component and subsystem supplier to its entire range of customers.

United Airlines

Fulfilling its commitment to excellence in air transportation

When United Airlines inaugurated daily DC-3 flights at Denver in May 1937, putting the city on the transcontinental map, the airline was already established as the industry's largest and leading company. Four predecessor companies that eventually became United had cut their teeth on the initial air mail routes that Congress had turned over to commercial operators beginning in 1926.

Even in those days, there were a few adventurers who wanted to travel across the continent by air. Uncomfortably seated in a small compartment in a Boeing 40B, two passengers could travel on Boeing Air Transport, one of United's predecessors, from San Francisco to Chicago at a cost of $200. Another United predecessor, National Air Transport, outfitted passengers with parachute, helmet and goggles, and a seat on top of sacks of mail for the open cockpit ride on to New York for an additional $200.

United began as a management company in 1931, with each of the four carriers conducting its own operations. Two years later, a reorganization converted United from a management to a full-fledged operating company and William A. Patterson became its president. "Pat" — as he was affectionately known — became known as the industry's innovator in the ensuing three decades.

The company was the first to introduce all-cargo flights and the first transcontinental airline to equip its fleet with radar. Patterson also was the leader in development of systematic and uniform flight operations and pilot training procedures.

The first operations by United at Denver were performed by a small force of twenty employees. Since that time, the work force has grown to more than 4,000.

When World War II came along, United formed a Victory Corporation to stave off government takeover. The company contracted to provide an air transport service for the government for cost plus $1 — insuring postwar commercial aviation freedom.

United Airlines put Denver on the transcontinental air route in 1937 when it linked the city into transcontinental Route One. Here, a local passenger chats with airline personnel at United's ticket counter in Denver.

In 1943 United began training its pilot crews at Denver and 25 years later dedicated a $30 million Flight Training Center at Stapleton International Airport.

Following World War II, United expanded its route structure. Pat Patterson foresaw the future impact of the Hawaiian market and his projections paid off following the awarding of a Hawaii route by the Civil Aeronautics Board. Today it is the airline's single most important air destination.

United became the largest U.S. airline with the acquisition of Capital Airlines in 1961. The merger opened new route opportunities, particularly in the southeastern United States.

As demand for commercial passenger travel grew after the war, more employees and planes were needed. More sophisticated ticketing and reservations services were required as well, and in June 1971, the airline formally opened its W. A. Patterson Computer Center in Denver. The complex houses the carrier's nationwide "Apollo" passenger reservations sytem.

In 1969 UAL, Inc. was formed and the airline became a wholly-owned subsidiary of the corporation. The following year, the holding company acquired Western International Hotels. "Eddie" Carlson moved over from WIH to become president later that year and noted that hotels and airlines have a strong common purpose — both are in the people business.

As United grew, so did its operations at Denver. The airline opened a flight kitchen at the airport in 1941 and constructed a new $2 million food services facility at Stapleton in 1973. A new air freight facility opened in 1977.

An important step in UAL, Inc.'s corporate development occurred in October 1975, with the purchase of GAB Business Services — the nation's oldest and largest independent insurance adjustment company.

The following year, the airline observed its 50th anniversary by recreating the original flight operated by predecessor company Varney Air Lines between Pasco, Washington and Boise, Idaho.

United took the lead in supporting legislation to deregulate the airline industry, and its efforts paid off with the passage of the Airline Deregulation Act of 1978. The new law gave airlines more

freedom to price competitively and greater leeway in selecting the routes they fly.

That same year, United was awarded its first major international route when President Carter approved the carrier for a route from the Pacific Northwest to Japan.

Three of United's female pilots receive a briefing from a flight instructor before beginning a training session in a flight simulator at the airline's Flight Training Center in Denver.

Today, United is recognized in Denver not only as the largest air carrier serving the community, but also as a prime contributor to the economy of the state and the city.

Richard J. Ferris, current chairman and chief executive officer, recently told United shareholders: "We know what we want to be. We want to run the kind of airline we know how to run — a quality, financially successful longhaul airline."

United Bank of Denver

Meeting the financial needs of the West for nearly a century

On January 1, 1959, two of Denver's oldest banks consolidated to form Denver United States National Bank, which is now known as United Bank of Denver. At that time the two banks had between them 130 years of banking experience and assets of $258 million, making the new bank the second largest in Denver.

The first and oldest bank of the pair was the Denver National Bank, founded in 1884 by a group led by Joseph Thatcher. The success of the venture may be seen in the fact that the Denver National was one of three Denver banks to survive the Panic of 1893, and in the growth of its assets from $400,000 in 1884 to $8 million in 1904.

From the beginning, the Denver National Bank served individual customers as well as Colorado mining and livestock industries. A glance at the early signature books shows, along with such firms as Stearns-Roger and the Denver Dry Goods Co., "Buffalo Bill" Cody, Dwight Eisenhower, Helen Bonfils, and the Boettcher family. Denver National introduced the first commercial bank installment loan department in Denver in 1931. The bank also was one of the first Denver banks to make oil loans in the early 1950s, when most loans were made by banks outside the state.

The background of the United States National Bank goes back beyond 1904 when its charter was issued. Its most direct antecedent is the Daniels Bank, founded in 1901 by William Daniels to serve employees and customers of the Daniels and Fisher Stores, now part of May D&F.

In 1904 a group of investors bought the Daniels Bank as the basis for "a national bank properly organized and conducted along progressive and con-

The lobby of the Denver National Bank, the first bank in the area to remove the tellers' cages. Designed by Fisher & Fisher, prominent Denver architects, it was completed in 1929 and is now on the National Register of Historic Places.

servative lines..." The new bank was an immediate success. Under W. A. Hover, the first president and chairman of the board, assets reached $1 million within a month of its opening.

In 1914 it opened a separate savings department, paying four percent interest, and in 1915 was the first national bank in the area to offer trust services. Continued expansion and growth required new quarters, and Fisher & Fisher were retained to design a building, up the street from the future home

of the Denver National Bank. Located at Seventeenth and Stout Streets, it was completed in 1921.

In 1954 United States National concluded an agreement to renovate the Sears Building at Seventeenth and Broadway. This would be the first new bank building in Denver in nearly 30 years and the first bank to move out of the center of downtown. The building was finished in 1956.

That these two banks, which were neighbors for so long, should have consolidated may seem inevitable, but this was not the case. The first attempt, announced in a *Denver Post* front-page story in 1921, was probably a rumor. More discussions in 1948 were scuttled

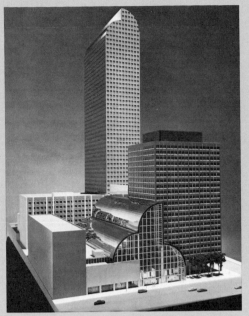

One United Bank Center, designed by Johnson/Burgee, rises behind the glass pavilion at Seventeenth and Broadway in this model.

by stockholders' hesitancies. Finally, in 1958, the details were worked out and the Denver National Bank moved to the Denver United States National Bank Center, at Seventeenth and Broadway.

One of the first statewide bank holdings in Colorado, the Denver U.S. Bancorporation, was established in 1964. By 1970 it had grown to include eight banks along the Front Range. To unify those banks, a new name and corporate symbol were adopted, and Denver United States National Bank became United Bank of Denver.

After consolidation, the combined strengths of both banks resulted in many service innovations. In 1964 what was then the world's largest motor bank was opened across Lincoln Street from the bank. Instrumental in bringing Master Charge to the region, United Bank of Denver now has more cardholder accounts than any other bank in the state. Its Guaranteed Check Card was the first such card in Denver. The

Personal Banker and Executive Banking programs originated at United Bank have been studied and imitated around the world.

Because involvement with the community was a tradition at both the U.S. National and the Denver National Bank, a Public Affairs Department was created. The bank sponsors two major regional sports events, the United Bank of Denver Marathon and the United Bank Tennis Classic. It co-sponsors with the Denver Commission on Community Relations and the Rocky Mountain News, the Minoru Yasui Community Volunteer Award. For more than 20 years the annual Fishing Derby has enabled exceptional children to experience the excitement of landing their own trout.

As the decade of the 1980s begins, United Bank of Denver, with more than 1,300 employees and assets of more than $1.5 billion, remains a forward looking bank with a sense of pride in its history.

University of Denver

Pioneer school meets changing needs of region, nation, world

The University of Denver began its 116-year history as a frontier private school of 35 students and two teachers. Today it is the largest private, independent university between Chicago and the west coast.

The University was chartered as Colorado Seminary by the Colorado territorial government on March 5, 1864. It began that fall in a single building at the corner of Fourteenth and Arapahoe Streets, near the home of its principal founder, Governor John Evans, also a principal founder of Northwestern University.

The University of Denver was established as the degree-granting body in 1880. Ten years later, the school began moving from downtown Denver to its present main campus in southeast Denver, near East Evans Avenue and South University Boulevard.

Once known as "Tramway Tech" because so many students came from Denver and either worked on or at least rode the streetcars, the university now attracts students from around the world, and Coloradoans comprise only 30 percent of its student body.

Its living alumni exceed 60,000 men and women, many of them leaders in business, the professions, education,

science, the arts and national life.

University programs have reflected the needs of a growing region. Law classes were begun in the 1890s, and now are embodied in a College of Law nationally known for natural resources, international and transportation law, and administration of justice programs.

The College of Law is the university's only remaining unit in central Denver, close to courts and agencies in which many students practice long before graduation.

The College of Business Administration, which began as did the law school in downtown buildings, is the nation's eighth oldest collegiate school of business. Founded in 1908, the college moved to the University Park campus in 1968.

One of two undergraduate colleges of the university today, the College of Business Administration includes the School of Hotel and Restaurant Management, ranked among the top three in the country, and one of the nation's first Schools of Accountancy.

The College of Arts and Sciences, the larger of the two, includes Schools of Art and Education and the Lamont School of Music.

Graduate programs are available in

Evans Memorial Chapel, surrounded by the Harper Humanities Gardens on the University of Denver's University Park campus, is the oldest Protestant church building in use in Denver. It was moved from its original downtown site stone-by-stone and reconstructed in 1959-60.

Graduate Schools of Arts and Sciences, Business and Public Management, Social Work, International Studies, and Librarianship and Information Management, as well as the College of Law and School of Professional Psychology, the latter one of only seven in the country.

More than 8,000 students currently enrolled in the University of Denver represent all 50 states, U.S. territories

241

and about 60 foreign countries. About half reside on or near the University Park campus. Annual enrollment in noncredit continuing education programs is about 8,246.

The full-time faculty totals 463, with 157 professors, 141 associate professors, 128 assistant professors, and 37 instructors. Eighty-four percent hold doctoral or terminal degrees in their areas. The student-faculty ratio is thirteen-to-one.

The University of Denver's 125-acre campus has more than 100 buildings housing laboratories, classrooms, faculty and staff offices, student residences and the million-volume Penrose Library.

Slated for 1981 completion is the $6 million Seeley G. Mudd Science Building. The Shwayder Art Building, completed in 1979, is another recent campus addition.

Two historic buildings, University Hall or "Old Main" (1890) and Mary Reed Building (1932), the main university library for 35 years, will soon undergo massive restoration and renovation. The university's Law Center downtown will expand with proceeds of the sale of alumnus Lowell Thomas' country home in Dutchess County, New York.

University research, both through the Denver Research Institute and in-

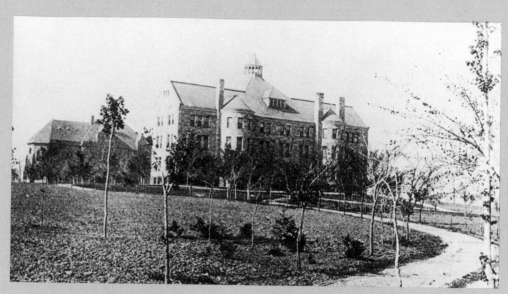

An early view of the University of Denver campus in southeast Denver shows University Hall and, in the background, Iliff School of Theology, now a separate educational institution.

dividual colleges and schools, solves problems of government and industry, discovers new knowledge and enhances and supports the educational process.

Community outreach of the university includes many free or low-cost entertainment events, exhibits and programs, and use of the community as a laboratory in new techniques and knowledge. Graduate and under-

graduate students intern with businesses, governments and community organizations. Hundreds of faculty and staff members as well as students participate as volunteers in community organizations and activities.

Dr. Ross Pritchard, former president of Hood College and Arkansas State University, is the university's fourteenth chancellor. The university is guided by a 28-member board of trustees and numerous volunteer advisory groups. Its current operating budget exceeds $64 million.

Van Schaack & Company

Seven decades of growth in Denver

In 1908, 21-year-old Henry Cruger Van Schaack rode a bicycle through the streets of downtown Denver, collecting rent for a local property management firm. From that pedestrian beginning, he went on to found Van Schaack & Company, now the Rocky Mountain region's largest multi-service real estate firm.

Born in Chicago in 1887 to a family of Dutch and English descent, Van Schaack came to Colorado when the flurry of growth and speculation spelled "opportunity" for enterprising young businessmen. In 1911, just three years after starting his job as a rent collector, Van Schaack was involved in the formation of his own company and soon was making a name for himself among Denver's leading businesses.

Van Schaack, by 1923, expanded the company's services to include insurance and mortgage loan activity, and within a few years he expanded its property management portfolio to include many of Denver's best known buildings — the

Equitable Building, the Continental Oil Building, the American National Bank Building, the Denver Hilton and others.

In 1929, Van Schaack & Company moved from its original offices in what is now the American National Bank Building at Seventeenth and Stout Streets, into the Ideal Cement Building at Seventeenth and Champa Streets. Headquarters were transferred to the Equitable Building at 724 Seventeenth Street in 1932. The company moved again, in 1949, to the Van Schaack Building at 624 Seventeenth Street, the first building to be constructed in Denver in twenty years, placing Van Schaack & Company in the headlines of local newspapers.

The company continued to expand throughout the 1950s, and in 1958 Van Schaack became chairman of the board — a position he held until his death in 1963 — and Thomas B. Knowles was named president.

Knowles, a Harvard University graduate, maintained an active interest

Henry Cruger Van Schaack, founder of Colorado's largest multi-service real estate firm, Van Schaack & Company.

Van Schaack & Company offices in the Equitable Building, 724 Seventeenth Street.

in civic as well as business endeavors. He led the drive to build the Denver Art Museum and was president of the Denver Art Museum, Mile High United Way, the Denver Building Owners and Management Association and Downtown Denver, Inc.

Knowles became chairman of the board in 1973, and John I. Hasselblad moved into the president's office. Under Hasselblad's leadership, Van Schaack & Company began developing its network of residential sales branch operations and moved to its present headquarters in the Colorado National Building at 950 Seventeenth Street.

Following Hasselblad's retirement in 1977, Grant T. Alley was elected president and chief executive officer. Under Alley's leadership, Van Schaack & Company has continued to expand its branch operations both in state and out of state. Today, this includes 24 residential sales

offices lining Colorado's Front Range, as well as offices in Albuquerque, New Mexico and San Diego, California.

Also under Alley's leadership, the company has expanded its services, which now include residential and commercial real estate brokerage, mortgage banking, insurance, development, national and international investments and relocation services through Van-Relco, a wholly-owned home buying subsidiary operating in 50 states. A number of VanRelco clients are Fortune 500 companies.

Van Schaack & Company is publicly held, grossing sales nearing $1 billion annually. A team of nearly 700 employees, demonstrating the personal desire to help others and the professional competence to get the job done, enables Van Schaack & Company to remain the same vital part of Denver's growth it has been for seven decades.

Watersaver Company, Inc.

From simple beginnings came leadership in saving water

The founding of Watersaver Company developed out of necessity. Just out of the Navy, in May 1948, W. Jay Slifer started a small burlap bag processing company at 3560 Wynkoop Street. Always looking for new uses for the age-old India jute cloth, Slifer conceived the idea of coating the burlap with asphalt and lining ditches to save water. This rather elementary beginning was followed by experimentation with new and revolutionary rubber and plastic materials that became available as a result of World War II technology. This venture was "plowing new ground" from the start.

The West was fighting back from a series of drouths and a war. Water was the difference between bountiful crops and crop failures. The control of dwindling water supplies was an old problem to be solved with modern ingenuity and new products. Watersaver Company had both. In the beginning it supplied the lining and supervised the installation of the earliest flexible ditch liners in the West, since the main idea at that time was water conservation for agriculture.

In 1980 giant panels 70 x 600' weighing 6000 pounds each were connected to form 192-acre-lined Uranium Tailings Pond. The completed liner weighed four million pounds.

Within a few years, it became apparent that the awareness of "water quality" had developed into a keen interest for pollution control and the need to stop seepage. Something had to be done to solve this long-range problem. Watersaver Company was quick to adapt the use of membrane liners to the problems of water conservation and

water pollution control. Working with engineers, governmental agencies, farmers and ranchers, industrialists and contractors, it was demonstrated how these problems of water control could be solved quickly, economically and permanently with the proper use of Watersaver's Flexible Membrane Lining Systems.

It was during the mid 1950s that Bill Slifer, son of the founder, and Bill Reetz, son-in-law, joined the company. Both of these men with engineering degrees, along with Jim Bryan, recently out of the University of Colorado, represented the second wave of talent arriving at the right time to give new input to the grow-

In 1952 the company began using the concept of lining irrigation ditches with asphalt-coated burlap to stop water loss.

ing company's progress. Today, these people constitute the management team that has stretched the family-owned business around the world.

In 1978 Watersaver International, Ltd. was founded to handle export sales overseas. Watersaver has achieved prominence worldwide for the development of efficient and economical membrane linings for the control of seepage. The company's linings and installation techniques meet state and federal requirements for water conservation, water quality and pollution control. Both products and systems have become standards in many countries now starting to solve their water problems.

With a history of more than 6,000 completed lining projects — many of which have been in service more than 20 years — Watersaver has established a unique viewpoint in the evaluation of new materials. Because the company is continually testing new lining membranes and materials. it bridges the important gap between laboratory technology and jobsite requirements for membrane liners of proven capability.

The concept of stopping seepage with membrane linings has been expanded now to include flexible membrane covers that float to protect water quality from pollution above. Also, specific rubber membranes are adapted to one-ply roofing systems for commercial buildings as a solution to leaking roofs.

The company continues to attract into its organization people with vision and talent who are capable of meeting the challenges set forth by its founder. From the very beginning, W. Jay Slifer was responsive to an important need that has since gained worldwide recognition, the necessity to save water. Throughout the years, the Watersaver Company has dedicated itself to excellence in both product and service. The result has been the growth and progress of a company far beyond the dreams of the man who started by coating burlap with asphalt to save water in irrigation ditches in the West.

Western Airlines

America's senior airline in Denver since 1927

A major airways hub today, Denver has an airline history that goes back to the mid '20s and the very beginnings of air mail service.

In early 1925, Congress gave the U.S. Post Office authority to contract with private companies for the carriage of air mail. This important development gave rise to a number of budding air carriers — including Colorado Airways. That carrier's founder — Anthony F. Joseph — bid successfully for a branch line to connect the Colorado cities of Denver, Colorado Springs and Pueblo with the government-operated transcontinental air mail route at Cheyenne.

Colorado Airways inaugurated service on May 31, 1926, using a fleet of

Hispano Suiza engined Standard biplanes. Like many of the fledgling carriers, Colorado ran into financial operational problems and on December 10, 1927, its route and air mail contract were taken over by Western Air Express.

Western Air Express, today's Western Airlines, got its start with an air mail contract route between Los Angeles and Salt Lake City via Las Vegas. It reported a profit at the end of 1926 and became the first airline in the nation to pay shareholders a dividend.

The move into Colorado was Western Air Express' first route expansion. With it, the small airline made its second major aircraft purchase — three Stearman open-cockpit biplanes which were

called "glowing examples of aeronautical engineering genius."

During the next few years, Western continued to grow and became known as a leader among airlines, truly an industry giant (by standards of the era).

Having grown to be the nation's largest airline in 1930, Western was forced by the powerful Postmaster General into a consolidation of most of its route system with Transcontinental Air Transport. The consolidated company, — first known as Transcontinental and Western Air Express — went on to become TWA. All that remained of Western Air Express was the historic Los Angeles-to-Salt Lake City route (to which had been added San Diego) and the Cheyenne to Pueblo via Denver and Colorado Springs segment.

Meanwhile there were other airlines stirring on the east slope of the Rockies and one of them — Wyoming Air Service — would play a major role in Western's future. Wyoming Air Service began operations in May 1930 and by the following year, it was operating scheduled passenger service between Casper and Denver. Air mail contracts were the lifeblood of early airlines, though, and without one, Wyoming Air Service struggled through the first years of existence.

The Air Mail Act of 1934 took air mail contracts away from most of the original air carriers and brought about the reorganization of all of them, but it was a bonanza for Wyoming Air Service. Founder Dick Leferink submitted a bid for Route 17, Cheyenne-Pueblo via Denver and Colorado Springs, and another one for Route 28 from Cheyenne to Billings via Casper and Sheridan. He won both, knocking Western at least temporarily out of the Colorado/Wyoming aviation picture.

Wyoming Air Service grew and changed its name to Inland Airlines, and in 1944 Inland became a part of Western Airlines, putting Western back into Denver after a ten year absence.

Western pioneered the first aerial route between Denver and Los Angeles in 1946, but postwar years were financially rocky and the airline ended up selling that route to United Airlines in 1947.

The airline continued to grow and expand its routes in and out of Denver. Today Western offers nonstop services between Denver and eleven cities plus direct service to dozens of other points including Hawaii. Denver has been chosen as the newest U.S. gateway city to London, England, and Western has received the nod to provide that new nonstop service.

As Denver reaches its centennial milestone, Western — the city's senior airline — will be turning 55 years old, and together the city and the airline look to new and broader horizons.

Western started service to Denver using Stearman bi-planes in December of 1927.

The eleven-passenger all-metal aircraft shown at Denver, was operated by Western Air Express for a few months in 1934.

Western Federal Savings

Since 1891 there's never been a doubt

Colorado entered the 1890s with a roar. The silver and gold camps were booming, the miners and businessmen were profiting and homes were springing up throughout the state. Then came the Panic of 1893 and the repeal of the Sherman Silver Purchase Act that led to the closing of many silver mines and smelters, widespread unemployment and a sharp drop in real estate values.

Colorado, the Silver State, felt the blow seriously. Of the nearly 40 savings and loan associations then operating in the state, only nine survived those hectic days.

The current 24-story home office of Western Federal Savings in downtown Denver.

Among the three Denver associations that survived was Industrial Federal Savings, today known as Western Federal Savings, the largest savings association in Colorado. Founded by Alfred John Bromfield on April 18, 1891, the firm established an early record of growth and safety. Through the Panic of 1893, wars and several depressions, earnings have been paid twice a year to depositors since 1891 without a single interruption.

An English journalist and friend of Mark Twain, Bromfield had come to Denver with his wife and daughter in search of opportunity and health. Recognizing Denver's growth potential and the need for home financing, he founded Industrial Federal Savings with total assets of $3,160. The firm's first office was located on the second floor of the Union Block Building at 1114 Sixteenth Street.

Assets grew continuously and by 1937, when Bromfield was succeeded as president by his son, A. J. Bromfield, total assets were just under $5 million. In the years following, the association expanded rapidly to reach $6.5 million in 1940, $114 million in 1960. In January of 1968, when Bromfield stepped aside and the presidency was assumed by Junius F. Baxter, assets had reached $300 million. In 1972 they had climbed to $500 million and $1 billion in 1977. By 1980 total assets had topped $1.25 billion and Western Federal Savings was ranked the 44th largest in the nation.

Along with the growth in business and assets, the firm faced the need for larger business quarters. In 1914 offices were moved to 338 Fifteenth Street and in 1928 to the Equitable Building at 740 Seventeenth Street. In 1938 the association built its own new office building at 1630 Stout Street and 22 years later revealed plans to build a 24-story skyscraper in downtown Denver. At the same time a major change was announced, Industrial Federal Savings would change its name to Western Federal Savings to keep pace with the times.

The change to the new 24-story building at Seventeenth and California Streets was made in 1962 and during 1980 administrative offices were split between the downtown office and a new ten-story Cherry Creek Building. In addition to its home office growth, the savings association was busy establishing branch offices throughout the state. In 1951 Western Federal Savings opened the first branch office in Colorado in Aurora. By 1980 the association had additional branch facilities in Cherry Creek, Lakeside, Westland, Englewood, East Denver, Stapleton, Bear Valley, Northglenn, Southglenn, Denver Tech Center, Arvada, Aurora Mall, Boulder, Colorado Springs, Fort Collins, Pueblo and La Junta. Plans were announced to open branches in University Hills, Loveland and Grand Junction.

Over the years the firm had become a consistent leader in mortgage lending and during the 1970s it moved to expand its services through subsidiaries. In 1970 Field Corporation was formed as a property management division and one year later Western Service Agency, Inc., a full service insurance agency, was acquired.

Institutional Investors Corporation was begun in 1975 as a consultant for financial institutions in the management of their liquidity portfolios. Shelter America Corporation was organized as a mobile home lender for VA, FHA and conventional financing in 1977. Within two years it became the nation's largest VA and FHA mobile home lender. Western Real Estate, formed in 1979, was created to handle property management of the association's office buildings.

"Our primary purpose will always be promoting thrift and home ownership," Baxter said. "But we also believe that both depositors and home owners are best served by a variety of financial services."

The Union Block Building, site of the first Industrial Federal Savings, predecessor to Western Federal Savings.

Wright & McGill Co.

A better idea got company hooked on growth and success

In the early 1920s the idea of how to make a better fishing fly inspired Andrew "Drew" McGill. McGill, convinced the product was a good one, started having the flies tied and selling them in the Rocky Mountains. Stanley M. Wright joined him in 1925 and the Wright & McGill Co. was formed.

From those humble beginnings, the Wright & McGill firm expanded into the manufacture of lures, increased its production of flies and became a major factor in the fishing fly market.

In the early days, the company rented space in downtown Denver in the Clayton Building. A major turning point in its growth developed around 1930 when Wright & McGill developed machinery to manufacture and sell its own fish hooks, under the trademark and now famous brand name — Eagle Claw. Shortly afterward, the company moved to a rented building at 1463 York Street and began a major expansion program.

With the supply of fish hooks to the free world practically stopped in the 1940s, the company manufactured fish hooks that enabled England and other lend/lease countries to continue their fish food supplies. Following World War

II, Wright & McGill developed fully automatic machinery to produce the Eagle Claw hooks. It then acquired the Goodwin Granger fishing rod manufacturing facility and began manufacturing fine grade Tonkin Cane fly rods. A new technique was added in the manufacture of fishing rods — by using glass fibers. Wright & McGill produced some of the first solid fiberglass rods in the country by instituting the new technique.

A first in the market place was the use of nylon monofilament in fishing, which Wright & McGill introduced with the manufacture of leaders and snelled hooks.

The company was fully acquired by Andrew McGill upon Stanley Wright's death in 1956.

In 1959 the company constructed a new, wholly-owned manufacturing facility at Fourteenth and Yosemite Streets in Aurora, Colorado. The new 70,000 square-foot building greatly increased efficiency and production.

In 1960, after McGill's death, the Wright & McGill Company came under the direction of McGill's wife, Madeline F. McGill.

The manufacture of Tonkin Cane rods was phased out during the '50s and the company became a major manufacturer of tubular fiberglass rods — constructed

in a new factory in Greeley, Colorado.

The famous Eagle Claw fish hooks became the firm's main product and gained the major share of the fish hook market in the U.S. Wright & McGill continued to expand its manufacturing facilities and to refine its automated equipment.

Another major step was taken in 1972 when the company purchased new manufacturing facilities — 200,000 square feet at the corner of I-70 and Colorado Boulevard. The manufacture of fishing rods was moved from the Greeley plant into the Fourteenth and Yosemite Street location.

Under the terms of Madeline McGill's will, the company has been privately held since her death in 1977.

Wright & McGill Co. has built its reputation over the years on high-quality fishing equipment. It is today not only a major factor in the United States fishing market, but also exports its products worldwide and is the second largest manufacturer of fish hooks in the world.

Wright & McGill actively pursues further expansion and new markets. It currently produces 1,500 different patterns and sizes of hooks and 200 different models of fishing rods, including the new rods made from graphite fibers and rods made of glass.

Early design fish hook making equipment, 1943.

Denver's horse-drawn street railway

Conclusion

It was not a likely location for a city.

The remote townsite was platted on a jumped gold claim
at the edge of the Great American Desert
and the foot of the soaring Colorado Rockies.

But from its earliest days, Denver's people had vision.
They were dreamers—and they were determined.
They backed their dreams with hard work, money and a handful of luck.
And they won—
The people carved a permanent place in the West and its history.
They won their name and a railroad.
They survived epidemics, the collapse of silver and staggering unemployment.
They established a community—
A place that has captured the hearts of adventurers, seekers and dreamers.
The riches those early miners sought were not just within the earth.
They were in the people themselves,
people who dreamed golden dreams and found that,
as the underground riches vanished,
a new wealth had grown up around them and within them.
They had become a city of natural and cultural beauty.
Denver was the real treasure so long sought—the true Rocky Mountain gold.

Denver: An Annotated Bibliography

Arps, Louisa Ward. *Denver in Slices.* Denver: Sage Books, 1959. 263 pp., illus., notes, index.

Delicious slices on Denver's drinking water, city ditch, Cherry Creek, the South Platte, both Denver mints, Tabor ghosts, the Windsor Hotel, the Baron of Montclair, Overland Park, Buffalo Bill, Elitch Gardens and Eugene Field. A delightfully written and diligently researched appetizer.

Athearn, Robert G. *Rebel of the Rockies: A History of the Denver and Rio Grande Western Railroad.* New Haven: Yale University Press, 1962. 395 pp., illus., notes, bib., index.

Of 100 Colorado railroads, this gritty narrow-gauge incorporated in 1870 is the only Denver-based survivor. Professor Athearn eloquently and authoritatively traces the D&RGW's long uphill route to profits, independence and fame through Rocky Mountain scenery still enjoyed by passengers on the Durango-Silverton, Cumbres-Toltec and Rio Grande Zephyr trains.

Ballast, David Kent. *Denver's Civic Center: A Walking Tour.* Denver: City Publishing Company, 1977. 30 pp., illus., maps.

Elegant photographs and words on the park-like center of city and state government.

Bancroft, Caroline. *Denver's Lively Past from a Wild and Wooly Camp to Queen City of the Plains.* Boulder: Johnson Publishing Company, 1952. 48 pp., illus.

One of two dozen lively booklets on Colorado history by the legendary descendant of a prominent pioneer family.

Barney, Libeus. *Letters of the Pike's Peak Gold Rush.* San Jose: the Talisman Press, 1959. 97 pp., map. Introduction by Thomas Hornsby Ferril.

Light, witty letters portraying Denver at the age of one, by the '59er whose saloon hall housed the Queen City's first attempts at self-government, theater and church-going.

Barth, Gunther Paul. *Instant Cities: Urbanization and the Rise of San Francisco and Denver.* New York: Oxford University Press, 1975. 310 pp., illus., notes, bib., index.

Speculative, stimulating scholarship.

Bean, Geraldine. *Charles Boettcher: A Study in Pioneer Western Enterprise.* Boulder: Westview Press, 1976. 220 pp., illus., notes, bib.

Biography of the co-founder of Great Western Sugar Company, Ideal Basic Cement Company, Capital Life Insurance Company and numerous other entrepreneurial activities as well as Colorado's greatest philanthropic foundation.

Bird, Isabella. *A Lady's Life in the Rocky Mountains.* London: John Murray, 1879. 296 pp., illus. (Widely reprinted in both paperback and hardback editions.)

Isabella rambled over much of Colorado in 1873 and left this memorable but unflattering account. Of Denver she wrote, "The great braggart city lay spread out, brown and treeless, upon the brown and treeless plain, which seemed to nourish nothing but wormwood and the Spanish bayonet."

Bleumel, Elinor. *The Golden Opportunity: The Story of the Unique Emily Griffith Opportunity School of Denver.* Boulder: Johnson Publishing Company 1965. 198 pp., index.

Elinor Bluemel has also written *Dr. Florence Sabin* and *Colorado Women of the Century* to demonstrate the importance of women in Denver's history.

Breck, Allen D. *John Evans of Denver: Portrait of a Twentieth Century Banker.* Boulder: Pruett Publishing Company, 1972. 249 pp., illus., notes, bib., index. *William Gray Evans: Portrait of a Western Executive.* Denver: The University of Denver, 1964. 290 pp., illus., notes, bib., index.

Biographies of Governor John Evan's son (William) and grandson (John) who continued with some of his many city-shaping enterprises. These are the definitive accounts by the long-time chairman of the University of Denver history department.

Brenneman, Bill. *Miracle on Cherry Creek: An Informal History of the Birth and Re-Birth of a Neighborhood.* Denver: Central Bank & Trust Company, 1973. 130 pp., illus., bib.

Lively history of Denver, focusing on the lower downtown blocks revitalized by Elwood Brooks' Central Bank and by Denver Urban Renewal's Skyline Project.

Brettell, Richard B., *Historic Denver: The Architects and the Architecture, 1858-1893.* Denver: Historic Denver, Inc., 1973. 240 pp., illus., notes, bib., index.

A gorgeously illustrated coffee-table tribute to the brick-and-brownstone city now bowing to glass, steel, cement and asphalt. The fine, brief overview of nineteenth-century Denver is followed by a more technical look at its leading architects, Frank E. Edbrooke, William Lang and Robert Roeschlaub.

Bollinger, Edward T. and Frederick Bauer. *The Moffat Road.* Chicago: Swallow Press, 1962. 359 pp., illus., bib., index.

Last and most famous of the Colorado railroaders' antics (we are still paying for it) surveyed in 430 illustrations and some text.

Casey, Lee, ed. *Denver Murders.* New York: Duell, Sloan and Pearce, 1946. 217 pp.

Eight different writers report on different and spectacular homicides from the Gordon case of 1860 to the Spider Man in 1942.

Children's Museum of Denver. *Denver City Games: For Explorers of All Ages.* 1977. 72 pp., illus.

A delightful way to explore Denver.

"The Colorado Magazine." Denver: State Historical Society of Colorado, 1923-present. Quarterly.

A scholarly magazine loaded with original research on Denver and Colorado. Preceded by *"The Trail"* and *"Sons of Colorado"* magazines. An invaluable, well-indexed gold mine of material.

Dallas, Sandra. *Cherry Creek Gothic: Victorian Architecture in Denver.* Norman: University of Oklahoma, 1971. 292 pp., illus., bib., index.

Intriguingly illustrated and written with a much broader historical value than the title suggests. *Yesterday's Denver.* Miami: E. A. Seeman Publishing Company, 1974. 160 pp., illus.

A pictorial history with minimal text.

Davis, Sally & Betty Baldwin. *Denver Dwellings and Descendants.* Denver: Sage Books, 1963. 250 pp., illus., bib., index.

Many photographs and informative text on leading families and their mansions.

Denver Chamber of Commerce. *Distinctive Denver: The Romance of An American Capital.* Denver: Chamber of Commerce, 1926. 63 pp., illus.

This is only one example of many publications on the Queen City by the Chamber of Commerce since its organization in 1884.

Denver City Directories. (Various Publishers.) 1873-present. Annual.

Invaluable for researching local history. Supplemental since 1925 with the Householders' Directory which is arranged by street address.

"Denver Municipal Facts." City and county of Denver, 1909-1931. (Initially a weekly, then a monthly magazine.)

A house organ begun by Mayor Speer to publicize Denver's problems and improvements. Many illustrations. A first-rate source for research on the city.

Denver Research Institute. *Economic Forces Behind Colorado's Growth, 1870-1962.* Denver: University of Denver, 1963.

The D.R.I. publishes a wealth of materials on Colorado, particularly growth studies.

The Denver Westerners. "Monthly Roundup." Denver: Denver Posse of Westerners, 1944-present. *Brandbook.* Annual.

A mother lode of original research on many aspects of Denver, Colorado and Western history.

Dorsett, Lyle W. *Queen City: A History of Denver.* Boulder: Pruett Publishing Company, 1977. 320 pp., illus., bib., index.

Surveys the political bosses, the power elite and the quality of life in the most important history of Denver since Jerome Smiley's classic was published in 1901.

Dunning, John. *Denver.* New York: Times Books, 1980. 407 pp.

A lusty historical novel that vividly portrays Denver journalism, politics and the Ku Klux Klan in the 1920s.

Etter, Don D. *Auraria: Where Denver Began.* Boulder: Colorado Associated University Press, 1972. *Denver Going Modern: A Photographic Essay on the Imprint of the International Style on Denver Residential Architecture.* Denver: Graphic Impressions, Inc., 1977. 132 pp., illus., index. *University Park: Four Walking Tours.* Denver: Graphic Impressions, Inc., 1974. 55 pp., illus.

Three elegant photographic studies by Historic Denver, Inc., activist instrumental in preserving Auraria's Ninth Street Park and the Curtis Park neighborhood.

Etter, Don D. and William D. West. *Curtis Park: A Denver Neighborhood.* Boulder: Colorado Associated University Press, 1980. illus.

Photography by Etter and prose by West, an English professor whose interest in all things Victorian prompted him to spearhead the renaissance of Denver's first streetcar suburb.

Fallis, Edwinia H. *When Denver and I Were Young.* Denver: Big Mountain Press, 1956. 198 pp., illus.

Childhood memories of a school marm born in Denver in 1876.

Ferril, Thomas Hornsby. *Words for Denver and Other Poems.* New York: Morrow, 1966. One of many anthologies by Colorado's celebrated poet laureate.

Graham, Lewis. *The Great I Am.* New York: Macaulay, 1933. 256 pp.

A fictional, unflattering biography of Frederick G. Bonfils, who tried to ban this book from Denver.

Fowler, Eugene. *Timberline: A Story of Bonfils and Tammen.* New York: Covici, Friede, 1933. 480 pp.

A gossipy account of the adolescence of the *Denver Post*, written with as much zest and a shade more accuracy than the former conman and bartender ever mustered for their outrageously sensational (and profitable) newspaper.

Hafen, LeRoy R., editor, *Colorado and Its People.* New York: Lewis Historical Publishing Co., 1948. 4 vols., illus., notes, bib., index.

The best, most authoritative history of Colorado edited by the most published Colorado historian. Two volumes of topically arranged coverage (e.g. chapters on mining, railroads, banking, etc.) and two volumes of biographical summaries of leading Coloradans.

Halaas, David F. *Fairmount and Historic Colorado.* Denver: Fairmount Cemetery Association, 1976. 104 pp., illus.

Dr. Halaas has made this potentially morbid tale an engrossing history not only of Fairmount, but of other early boneyards and the city on which they have thrived.

Haywood, William D. *Big Bill Haywood's Book.* New York: International Publishers, 1938. 368 pp.

Uproarious autobiography of the one-eyed, heavy-drinking socialist union organizer who used to terrorize the Oxford Hotel bar and the Mining Exchange Building before he went to the Soviet Union in 1919. Big Bill was the star promoter of the Western Federation of Miners and the Industrial Workers of the World.

Hosokawa, Bill. *Thunder in the Rockies. The Incredible Denver Post.* New York: William Morrow & Co., 1976. 447 pp., illus., index.

A candid, insider's peek at the paper that has done so much to shape twentieth-century Denver. A sequel to Fowler's *Timberline.*

Johnson, Charles A. *Denver's Mayor Speer.* Denver: Green Mountain Press, 1969. 255 pp., illus., bib., index.

A eulogy to Denver's greatest mayor and city boss who converted the Queen City to a city beautiful.

Jones, William C. & Kenton Forrest. *Denver: A Pictorial History.* Boulder: Pruett Publishing Co., 1974. 334 pp., illus., bib.

A good introduction.

Jones, William C. & F. Hol Wagner, Jr. *Mile-High Trolleys.* Boulder: Pruett Publishing Co., 1974. 120 pp., rev. ed. of a 1955 work, illus.

Eighty-year history of the street cars with over 200 photos, drawings, timetables and maps.

Karnes, T. L. *William Gilpin: Western Nationalist.* Austin: University of Texas Press, 1970. 382 pp., illus., notes, bibl., index.

Biography of the speechifying booster of pioneer Colorado, appointed by President Lincoln to be the first governor of Colorado territory.

Kelly, George V. *The Old Gray Mayors of Denver.* Boulder: Pruett Publishing Co., 1976. 266 pp., illus., index.

An insider describes the mayoral regimes of Stapleton, Newton, Nicholson, Batterton, Currigan and McNichols.

Kelsey, Henry E., Jr. *Frontier Capitalist: The Life of John Evans.* Boulder: Pruett Publishing Company and Colorado Historical Society, 1969. 372 pp., illus., notes, bib., index.

Definitive portrait of the key man in nineteenth-century Denver.

King, Clyde I. *The History of the Government of Denver with Special References to Its Relations with Public Service Corporations.* Denver: Fisher Book Co., 1911. 322 pp., notes, index.

A progressive reformer attempts to document the sometimes shady development of Denver's municipal government and public utilities.

Kohl, Edith E. *Denver's Historic Mansions: Citadels to the Empire Builders.* Denver: Sage Books, 1957. 268 pp., illus.

Photographs and descriptions of 31 mansions.

Larimer, William H.H. *Reminiscences of General William Larimer and of His Son, William H.H. Larimer.* ed. by Herman S. Davis. Lancaster, Pennsylvania: The New Era Printing Co., 1918. 256 pp., illus., notes, index.

Entertaining recollections of the claim jumpers who founded Denver.

Larsen, Charles. *The Good Fight: The Life and Times of Ben B. Lindsey.* Chicago: Quadrangle Books, 1972. 307 pp., bib., index.

Good biography of Colorado's greatest reformer who was run out of the state in the 1920s.

League of Women Voters of Denver. *Know Your Denver Government.* Denver: L.W.V., 1979. 80 pp., illus.

This booklet outlines everything from Denver history to the water system, from the tennis courts to the judicial system, from public housing to population trends. Wonderfully concise and systematic coverage of the myriad arms of city government. Fifteen maps and charts help make this an invaluable handbook for every Denverite. The League also publishes neighborhood guides in connection with their annual tours of Denver neighborhoods.

Lindsey, Judge Benjamin Barr and H.J. O'Higgins. *The Beast.* New York: Doubleday, Page & Company, 1910. 340 pp. (various reprints).

Chilling exposé by the celebrated juvenile court judge and muckraking reformer who blackened Denver's power elite—Evans, Moffat, Hughes, Cheesman, Buchtel—sparing not even the clergy. The trail of the beast in Denver led, according to the Judge, "step by step, from the dives to the police board, from the police board to the lower courts, from the courts to the political leaders who nominated the judges, and from the political leaders to the corporation magnates who ruled all. The trail leads from the offices of the corporations to the doors of the Capitol; it ascends the steps of the State House; it enters the sacred precinct of the Supreme Court itself."

Mazzulla, Fred (with Max Miller, Jo Mazulla and Margaret Miller). *Holladay Street.* New York: Ballentine Books, 1962. 224 pp., illus.,

Index

index.
Titillating tour of Denver's red-light district that has since been cleaned up and re-named Market Street.

Morris, Langdon E., Jr. *Denver Landmarks.* Denver: Charles W. Cleworth, 1979. 324 pp., illus., index.
A handy handbook listing most of the designated landmarks and historic districts in the city and county of Denver with a one- or two-sentence description, construction date, architect, style and photograph of each site.

McPherson, Alan & Sue. *Edible and Useful Wildplants of the Urban West.* drawings & photos by Jim Knopf. Boulder: Pruett Publishing Company, 1980. 330 pp., illus., index., bib.
Unique cookbook that grew out of the author's course at Denver Free University where students sampled recipes ranging from sunflower seed coffee to dandelion flower muffins. This handbook transforms Denver's weedy asphalt jungle into a fascinating and nutritious wilderness.

McCarthy, G. Michael. *Hour of Trial: The Conservation Conflict in Colorado and the West, 1891-1907.* Norman: University of Oklahoma Press, 1977. 327 pp., illus., endnotes, bib., index.
Remarkably dispassionate, scholarly treatment of early efforts to preserve Colorado as it once was.

Mumey, Nolie. *History of the Early Settlements of Denver, 1859-1860; with Reproductions of the First City Directory, the 1859 Map, the First Issue of the Rocky Mountain News and the Rare Cherry Creek Pioneer.* Glendale, California: Arthur H. Clark, 1942. 213 pp., illus., notes, bib., index.
A Denver physician, Dr. Mumey is living proof of his theory that human beings need only four hours of sleep a day. With all his spare time, the doctor has produced this and several dozen other books and reprints on Denver and Colorado.

Noel, Thomas J. *Richthofen's Montclair: A Pioneer Denver Suburb. A Brief History, Illustrated Walking Tour and Research Guide to Denver House and Neighborhood History.* Boulder: Pruett Publishing Company, 1978. 116 pp., illus., bib., index.
Longwinded title for a short book on the 1880's east Denver suburb that futilely hoped to elude the clutches of the Queen City.

Parkhill, Forbes. *The Wildest of the West.* New York: Henry Holt and Company, 1951. 310 pp., index., bib.
Perhaps the best book on Denver's 19th-century demimonde.

Mister Barney Ford: A Portrait in Bistre. Denver: Sage Books, 1963. 218 pp., illus., bib., index.
Another of Parkhill's half-dozen books on Denver, this one focuses on Denver's leading black entrepreneur.

Perkin, Robert L. *The First Hundred Years: An Informal History of Denver and the Rocky Mountain News, 1859-1959.* New York: Doubleday, 1959. 624 pp., notes, bibl., index.
Witty, highly readable account of the *Rocky Mountain News* and Denver. A splendid complement to *Timberline* by Gene Fowler, who wrote the introduction for this treasure trove of knowledge and trivia.

Reps, John W. *Cities of the American West: A History of Frontier Urban Planning.* Princeton: Princeton University Press, 1979. 827 pp., illus., notes, bib., index.
A monumental, lavishly illustrated 8½-pound grand tour of the graceless grids sprinkled across the West by town boomers.

Sinclair, Upton. *Mountain City.* New York: Albert & Charles Boni, 1930. 399 pp.
Denver inspired one of Sinclair's worst novels, but his worst is still one of the best novels so far about our town.

Smiley, Jerome C. *History of Denver.* Denver: Western Americana Publishing Company, 1978. (Reprint of original 1901 edition). 1,115 pp., illus., index.
Centuries from now this five-pound bible will still be the definitive history of nineteenth-century Denver. Superb index and 800 pic-

tures. A booster history written with amazing grace, wit and intelligence. If you really want to know about nineteenth-century Denver, Smiley is better than all the other books stacked together.

Smith, Barbara A. *Historic Denver for Kids.* Denver: University of Denver, Center for Teaching International Relations, 1978. 87 pp., illus., index.
A very helpful and informative guide to 71 historic sites, including many little-known suburban attractions.

Smith, Duane A. *Horace Tabor: His Life and the Legend.* Boulder: Colorado Associated University Press, 1973. 395 pp., illus., notes, bib., index.
The best account of Tabor's personal, business and political life by the much published professor at Fort Lewis College.

Spencer, Elma Dill Russell. *Green Russell and Gold.* Austin: University of Texas Press, 1966. 239 pp., illus., bib., index.
Definitive account of the Georgian whose gold discovery created Denver. Written by a descendant who partly relies on family oral history.

Uchill, Ida Libert. *Pioneers, Peddlers and Tsadikim.* Denver: Sage Books, 1957. 327 pp., notes, bib., index. (reprinted in 1979 by the author)
Splendid history of the Jews in Colorado.

Van Cise, Philip S. *Fighting the Underworld.* Boston: Houghton Mifflin, 1936. 369 pp., illus., index.
An exposé of Denver during the Prohibition period by the district attorney who finally nailed underworld czar Lou Blonger.

Vickers, W. B. *History of the City of Denver.* Chicago: O. L. Baskin, 1880. 652 pp., illus., index in the reprint.
A lavish booster history written when Denver was a 22-year-old adolescent. Wonderful drawings of bushy-bearded pioneers and their Victorian homes.

Wharton, J.E. & D.O. Wilhelm. *History of the City of Denver from Its Earliest Settlement to the Present Time, to which is added a Full and Complete Business Directory of the City.* Denver: Byers and Dailey, 1866. 184 pp., illus., (1901 reprint by D.O. Wilhelm).
Invaluable first history of Denver with the best 1860s city directory to boot. A rare find in used bookstores and a closely guarded rarity in libraries.

Wiberg, Ruth Eloise. *Rediscovering Northwest Denver: Its History, Its People, Its Landmarks.* Boulder: Pruett Publishing Company, 1976. 212 pp., illus., notes, bib., index.
Northwest Denver is a fascinating, neglected quadrant of the Queen City. This readable, highly informative book collects in words and numerous illustrations the forgotten history and charm of Highlands, Argo, Sloan's Lake, Berkeley and other neighborhoods.

Winter, Margaret Appel. *Exploring Denver with Children Young and Old.* Boulder: Lexicon, 1971. 137 pp., illus.
An excellent guide to the myriad delights of the city, through every nook and cranny from Dale's Rabbitry to the Western Union Telegraph Company, from City Park pedal boats to the Buckhorn Exchange Restaurant. When Uncle John and Aunt Matilda come in from Iowa with the kids, just give them this!

Wolfe, F.L. *Bicycle Denver: 107 Bicycle Tours.* Denver: Graphic Impressions, Inc., 1976. 264 pp., illus.
Details an alternative way to explore Denver, which has one of North America's finest bike path networks.

*The Holladay Overland Mail and Express
Company Depot on Market Street became
Wells, Fargo & Company in 1866.*

Author's Acknowledgements

A city's history is its people and I am fortunate that so many people have shared their knowledge of Denver with me.

Louisa Ward Arps, Maxine Benson, Sue Blakey, Nels Carman, Bill Center, Alan Culpin, Lyle Dorsett, Sharon Elfenbein, Jay Fell, Mark Foster, Dennis Gallagher, Eleanor Gehres, David F. Halaas, Phil Hernandez, Margaret Jacob, Steve Leonard, Mike McCarthy, Augie Mastrogiuseppe, Rebecca Miller, Jack Murphy, Jim Noel, Louise Noel, Vi Noel, Barbara Norgren, Margaret Picher, Gene Rakosnick, Jerry Sheely, Leona Rozinski, Bill Vaile, Dave Halaas, Bill West, Rodd Wheaton, Chris Whitacre, Ronna Widener and Fred Yonce are among those who read all or parts of the manuscript and made hundreds of helpful corrections and suggestions.

Elwyn Arps, Marc Applebaum, Tom Carr, Bill Ellswick, Winnie Ewalt, Sam Morrison, Florine O'Connell, Bob and Jonathan Shikes, Shari Stotts, Al Wuth and others helped to provide photographs. For help in obtaining illustrations, I am also indebted to Ron Tyler of the Amon Carter Museum, the Bancroft Library at the University of California at Berkeley, Jack Brennan of the Western Historical Collections at the University of Colorado at Boulder, the Henry E. Huntington Museum, the Newberry Library, Lynn Spendst of the Astor House Museum in Golden, Ginny Roberts Steele of the Aurora History Center, Kyla Allis of Children's Hospital, Harold Kountze of Colorado National Bank, the Denver Housing Authority, Jack Murphy and Bob Wright of the Denver Museum of Natural History, Barclay Howarth of the *Denver Post* library, Bob Cameron and Galen McFadyn of the Denver Urban Renewal Authority, Duane Bonham of the Denver Water Department, Krebs Uptown Photography, Bob McQuarrie of

the Littleton Historical Museum, Ida Hooker and Ted Sanquist of Mountain Bell, Martin-Marietta, Jim Kunkle and Gary Robertson of the Regional Transportation District, Belle Marcus of the Rocky Mountain Jewish Historical Society, John Holtz and Barb Porter of St. Joseph Hospital and Willard Simms and Chuck Sylvester of the National Western Stock Show. My former collegues at the State Historical Society of Colorado Library and splendid staff of Denver Public Library's Western History Dept. have been most helpful.

My Colorado and Denver history students, who have produced many splendid original research papers over the years, have taught me more than I have taught them.

Publishers acknowledgements

The editors and publishers of *Denver: Rocky Mountain Gold* are also indebted to a number of people, who by their continuous interest and guidance, have contributed to this volume that salutes the city and her people.

Our special thanks go, of course, to author Dr. Thomas J. Noel, for his commitment to this project.

In addition, we thank the staff and volunteer leadership of the Denver Chamber of Commerce for their continuing support and assistance, including Lael S. DeMuth, chairman; John D. Hershner, immediate past chairman; Rex Jennings, president; Georgia Ann Hale, staff project manager and Becky Miller, Staff Writer and Chamber volunteers Jerry Sheely, Bill Vaile and

Gordon Parker. Chamber staff members Dave Anderson, Jeanne Appareti, Linda Bagby, Kelli Callison, Cindy Garcia, Laura Gindro, Jim Guilfoyle, Chuck Kangas, Rick Leech, Mary Ellen Rawley, Jerry Robison, Marcia Rolander, Jan Rothfuss, Dave Sondag, Joni Stransky, Joan Thomson, and Jean White were also helpful.

A special note of thanks to Bill Center, former vice president of the Denver Chamber, now executive vice president of the Virginia Beach, Virginia Chamber of Commerce for his sensitive counsel and support.

We are sincerely grateful to Lois Lusky, senior vice president and chief operating officer, Hill and Knowlton/Denver, for her unabashed support, keen interest and special considerations toward this community project.

Greg, Joye and Heidi Jenson provided a fine sampling of Colorado hospitality for which we are sincerely indebted. We are grateful to Teresa Hauschel, Trudy Hauschel, Tina and Todd Hauschel who inspired an atmosphere of stimulation and creativity. Thanks to Aaron and Vicki Fontinel for their continued interest in *The American Portrait Series*. A special thanks to Mary Colwell for her significant interest in Denver and support for this publication.

Others who contributed to the book's success include:

Marie Flagg, Paula Sullivan, Missy Kruse, Caroline Johnson, and CHP staff members Barbara Jameson, Pat Briggs, Darlene Rudd, Lin Mullis, Nancy Coats, Nina LeMaire, Linda Logdson, Sabrina Hong and Wally King.

Credits

Sources of photographs, maps and art appearing in this book are noted here in alphabetical order and by page number (location on the page is noted). Those photographs appearing in the chapter *Partners in Progress*, pages 186 through 247, were provided by the represented firms.

Amon Carter Museum: 2/3, 4/5, 10/11, 36 center left, 36 bottom left, 49 top, 71 bottom, 99 middle left, 104 bottom left, 106 top, 109 top and bottom.

Applebaum, Marc: 110.

Arps, Elwyn: 47 right middle, 80.

Astor House Museum: 59 middle inset.

Bernstein, Ed: 172 bottom right.

Birlauf & Steen: 125 top right.

Carr, Tom: 122 top.

Colorado Visitors Bureau: 170 middle right inset.

Denver Broncos: 172 top.

Denver Chamber of Commerce: 172 top left, 173, 182, 184 center and top right.

Denver, City of, Mayors Office: 179 top right.

Denver Housing Authority: 141 top right and middle right, 142 top left and middle left.

Denver Museum of Natural History: 8/9, 98 top left

Denver Planning Office: 96 bottom.

Denver Post, The: 71 top left and inset, 120 top, 150 top left and middle left, 151 top right and bottom right, 155 top right and bottom right, 157 bottom right, 162 top left, 168 bottom left.

Denver Public Library, Western History Department: 36 top center, 38 bottom left, 39 bottom inset and top center, 54 lower left middle, 55 middle and top right, 61 middle right, 62 inset, 67, 70 top left, 72 top and bottom right, 73 inset and top right, 74 top left, 75 top left and bottom right, 82 top and bottom, 85 bottom right, 86 bottom left, 87 middle right and bottom left inset, 92 top, top

inset, bottom left and bottom right, 93 top, 96 top left, 97 top right, 99 top left and top right, 100 top left, middle left, middle right and bottom left, 102 top, 103 top left, top middle and top right, 104 top and bottom right, 105 top left, 112 middle left, 114 top right inset, 117 middle right, 127 middle left, 129 bottom left, 130, 134 top left, 136 bottom left, 139 top, 140 inset, 142 top right and middle right, 144 inset, 155 top left, 158 middle left, 163 top, 248, 256, dust jacket back.

Denver Urban Renewal Authority: 88 top left, 127 top left.

Denver Water Board: 52 top left and right, 63 top right, 119 middle right, 127 top right.

Elswick, Bill: 50 middle left.

Greenway Foundation, The: 169 top right.

Huntington, Henry E., Library & Art Gallery: 55 bottom left.

Jewish Historical Society: 116 top left.

Kountze, Harold, Colorado National Bank: 62 top center.

Kunkle, James E.: 94 top, 127 bottom left.

Littleton Historical Museum: 118 bottom right, 119 bottom right, 120 top left inset.

Morrison, Sam: 76 circle, 129 circle.

National Western Stock Show: 78, 79.

Noel, Thomas J.: 16 left, 18 bottom right, 24 bottom left, 27 top and bottom left, 29 center right, 30, 32 top left, 32/33, 39 top inset, 40 bottom left, 45 right middle inset, 46 top left, 48 inset middle left, 50 top left, 51 top right, 54 top left, 55 top left corner, left middle top, top right middle and upper middle left inset, 58 middle right, 59 top right and middle right, 61 middle center, 63 top left, 65 top left and right, 75 top right, 76 bottom right, 84 top

left, 85 left middle, 87 top left, top right and bottom left, 89 top right, 90 top left, 101 top right, 102 middle left, 103 middle right, 105 middle right, 108 top, 112 bottom left, 114 top left inset, 116 top right, 121 middle right and left, 124 bottom right, 125 top left, 128 bottom right, 133 top left, 154 top left and middle left, 184 middle right, 185 top center and bottom right.

O'Connell, Florine K.: 129 top and top right inset.

Public Service Company of Colorado: 147.

Regional Transportation District: 178 top and bottom left.

Shikes, Bob and Jonathan: 90 bottom left, 93 bottom left.

St. Joseph Hospital: 49 lower left, lower right middle and bottom middle inset.

State Historical Society of Colorado: 14, 17 right, 18 bottom center, 18 top left and top right, 19 top left, 20, 23 top right, 25 center right, 24 top, 26 bottom left, 27 bottom right, 28 top left, center right and top right, 29 top left, 38 center left, 40 top center, 41 top right, top extreme right, bottom right and center, 44 center left, 45 top right, top middle, top left, left middle, and right bottom, 46 top right, 47 top left and top right, 48 bottom left, lower middle right and bottom right, 49 top right inset, bottom left and bottom center right, 51 left middle, 53 top and right middle, 56, 60 top right, 61 middle left and bottom inset, 61 top, top inset and bottom right, 64, 65 middle left and lower left, 66, 68, 70, 73 center, 77, 84 left middle, bottom left and bottom right, 85 left top and middle top, 87 top left inset, 88 middle, 89 bottom right, 91 bottom left, 93 bottom, 101 middle right, 107 bottom left and middle right, 108

bottom left, 113, 118 top, 121 center, 126 top, 132 middle right and bottom right, 135 top, 137 middle left, 143 top right, 151 top left, 158 top left, 168 middle left, 6, 19, 23 bottom and center right, 25 bottom left, 26 top left and center left, 28 center, 34 (map), 35 (map), 37, 38 top left, 39 bottom left, 42 top, 48 top left, 51 top left, 59 top left, 61 middle left, 71 top right, 72 top left and bottom right, 73 top middle and bottom, 74 top right and bottom, 76 top left and right, 86 bottom left, 97 middle right, 108 middle left, 114 top, 132 middle left, 136 top right, middle right, top left and middle left, 158 top left and top right.

Stotts, Shari M.: 123 top left.

University of Colorado at Denver: 128 top left.

Whitacre, Roger: 44 bottom left, 46 middle right, bottom right and bottom right inset, 63 middle right, 81 top and bottom right, 100 bottom right, 115 top right, 116 middle left and middle right, 117 top left, 137 top left, 140, 141 bottom right, 144, 145 top right and bottom right, 148 all and inset, 152 all and inset, 153 top left, bottom left and bottom right, 156 top, bottom left and bottom right inset, 157 top, 158 bottom right, 159 middle left, top right, middle bottom and middle right, 160 top, bottom left and bottom right, 161 top, middle right and bottom right, 163 top right inset, 164 top, bottom left, bottom middle and bottom right, 165 top right, 170 top, 171 bottom, 173 bottom inset, 174 top left, 175 top right, 176 top left, top center, top right, middle left, middle right, bottom center and bottom right, 177 top and top left inset, 180 top, 181, dust jacket front.

Larimer Street before the turn of the century.

Concept and design by Continental Heritage Press, Tulsa.
Printed and bound by Kingsport Press, Kingsport, Tennessee.
Type set in Century Expanded.
Text sheets are Warrenflo by S. D. Warren Company.
Endleaves are Multicolor Offset by Process Materials.
Cover is Kingston Linen by Holliston Mills.